John's Use of Ezekiel

John's Use of Ezekiel

Understanding the Unique Perspective of the Fourth Gospel

Brian Neil Peterson

Fortress Press
Minneapolis

JOHN'S USE OF EZEKIEL

Understanding the Unique Perspective of the Fourth Gospel

Copyright © 2015 Fortress Press. All rights reserved. Except for brief quotations in critical articles or reviews, no part of this book may be reproduced in any manner without prior written permission from the publisher. Visit http://www.augsburgfortress.org/copyrights/ or write to Permissions, Augsburg Fortress, Box 1209, Minneapolis, MN 55440.

Cover image: Detail of Predella panel, Altar-Piece of Maesta di Siena. (oil on Board)., Duccio di Buoninsegna, (c.1278-1318) / National Gallery of Art, Washington DC, USA / Bridgeman Images

Military Parade at Campo di Marte, 1308 – 1311 (tempera on panel, with gold ground), Duccio di Buoninsegna, (c.1278-1318) / Duomo, Siena, Italy / Mondadori Portfolio/Electa/Antonio Quattrone / Bridgeman Images

Cover design: Laurie Ingram

Library of Congress Cataloging-in-Publication Data

Print ISBN: 978-1-4514-9031-2

eBook ISBN: 978-1-5064-0038-9

The paper used in this publication meets the minimum requirements of American National Standard for Information Sciences — Permanence of Paper for Printed Library Materials, ANSI Z329.48-1984.

Manufactured in the U.S.A.

This book was produced using PressBooks.com, and PDF rendering was done by PrinceXML.

I dedicate this book to my patient and encouraging wife, Christine. It is only through her willingness to carry much of the burden of the raising of our children at this time that I have been able to focus my efforts on research and writing. I know that this sacrifice is not always easy but I appreciate her support and love as I fulfill one of my passions in life—to educate this generation of students in the Sacred Text.

You share in my successes, Christine:

אֲהַבְתִּיךְ

Contents

Acknowledgements ix
Abbreviations xi
Introduction 1

1. The Uniqueness of John's Gospel 5
2. John 1 and Ezekiel 1–3 Juxtaposed 33
3. John's Use of Signs and Ezekiel's Sign Acts 65
4. John's Placement of the Cleansing of the Temple in Light of Ezekiel 8–11 99
5. John's "I Am" Sayings in Light of Ezekiel 129
6. John 17, 20, and Ezekiel 37 165
   Unity, Resurrection, and the Insufflation
7. Jesus' Rebuilt "Temple" and Ezekiel 40–43 187
8. Conclusions and Implications 201

Index of Subjects 207
Index of Scripture References 213

Acknowledgements

I wish to express my gratitude to the administration of Lee University for the generous financial support given to me over the past three summers in order to pursue my research interests. These grants have enabled me to complete this work, as well as others, in a timely fashion. More specifically, I wish to express my appreciation to Dr. Paul Conn for awarding me a summer 2014 Presidential Faculty Development Grant for this project. I would also like to thank the faculty council at Lee University for believing in this project and voting to award me a summer 2014 Research Grant through the office of Dr. Debbie Murray, Vice President of Academic Affairs.

Abbreviations

AB	Anchor Bible
ABR	*Australian Biblical Review*
ABRL	Anchor Bible Reference Library
AMD	Ancient Magic and Divination
ANRW	*Aufstieg und Niedergang der römischen Welt*
BA	*Biblical Archaeologist*
BASOR	*Bulletin of American Schools of Oriental Research*
BBR	*Bulletin for Biblical Research*
BCBC	Believers Church Bible Commentary
BDAG	Frederick W. Danker et al., *A Greek-English Lexicon of the New Testament and Other Early Christian Literature*. third ed. Chicago: Chicago University Press, 2000.
BECNT	Baker Exegetical Commentary on the New Testament
BETL	Bibliotheca Ephemeridum Theologicarum Lovaniensium
Bib	*Biblica*
BibInt	*Biblical Interpretation*
BIS	Biblical Interpretation Series

BLS	Bible and Literature Series
BSac	*Bibliotheca Sacra*
BSR	Biblioteca di Scienze Religiose
BWANT	Beiträge zur Wissenschaft vom Alten und Neuen Testament
CBET	Contributions to Biblical Exegesis and Theology
CBQ	*Catholic Biblical Quarterly*
CTM	Currents in Theology and Mission
EgT	*Église et théologie*
EvQ	*Evangelical Quarterly*
ExpTim	*Expository Times*
FCBS	Fortress Classics in Biblical Studies
FRLANT	Forschungen zur Religion und Literatur des Alten und Neuen Testaments
HBT	*Horizons in Biblical Theology*
HTCNT	Herder's Theological Commentary on the New Testament
HUCA	*Hebrew Union College Annual*
Int	*Interpretation*
JANES	*Journal of the Ancient Near Eastern Society*
JAOS	*Journal of the American Oriental Society*
JBL	*Journal of Biblical Literature*
JCHS	Jewish and Christian Heritage Series
JCTCRS	Jewish and Christian Texts in Contexts and Related Studies
JETS	*Journal of the Evangelical Theological Society*
JNSL	*Journal of Northwest Semitic Languages*
JSNT	*Journal for the Study of the New Testament*
JSNTSup	Journal for the Study of the New Testament Supplement Series
JSOTSup	Journal for the Study of the Old Testament Supplement Series
JTS	*Journal of Theological Studies*

ABBREVIATIONS

KAT	Kommentar zum Alten Testament
LNTS	Library of New Testament Studies
NCBC	The New Century Bible Commentary
NCCS	New Covenant Commentary Series
Neot	*Neotestamentica*
NICNT	New International Commentary on the New Testament
NICOT	New International Commentary on the Old Testament
NIDB	New International Dictionary of the Bible
NovT	*Novum Testamentum*
NovTSup	Novum Testamentum Supplement Series
NTC	New Testament Commentary
NTG	New Testament Guides
NTM	New Testament Monographs
NTS	*New Testament Studies*
OBO	Orbis biblicus et orientalis
OIUC	Oriental Institute of the University of Chicago
PFES	Publications of the Finnish Exegetical Society
PNTC	The Pillar New Testament Commentary
PTMS	Princeton Theological Monograph Series
RB	*Revue Biblique*
SBFA	Studium Biblicum Franciscanum Analecta
SBL	Society of Biblical Literature
SBLDS	Society of Biblical Literature Dissertation Series
SBLit	Studies in Biblical Literature
SBLStBl	Society of Biblical Literature Studies in Biblical Literature
SBLSS	Society of Biblical Literature Semeia Studies
SBLSP	Society of Biblical Literature Seminar Papers
SBLSymS	Society of Biblical Literature Symposium Series

SBT	Studies in Biblical Theology
SNTI	Studies in New Testament Interpretation
SNTSMS	Society for New Testament Study Monograph Series
TCC	The Communicator's Commentary
TDNT	*Theological Dictionary of the New Testament*. Edited by G. Kittel and G. Friedrich. Translated by G. Bromiley. 10 vols. Grand Rapids: Eerdmans, 1964–1976.
TJ	*Trinity Journal*
UCOIS	University of Chicago Oriental Institute Seminars
VD	*Verbum domini*
VE	*Vox Evangelica*
VT	*Vetus Testamentum*
VTSup	Supplements to Vetus Testamentum
WBC	Word Biblical Commentary
WBCom	Westminster Bible Companion
WMANT	Wissenschaftliche Monographien zum Alten und Neuen Testament
WUNT	Wissenschaftliche Untersuchungen zum Neuen Testament
ZAW	*Zeitschrift für die alttestamentliche Wissenschaft*
ZNW	*Zeitschrift für die neutestamentliche Wissenschaft*

Introduction

To what extent Ezekiel rather than another OT source has channeled to John his characteristic concepts would be a profitable area for study.[1]

When studying the Gospel of John from a scholarly perspective, a number of questions concerning his authorial methodology and purpose inevitably arise. For example: Why is the Fourth Gospel so different vis-à-vis the Synoptic Gospels? Why did the author include certain events while excluding others? What agenda drove him to write with such a radically different outlook on Jesus' life? Is it even possible to discern that agenda? Did the fact that he had a particular audience in mind govern his unique presentation? What sources were utilized by the author? And is his use of sources—perhaps unique to him—an explanation for his distinctive presentation?

---

1. Bruce Vawter, "Ezekiel and John," *CBQ* 26, no. 4 (1964): 450–58 (450). Based upon my research, in the past fifty years only one monograph has been published that has attempted to do a thorough analysis on the Ezekiel//John connections and even then it has a tripartite focus: Ezekiel's influence on John *and* the Dead Sea Scrolls and the Second Temple Period. See Gary T. Manning, *Echoes of a Prophet: The Use of Ezekiel in the Gospel of John and in Literature of the Second Temple Period* (London: T & T Clark, 2004), esp. 100–49. Unfortunately, when dealing with the actual Ezekiel//John parallels, Manning spends most of his time addressing only the obvious connections (i.e., John 10//Ezekiel 34 and John 15// Ezekiel 15). Similarly, the work by Henk Jan de Jonge and Johannes Tromp (*The Book of Ezekiel and Its Influence* [Farnham, Surrey, England: Ashgate, 2007]), fails to draw any significant connections either. Conversely, the unpublished dissertation of William Glenn Fowler ("The Influence of Ezekiel in the Fourth Gospel: Intertextuality and Interpretation" [PhD diss., Golden Gate Baptist Theological Seminary, 1995]), does offer many more inter-textual insights, which I incorporate throughout this work.

These and a plethora of other questions have propelled the Johannine discussion for decades, if not centuries. Scholars have posited answers to these question, some of which are satisfying while others not so much so. Other scholars have also proposed theories that have held the day for a generation or two only to be replaced by a newer hypothesis when the older hypothesis has run its course.[2] In such tempestuous scholarly waters, it would indeed be presumptuous on my part to think that I could answer all the questions noted above in such a short monograph. Nonetheless, it may be possible to shed some light on the discussion, and perhaps even answer a couple of these nagging queries.

Furthermore, I do not claim to be a Johannine "scholar," in the strictest sense of the term. To be sure, in many cases I would defer to those whose life's work has been devoted to such a fundamental Christian text.[3] Yet, sometimes it takes an outside observer to see things that others, in the heat of the debate, fail to notice. It is from this vantage point that I seek to enter the scholarly fray, all the while maintaining a level of humility as I write in the shadow of some of the greatest Johannine scholars known to biblical studies. At the same time I must offer a word of apology for perhaps overlooking a

2. A good example of this is the theory that the book of John was a second-century Greek composition; a position that has changed radically in light of archaeological findings (i.e., the John Rylands Papyrus). In light of this discovery, John is now seen as a late first-century Jewish work. See James H. Charlesworth, "The Dead Sea Scrolls and the Gospel according to John," in *Exploring the Gospel of John: In Honor of D. Moody Smith*, ed. R. Alan Culpepper and C. Clifton Black (Louisville: Westminster John Knox, 1996), 65–97 esp. 65–68. See a similar assessment by David Wenham, "The Enigma of the Fourth Gospel: Another Look," in *Understanding, Studying and Reading: New Testament Essays in Honour of John Ashton*, ed. Christopher Rowland and Crispin H. T. Fletcher-Louis, JSNTSup 153 (Sheffield: Sheffield Academic, 1998), 102–28 (103). Also, the once-popular "Johannine Community Hypothesis" has now been abandoned even by some of its most ardent supporters. On the latter point, see the discussion by Andreas J. Köstenberger, "The Destruction of the Second Temple and the Composition of the Fourth Gospel," in *Challenging Perspectives on the Gospel of John*, ed. John Lierman, WUNT 2.219 (Tübingen: Mohr Siebeck, 2006), 69–108 (72–76).
3. For a good representation of current Johannine scholars and their positions, see Tom Thatcher, ed., *What We Have Heard from the Beginning: The Past, Present, and Future of Johannine Studies* (Waco, TX: Baylor University Press, 2007).

particular scholar's article or monograph. When researching a topic such as this, one quickly realizes that the research is voluminous—for both Ezekielian and Johannine studies. Therefore, in the discussion that follows I have attempted to offer only a cross-section of scholarship from both camps.

With this caveat, I look for answers to some of the nagging questions noted above in a source every New Testament author would have been familiar with—the Hebrew Bible/LXX.[4] More specifically, I wish to draw upon my previous work on the book of Ezekiel,[5] a biblical book that I believe may hold answers to many of the questions listed above than many realize. When read in light of the Old Testament book of Ezekiel, the Gospel of John takes on new meaning, especially when we begin to discuss *John's use of Ezekiel*.

---

4. So too Peter M. Phillips, *The Prologue of the Fourth Gospel: A Sequential Reading*, LNTS 294 (London: T & T Clark, 2006), 147; Saeed Hamid-Khani, *Revelation and Concealment of Christ: A Theological Inquiry into the Elusive Language of the Fourth Gospel*, WUNT 120 (Tübingen: Mohr Siebeck, 2000), 132–39 esp. 133, 136; and D. E. H. Whitely, "Was John Written by a Sadducee?," *ANRW* II.25.3 (Berlin/New York: de Gruyter, 1985), 2481–2505 (2483).
5. Brian Neil Peterson, *Ezekiel in Context: Ezekiel's Message Understood in Its Historical Setting of Covenant Curses and Ancient Near Eastern Mythological Motifs*, PTMS 182 (Eugene, OR: Pickwick Publications, 2012).

1

The Uniqueness of John's Gospel

Ezekiel, prophet in exile, is perhaps destined in Biblical scholarship to remain in a foreign land. From time to time he has been transported by a venturesome scholar from dismal Babylonia to the scholastic elevations of Jerusalem. There he has glimpsed the world of scholarly scrutiny that Isaiah and Jeremiah have known so well. But he always seems to end up again in Babylonia. One may wonder if those three hundred barrels of oil were well spent by Chananiah ben Hezekiah when he composed his commentary on Ezekiel to prevent the book from sinking into canonical obscurity (*b. Sabb.* 13b). In fact, the prophecy of Ezekiel has largely been viewed as an apocalyptic resource. And we may admit the truth of that without disparaging the book in the least. In that respect the influence of Ezekiel on the NT has most readily been detected in the Apocalypse of John.[1]

Hassell Bullock's assessment of how the book of Ezekiel is used in New Testament studies highlights well the major lacuna, which this present work seeks to address. I believe that many of its unique

---

1. Hassell Bullock, "Ezekiel: Bridge between the Testaments," *JETS* 25, no. 1 (1982): 23–31 (23).

literary features will make sense when the Fourth Gospel is viewed through the lens of Ezekiel.

That the Gospel of John is unique goes without saying. Some of this uniqueness rests in the reality that John "discusses only about twenty days in the life of Jesus, a story encompassing more than thirty years of time...."[2] Conversely, throughout the Synoptic Gospels we find accounts covering Jesus' birth to his death, albeit selectively.[3] But John has fashioned his Gospel in more distinctive ways than just the chronology of Jesus' life: John has also included accounts unique to his Gospel, while eliminating key features present in the Synoptics.[4] In some cases, the ordering of the material within his book finds no parallels in the Synoptics. There is also the issue of Johannine theology/Christology and the author's rhetorical outlook. These are just a few of the larger literary features peculiar to John's Gospel. When one begins to focus on pericopae germane to all four gospels, we will see that, even on the micro level, there are variations in how John relates his accounts vis-à-vis the Synoptics.

In light of these peculiarities related to the Gospel, in this opening chapter I want to briefly introduce the reader to some of these specific literary "problems" associated with John's Gospel.[5] Here I will refrain

---

2. Kenneth K. Maahs, *The John You Never Knew: Decoding the Fourth Gospel* (New York: Peter Lang, 2006), 1. Maahs appears to be focused on the last portion of Jesus' ministry. According to the appearance of three Passover feasts in John, John, unlike the Synoptic Gospels, covers three years of Jesus' ministry as opposed to one to one-and-a-half years. For a detailed chart covering the period of Jesus' Johannine ministry, see Andreas J. Köstenberger, *John*, BECNT (Grand Rapids: Baker, 2004), 11–13.
3. Although Mark's treatment of Jesus' life is the closest to the Fourth Gospel, it still has the rhetorical flare of the Synoptics in its presentation of the ministry of Jesus. Indeed, the theories of Markan priority and a Q source derive from a close study of the Synoptics.
4. While there is some debate over whether John used, or was familiar with, the Synoptics, some scholars, myself included, believe that it is indeed possible that the author of the Fourth Gospel knew of these accounts (see more in discussion below). See also the discussion by John Marsh, "John: A Very Different Gospel?," in *A Companion to John: Readings in Johannine Theology (John's Gospel and Epistles)*, ed. Michael J. Taylor (New York: Alba, 1977), 3–31.
5. For a discussion on the theological differences/similarities between the Synoptics and John, see James D. G. Dunn, "John and the Synoptics as a Theological Question," in *Exploring the Gospel*

from entering into a detailed discussion on the numerous proposed solutions to these apparent enigmas, as I will handle the most relevant of these proposed solutions in the chapters that follow. In this chapter, I will also outline in broad strokes the solution I am proposing in this work. I am convinced that many of these differences can be attributed to John's theological and rhetorical purposes in light of his use of the book of Ezekiel.[6]

Finally, while scholars have attempted to account for the unique features of the Fourth Gospel by utilizing source-critical theories—John did not know about or use the Synoptics, or John had his own written and/or oral sources—this perspective is now being reexamined within Johannine scholarship. This is in large part due to close linguistic analyses, which have demonstrated an apparent mutual dependence on a similar source(s) or at least a similar tradition. Therefore, many Johannine scholars are now coming to the conclusion that John was aware of the Synoptic Gospels and/or the similar source material of Mark and Luke.[7] As such, the theory that John is less historical than the Synoptics is being challenged. As I will note below, in some cases, the Gospel is actually the preferred perspective when trying to recreate the events of Jesus' life.

---

of John: In Honor of D. Moody Smith, ed. R. Alan Culpepper and C. Clifton Black (Louisville: Westminster John Knox, 1996), 255–73.

6. Contra Barnabas Lindars, *The Gospel of John*, NCBC (Grand Rapids: Eerdmans, 1982), 27.

7. Ibid., 27. So too Richard Bauckham, "John for Readers of Mark," in *The Gospels for All Christians: Rethinking the Gospel Audiences*, ed. Richard Bauckham (Grand Rapids: Eerdmans, 1998), 147–71 esp. 159–60. See also the work of Thomas L. Brodie, *The Quest for the Origins of John's Gospel: A Source-Oriented Approach* (New York: Oxford University Press, 1993), 67–120; Howard M. Teeple, "Methodology in Source Analysis in the Fourth Gospel," *JBL* 81, no. 3 (1962): 279–86 (282); Edwin D. Freed, "The Entry into Jerusalem in the Gospel of John," *JBL* 80, no. 4 (1961): 329–38; and Edwyn Hoskyns, *The Fourth Gospel Vol. 1* (London: Faber and Faber Limited, 1940), 87.

Features Peculiar to John's Gospel

As just noted, the uniqueness of John's record of Jesus' life and ministry when compared to the Synoptic Gospels has fostered a number of debates and theories as to why the author organized his material in such a distinct fashion. Even though I will be handling these topics in more detail in the chapters to follow, a few of the most notable examples of these literary anomalies can be categorized under three main headings: 1) material in John and the Synoptic Gospels, but presented differently in the Fourth Gospel (points 1 and 2 below); 2) material that is absent in the Fourth Gospel but present in the Synoptics (points 3-5 below); and 3) content unique only to the Fourth Gospel (points 6-13 below).

1. The abrupt and exalted introduction of Jesus in John 1 stands in stark contrast to Matthew's and Luke's presentations, which begin with Jesus' early life (Mark comes the closest to John's abrupt beginning but that Gospel falls far short of the explicit promotion of Jesus' divinity).
2. The cleansing of the temple appears early in the ministry of Jesus in the Fourth Gospel as opposed to its appearance late in the Synoptics (John 2:13-22; cf. Matt. 21:12-17; Mark 11:15-17; Luke 19:45-46) (note John's use of ten verses to describe the temple cleansing as opposed to the use of two or three in the Synoptics).
3. The absence of Jesus' temptation and transfiguration is striking when compared to the Synoptics (Matt. 4:1-11; Mark 1:11-13; Luke 4:1-13 and Matt. 17:1-9; Mark 9:2-8 respectively).
4. The failure to include an exorcism by Jesus[8] in the Fourth Gospel

---

8. Cf. Robert T. Fortna, *The Gospel of Signs: A Reconstruction of the Narrative Source Underlying the Fourth Gospel*, SNTSMS 11 (Cambridge: Cambridge University Press, 1970), 100. The absence of "narrative" parables, perhaps with the exclusion of John 15:1-8, also falls into the category of

is surprising compared to the prevalence of exorcisms in the Synoptics.
5. The absence of the institution of the communion meal (cf. Matt. 26:26-29; Mark 14:22-25; Luke 22:17-20).[9]
6. The narrative content of John 2–4 is absent from the Synoptics.
7. The "I Am" Sayings are distinctive to the Fourth Gospel.
8. John's reliance on signs to prove Jesus' divinity is unique to John.
9. In John, Jesus makes three trips to Jerusalem for Passover as opposed to one in the Synoptics (John 2:13; 6:4; 11:55—12:1 cf. Matt. 26; Mark 14; Luke 22).
10. The raising of Lazarus in John 11 is absent from the Synoptics.
11. The extended treatment of Jesus' last few hours and the Farewell Discourses do not find parallels in the other gospels (John 13–17).
12. John's insufflation[10] in chapter 20 and the putative appendix of John 21 is glaringly absent from the Synoptics.
13. The post-cross call of Peter in John 21[11] is only recorded by John.

As noted, these are just a few of the more blatant literary peculiarities. If one were to include all the micro-level comparisons, the list would stretch on for pages. Now to be sure, John's uniqueness certainly did

---

unique features in John. On this latter issue, see Eduard Schweizer, "What about the Johannine 'Parables'?," in *Exploring the Gospel of John: In Honor of D. Moody Smith*, ed. R. Alan Culpepper and C. Clifton Black (Louisville: Westminster John Knox, 1996), 208–19.

9. Jesus' call in John 6:48-66 for the people to eat his body and drink his blood should not be seen as an allusion to the Eucharist as much as it is an allusion to Deut. 8:3. Jesus is thus speaking in a metaphor about trusting God for their provision and spiritual wellbeing.

10. "Insufflation" is a technical term used to denote an act of blowing on or into something or someone. The word is used frequently in the discussion of John 20:22.

11. For a list of the unique features of the Fourth Gospel, see Paul N. Anderson, *The Riddles of the Fourth Gospel: An Introduction to John* (Minneapolis: Fortress Press, 2011), 12–18; and Maahs, *The John You Never Knew*, 12–14. See also the discussion by Craig L. Blomberg, *The Historical Reliability of John's Gospel: Issues and Commentary* (Downers Grove, IL: InterVarsity, 2001), 19–22, 46–52.

not stem from merely a reordering of a pre-set group of pericopae employed by the Synoptic writers—John 21:25 dispels that belief.[12] John certainly had numerous events from Jesus' ministry to choose from when fashioning his Gospel. However, many of these omissions or re-orderings may be connected to the influence that the book of Ezekiel had on John.[13]

A Proposed Alternative Solution

The increased interest in the topic of the New Testament authors' use of the Old Testament, as well as Jewish Intertestamental literature, has paved the way for a fresh understanding of many New Testament passages.[14] In this vein, Johannine scholars have looked at a wide array of literary and non-literary influences in an attempt to explain the uniqueness of the Fourth Gospel. These include, but are not limited to, the Essene community from Qumran, various Second Temple and first-century C.E. literature (e.g., Hermetica, the Gospel of Thomas, the Palestinian Targumim), oral tradition, rhetorical needs based

---

12. Others have also noted the independent nature of the Johannine content. See, for example, Craig A. Evans, "The Function of Isaiah 6:9-10 in Mark and John," *NovT* 24, no. 2 (1982): 124–38, esp. 125–26; and idem, "The Hermeneutics of Mark and John: On the Theology of the Canonical Gospel," *Bib* 64, no. 2 (1983): 153–72, esp. 158n22, and the bibliographic entries there.
13. For a discussion that focuses on Exodus as the literary influence on John, see Jacob J. Enz, "The Book of Exodus as a Literary Type for the Gospel of John," *JBL* 76, no. 3 (1957): 208–15 esp. 209–11. While some of Enz's parallels are noteworthy (e.g., the use of signs), the majority of the connections are not as convincing as they are when compared to the book of Ezekiel. Cf. also the theory by Harald Sahlin, *Zur Typologie des Johannesevangeliums* (Uppsala: Lundequistska bokhandeln, 1950). For a critique of both, see Robert Houston Smith, "Exodus Typology in the Fourth Gospel," *JBL* 81, no. 4 (1962): 329–42, esp. 329–33.
14. The bibliography for this topic is immense. See, for example, Andreas J. Köstenberger, "John," in *Commentary on the New Testament Use of the Old Testament*, ed. G. K. Beale and D. A. Carson (Grand Rapids: Baker, 2007), 415–512; and D. A. Carson and H. G. M. Williamson eds., *It is Written: Scripture Citing Scripture: Essays in Honor of Barnabas Lindars* (Cambridge: Cambridge University Press, 1988), esp. 245–64 for an essay dealing with John. For a fuller bibliography, see Stefanos Mihalios, *The Danielic Eschatological Hour in the Johannine Literature*, LNTS 436 (London: T & T Clark, 2011), 1n1.

upon anti-Christian hostilities in the synagogues, pro-Samaritan sympathies, and anti-Gnostic agendas.

There can be no doubt that some of these theological needs of the first century shaped the Gospel, but this does not necessarily answer the host of literary peculiarities in John. As such, I propose that Johannine scholars may need to look in another direction concerning John's methodology and literary style. By scrutinizing only the literary style of earlier gospels and the socio-religious peculiarities and genres of the first century to find an answer to this dilemma, scholars have handicapped themselves to a large degree. It is perhaps best to look to the dominant piece of literature that shaped first-century Judaism, namely, the Hebrew Bible and its Greek translation (Septuagint/LXX).[15]

It goes without saying that the Hebrew Bible/LXX served as the primary literary influence for the Gospel writers.[16] Furthermore, while they may have utilized the Greek text of the LXX, the author of the Fourth Gospel appears to have been limited in his ability to use Greek.[17] As such, the Hebrew text would have been the most

---

15. See, for example, the comments by Gail R. O'Day, "The Gospel of John: Introduction, Commentary and Reflections," in *New Interpreter's Bible: A Commentary in Twelve Volumes*, ed. Neil Alexander (Nashville: Abingdon, 1995), 9:491–865 (505). I am aware that scholars do in fact interact with Old Testament literature when studying the Gospels; however, more often than not, this only goes as far as drawing scriptural allusions and commentary on explicit prophetic utterances and the like. For the range of Old Testament quotations and allusions in the Fourth Gospel compared to the LXX and MT, cf. Johannes Beutler, S. J., "The Use of 'Scripture' in the Gospel of John," in *Exploring the Gospel of John: In Honor of D. Moody Smith*, ed. R. Alan Culpepper and C. Clifton Black (Louisville: Westminster John Knox, 1996), 147–62.
16. See T. F. Glasson, *Moses in the Fourth Gospel*, SBT 40 (London: SCM, 1963); D. A Carson, "John and the Johannine Epistles," in *It is Written: Scripture Citing Scripture*, ed. D. A. Carson and H. G. M. Williamson (Cambridge: Cambridge University Press, 1988), 245–64; Craig A. Evans, *Word and Glory: On the Exegetical and Theological Background of John's Prologue*, JSNTSup 89 (Sheffield: JSOT, 1993), 172–84, esp. 174–75; and Saeed Hamid-Khani, *Revelation and Concealment of Christ: A Theological Inquiry into the Elusive Language of the Fourth Gospel*, WUNT 120 (Tübingen: Mohr Siebeck, 2000), 132–39.
17. So Teeple, "Methodology in Source Analysis," 281. W. D. Davies, "Reflections on Aspects of the Jewish Background of the Gospel of John," in *Exploring the Gospel of John: In Honor of D. Moody Smith*, ed. R. Alan Culpepper and C. Clifton Black (Louisville: Westminster John Knox,

likely option for a reference work.¹⁸ Thus, when John uses the terms γραφή (*graphē* "Scripture" cf. John 2:22; 7:38, 42; 10:35; 13:18; 17:12; 19:24, 28, 36, 37; 20:9) or γράμμα (*gramma* "writings" [of Moses] cf. 5:47); they almost exclusively refer to the "Holy Scripture."¹⁹ John's frequent use of these terms serves as a clue as to his literary purview as he is writing, namely, that he has a view to the Hebrew Bible when he is writing his gospel.

Now, I do not mean to suggest that scholars have failed to see parallels between the Gospels—the Gospel of John in particular—and the Old Testament, for these are legion. For example, C. K. Barrett notes that in Matthew there are 124 references to Old Testament passages, seventy in Mark; and in Luke 109; with only twenty-seven direct references in John.²⁰ Regarding this anomaly for the Fourth Gospel, Barrett goes on to note that "John is unquestionably using the O.T., but . . . his use is very far from the simple 'proof-text' method of, say, Matthew . . . and we may again draw the conclusion that though John uses the O.T. he uses it in a novel manner, collecting its sense rather than quoting."²¹ Similarly, Martin Hengel comments, "In accordance with his esoteric, indirectly suggestive style, the emphasis in John (in contrast to Matthew) is on 'allusions.' He prefers the bare, terse clue, the use of a metaphor or motif more than the full

---

1996), 43–64, suggests that "the Greek he [John] wrote was influenced by a Hebraic-Aramaic idiom and connotation" (44).

18. Beutler, "The Use of 'Scripture'," 158, points to the comparative analyses that have been done showing John's use of the LXX in quoting Old Testament texts. Raymond E. Brown, *An Introduction to the Gospel of John*, ed. Francis J. Moloney, ABRL (New York: Doubleday, 2003), 136, notes John's use of Hebrew and the Targumim as well.

19. Beutler, "The Use of 'Scripture'," 148. See also, Francis J. Moloney, *The Gospel of John Text and Context*, BIS 72 (Boston: Brill, 2005), 342–45; and idem, "The Gospel of John as Scripture," *CBQ* 67, no. 3 (2005): 454–68. In the latter work Moloney concludes that the author of John not only referenced the Old Testament as "Scripture," but also understood the very words of Jesus to be "Scripture"; namely, the words that the author of the Gospel of John was writing!

20. Charles K. Barrett, "The Old Testament in the Fourth Gospel," *JTS* 48, no. 2 (1947): 155–69 (155). Barrett draws his frequency list from the appendixes of Westcott and Hort's edition of the New Testament. See also Carson, "John and the Johannine Epistles," 246.

21. Barrett, "Old Testament in the Fourth Gospel," 156.

citation."[22] Finally, George J. Brooke points up that John's use of the Jewish Scriptures "appears veiled to us . . . because the Jewish or Jewish-Christian audience would have been more attuned to what was said than we can be. . . ."[23] Barrett, Hengel, and Brooke are indeed correct in noting John's use of veiled allusions to the Old Testament as opposed to direct quotations.[24] And while this is true, I would add that Ezekiel seems to have been the biggest influence on John. As Bruce Vawter aptly notes, "By influence is meant, rather, the exploitation of certain themes or concepts which John is more likely to have taken from Ezekiel than from any other source."[25]

Now to be sure some may contend that if Ezekiel plays such a dominant role in shaping the Fourth Gospel, why does John fail to quote the prophet directly? While I cannot be certain of John's reasoning for such a lacuna, few would doubt the clear Ezekielian parallels in John. The vine imagery of Ezek. 15 vis-à-vis John 15 and the shepherding language of Ezek. 34 and John 10 immediately come

---

22. Martin Hengel, "The Old Testament in the Fourth Gospel," *HBT* 12, no. 1 (1990): 19–41 (31–32).
23. George J. Brooke, "Christ and the Law in John 7–10," in *Law and Religion: Essays on the Place of the Law in Israel and Early Christianity*, ed. Barnabas Lindars (Cambridge: James Clarke & Co., 1988), 102–12 (102).
24. So too J. A. Draper, "Temple, Tabernacle and Mystical Experience in John," *Neot* 31, no. 2 (1997): 271; and Hengel, "Old Testament in the Fourth Gospel," 31–32. See further Köstenberger, "John," 419–20. For studies on the explicit Old Testament citations in John, see Bruce G. Schuchard, *Scripture within Scripture: The Interrelationship of Form and Function in the Explicit Old Testament Citations in the Gospel of John*, SBLDS 133 (Atlanta: Scholars, 1992); Maarten J. J. Menken, *Old Testament Quotations in the Fourth Gospel: Studies in Textual Form*, CBET 15 (Kampen: Kok Pharos, 1996); Barrett, "Old Testament in the Fourth Gospel," 155–69; Edwin D. Freed, *Old Testament Quotations in the Gospel of John*, NovTSup 11 (Leiden: Brill, 1965); Anthony T. Hanson, *The Prophetic Gospel: A Study in John and the Old Testament*, second ed. (Edinburgh: T & T Clark, 2006); Frederic Manns, *L'Evangile de Jean à la Lumière du Judaïsme*, SBFA 33 (Jerusalem: Franciscan Printing Press, 1991); Claus Westermann, *The Gospel of John in the Light of the Old Testament*, trans. Siegfried S. Schatzmann (Peabody, MA: Hendrickson, 1998); and Raymond E. Brown, *An Introduction to the Gospel of John*, ed. Francis J. Moloney, ABRL (New York: Doubleday, 2003), 115–50 esp. 133–38. These last seven sources are noted by Francis J. Moloney, "The Gospel of John: The 'End' of Scripture," *Int* 63, no. 4 (2009): 357n6.
25. Bruce Vawter, "Ezekiel and John," *CBQ* 26, no. 4 (1964): 450–58 (450).

to mind (see more in chapter 5 below).²⁶ As will be demonstrated throughout the following chapters, it appears that John tends to work on a macro level when it comes to themes and motifs. He uses these allusions in an attempt to draw connections between the Old Testament, the prophets, and Jesus' life.²⁷ Nevertheless, at particular moments, John narrowed his focus by clear inter-textual clues (e.g., similar words and phrases) to draw the reader's attention to a specific account, many of which find affinity with Ezekiel.

In this regard, clearly John had a strong understanding of prophetic literature, and more specifically, that of the prophet Ezekiel.²⁸ When one steps back for a moment and considers the fact that almost every person, even today, has a favorite book(s)/pericope(ae) from the Bible, then it is not too hard to imagine that the New Testament authors had their favorites as well (consider the author of Hebrews and his use of Leviticus). Indeed, are we to think that the authors of the first century were any less human in this regard? I think not! With this in mind, I wish for my readers to stop and consider the possibility that John saw something in the life of Jesus that caused him to draw connections to the life and prophetic work of Ezekiel; specifically, Ezekiel's presentation of the majesty and divinity of Yahweh.²⁹

---

26. The recent work of Mihalios (see *The Danielic Eschatological Hour in the Johannine Literature*) is one example of a study that looks at the Old Testament allusions that may have influenced John. Here Mihalios looks at the influence of Daniel on John from the perspective of the "eschatological hour."
27. For example, Carson, "John and the Johannine Epistles," 253, notes that a specific allusion to Ezek. 36:25-27 may be the background for John 3.
28. I am not suggesting that John did not use other Old Testament works; they are numerous in the Gospel. What I am arguing is that the dominant structural parallels and motifs on the macro level point to John's use of the book of Ezekiel. Cf. Beutler, "The Use of 'Scripture'," 147–62.
29. Throughout this book I use Yahweh—the covenantal name of God in the Hebrew Bible—as opposed to the more generic term "God" in order to draw attention to Ezekiel's similar covenantal use and John's desire to show Jesus as parallel to Yahweh when he inaugurates the new covenant of peace. It is true that Ezekiel uses other terms for God, but the predominant term used throughout his prophetic text is Yahweh, which appears approximately 418 times, compared to the paltry thirty-five appearances of Elohim ("God"). Even the use of Adonai ("Lord") only appears ninety times but of those, eighty-seven are used as a compound name with Yahweh.

A clear example of this is John's use of extended discourse and dialogic material as opposed to pithy sayings and shorter pericopae, as is the approach of the authors of the Synoptics. This literary feature of John is more reflective of the oracles of the Old Testament prophets (see John 3; 4; 6; 8; 10; 13–17 etc.).[30] Interestingly, even within the larger prophetic corpus, the extended oracles and metaphors in Ezekiel set his message apart as unique among the classical prophets.[31] Therefore, this literary approach used by the prophets, Ezekiel in particular, could easily have been adopted by John in order to relate the life of Jesus to a first-century audience. This "Old-Testament" style fits well within the larger message of John as he attempts to connect the life and ministry of Jesus with the God of the Hebrew Bible—the God that believing Jews should have recognized in Jesus (cf. John 5:37; 14:9; 15:24).

What is more, Ezekiel, like many of the classical writing prophets, ministered directly to the people. However, Ezekiel's ministry stands out as even more noteworthy in that he ministered to the exiles/outcasts in a *foreign* land. Of course one could immediately make any number of connections between Jesus being a "Foreigner" on the earth and Ezekiel's being a foreigner in Babylon. While this may be legitimate, it is not the connection I want to make. John's Jesus speaks directly to the most unlikely of people; people such as Nicodemus (John 3), the woman at the well, Samaritans, and foreign(?) officials (John 4). In this regard, Craig R. Koester makes a forceful linguistic argument that Nicodemus and the woman at the well are actually

---

30. See Maarten J. J. Menken, "Observations on the Significance of the Old Testament in the Fourth Gospel," in *Theology and Christology in the Fourth Gospel: Essays by the Members of the SNTS Johannine Writing Seminar*, ed. Gilbert van Belle, Jan G. Van Der Watt, and Petrus J. Maritz, BETL 184 (Leuven: Leuven University Press, 2005), 155–76. See 155n1, for an extensive bibliography on the Old Testament use in John.

31. See also Brian Neil Peterson, *Ezekiel in Context: Ezekiel's Message Understood in Its Historical Setting of Covenant Curses and Ancient Near Eastern Mythological Motifs*, PTMS 182 (Eugene, OR: Pickwick Publications, 2012), 173–225.

characterized not only as individuals, but also as representations of their communities/people groups. Thus, Nicodemus represents the religious elite and the woman at the well the Samaritans.[32] This of course could be expanded to the royal official (4:48) as being representative of foreign/political groups.[33] Now, whereas Ezekiel ministered to his own people in exile, the greater connection to be made is that Yahweh came and ministered to his people in a foreign land. Yahweh was not bound by borders—a revolutionary perspective in Ezekiel's era and earlier (cf. 1 Kgs. 20:23, 28). Similarly, even though Jesus, God's divine Son, came to minister to his own people (John 1) in the Fourth Gospel, Jesus was able to go beyond these ethnic and geographical boundaries and minister to those on the "outside."[34]

When Jesus does try to minister to those of his region and the elite in the Fourth Gospel, he is rejected.[35] Jesus even went so far as to acknowledge that a prophet is not without honor save in his home country (John 4:44). Similarly, Ezekiel ministered in Babylon to an equally hard-hearted people in the religious elite/elders (Ezek. 3:8; 20:3, 31; 33:32), and, when they would not listen, he took his message to the common folk through sign acts in particular (e.g., Ezek. 4; 5; 12; 24), a picture strikingly similar to the use of signs (σημεῖα *sēmeia*) in John! Sadly, even then neither Ezekiel's nor Jesus' audiences would listen (cf. Ezek. 33:32; John 12:37).

---

32. Craig R. Koester, "Theological Complexity and the Characterization of Nicodemus in John's Gospel," in *Characters and Characterization in the Gospel of John*, ed. Christopher W. Skinner, LNTS 461 (London: T & T Clark, 2013), 169–72, esp. 169.
33. Ibid., 169n13. Here Koester adds Nathaniel (John 1:50-51) to this list.
34. Dorothy A. Lee, "Martha and Mary: Levels of Characterization in Luke and John," in *Characters and Characterization in the Gospel of John*, ed. Christopher W. Skinner, LNTS 461 (London: T & T Clark, 2013), 197–220 (207), labels the Samaritan woman as "representing outsiders who respond positively and unexpectedly. . . ." She goes on to include Nicodemus as representative of a group who are "ambivalent" in response to Jesus.
35. Unless otherwise noted, when I speak of the "Gospel" I am referring to the Gospel of John.

Thus, it is my contention that when one begins to do a close analysis of the Gospel of John vis-à-vis the book of Ezekiel, both at the macro level, and at particular junctures, at the micro level, some interesting rhetorical and structural parallels become apparent.[36] The reason John's writing style and ordering of his material is so unique in light of the Synoptics has more to do with his emulation of Ezekiel than some literary agenda by which John sought to be different from his colleagues or the status quo of the first century. Again, it must be stressed that John used the entire corpus of the Hebrew Bible to prove his point that Jesus in fact fulfilled many of the covenantal roles assigned to Yahweh, but most specifically in the book of Ezekiel. Again as Barrett notes, "For him the O.T. was itself a comprehensive unity, not a mere quarry from which isolated fragments of useful material might be hewn. It was not (in general) his method to bolster up the several items of Christian doctrine and history with supports drawn from this or that part of the O.T.; instead the whole body of the O.T. formed a background, or framework, upon which the new revelation rested."[37] Barrett's assertions are correct although I would narrow his understanding of what constituted a guiding "framework" for John's work. It seems apparent that John's message and literary ordering had a guiding structural pattern replete with themes and motifs. This is where I believe the book of Ezekiel comes to the fore.[38]

---

36. Hamid-Khani, *Revelation and Concealment*, 139, rightly notes that John's use of the Old Testament goes beyond ideas to include influencing his "literary style."
37. Barrett, "Old Testament in the Fourth Gospel," 168. For a treatment of many of these Old Testament allusions, see ibid., 162–68.
38. Elizabeth W. Mburu, *Qumran and the Origins of Johannine Language and Symbolism*, JCTCRS (London: T & T Clark, 2010), vii–vii, suggests that the Qumran Community Rule may be the backdrop for the "truth terminology" in John. See also the suggested Essene influence by James H. Charlesworth, "The Dead Sea Scrolls and the Gospel according to John," in *Exploring the Gospel of John: In Honor of D. Moody Smith*, ed. R. Alan Culpepper and C. Clifton Black (Louisville: Westminster John Knox, 1996), esp. 81–87.

The Structure of Ezekiel Juxtaposed with the Fourth Gospel

A number of structural patterns have been proposed for the book of Ezekiel. Three of the most common are:

1. A chronological structure based upon the specific dating sequences throughout the book,[39] which include: Ezek. 1:1, 2; 3:16; 8:1; 20:1; 24:1; 26:1; 29:1, 17; 30:20; 31:1; 32:1, 17; 33:21; 40:1a, 1b.

2. A structure based upon the literary content (i.e., the changes in basic themes and content),[40] outlined as follows:

   i. Chapters 1–11: The call of the prophet and the plight of the people of Jerusalem in light of their sin and rebellion;
   ii. Chapters 12–24: Oracles against Judah for covenant violations;
   iii. Chapters 25–32: Oracles against the nations;
   iv. Chapters 33–39: Oracles of hope for both Israel and Judah;
   v. Chapters 40–48: Ezekiel's vision of the new temple.[41]

---

39. For example, K. Freedy and D. B. Redford, "The Dates in Ezekiel in Relation to Biblical, Babylonian and Egyptian Sources," *JAOS* 90 (1970): 462–85; and J. E. Miller, "The Thirtieth Year of Ezekiel 1:1," *RB* 99 (1992): 499–503.
40. For example, Daniel Block, *The Book of Ezekiel: Chapters 1–24*, NICOT (Grand Rapids: Eerdmans, 1998), 23.
41. This perspective has also been argued from a three-part structure: i. Chapters 1–24: Judgment on the house of Israel; ii. Chapters 25–32: Oracles against the nations; iii. Chapters 33–48: Restoration for the house of Israel. For example, see Ellen S. Davis, *Swallowing the Scroll*, BLS 21 (Sheffield: Sheffield Academic, 1989), 11; and S. R. Driver, *Introduction to the Literature of the Old Testament* (New York: Scribner, 1910), 279. On the other hand, some scholars such as Ronald E. Clements, "The Ezekiel Tradition: Prophecy in a Time of Crisis," in *Israel's Prophetic Tradition: Essays in Honour of Peter Ackroyd*, ed. Richard Coggins, Anthony Phillips, and Michael Knibb (Cambridge: Cambridge University Press, 1984), 127; and Brevard Childs, *Introduction to the Old Testament as Scripture* (Philadelphia: Fortress Press, 1979), 365, divide Ezekiel into four sections (e.g., chs. 1–24; 25–32; 33–39; 40–48). There are also those who use a five-fold division (e.g., chs. 1–3; 4–24; 25–32; 33–39; 40–48); cf. Charles R. Biggs, *The Book of Ezekiel* (London: Epworth, 1996), xiv.

3. A structure based upon the visionary sequences, which divide the book in two parts (see chart below),[42] outlined thus:

I. Chapters 1–24—Impending Judgment;

    A. The inaugural chariot-throne vision of Yahweh's glory: Chapters 1–3;
    B. The first temple vision followed by the departure of Yahweh's glory: Chapters 8–11;

II. Chapters 25–48—Restoration and Hope;

    A. The vision of the valley of dry bones: Ezek. 37:1-14;
    B. The second temple vision, the return of Yahweh's glory, and the renewal of the land of Israel: Chapters 40–48.

---

42. Walther Zimmerli, *The Fiery Throne: The Prophets and Old Testament Theology*, FCBS, ed. K. C. Hansen (Minneapolis: Fortress Press, 2003), 59, offers a variation of this structure.

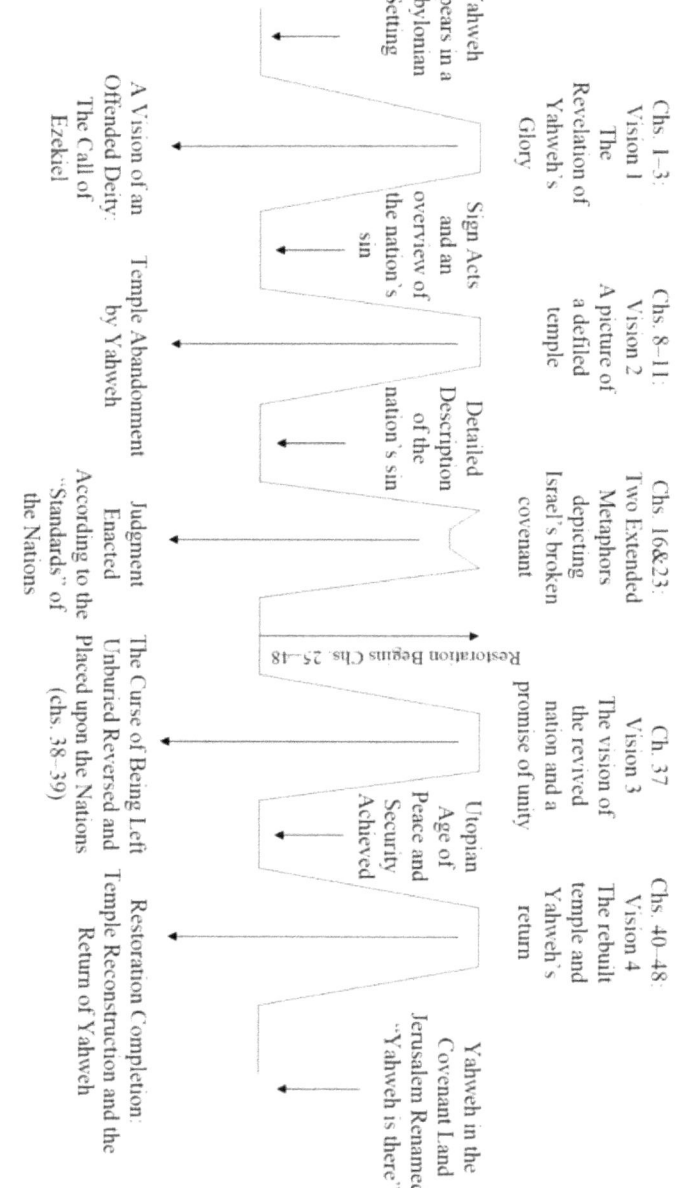

Of all of these suggestions, the structure that best fits Ezekiel's rhetorical agenda appears to be based upon the third presentation: four strategically placed visions with two in the section containing oracles of doom and two in the section containing oracles of hope.[43] In the chart, I have labeled these "peaks" and will at points refer to these visions as such.[44]

It is my contention that John was very much aware of the importance of these visions and has fashioned his Gospel structurally around the theological message connected to the visions of Ezekiel. Thus, Ezekiel's first two visionary sequences are connected to Jesus' period of public ministry (John 1–12) whereas Ezekiel's second two visions

---

43. I have argued this elsewhere. See Peterson, *Ezekiel in Context*, 88–91.
44. I do not handle the third "peak" (i.e., the extended metaphors of Ezek. 16 and 23) in my discussion, although the oft-debated pericope of the woman taken in adultery (John 7:53—8:11) fits nicely with the theme of the metaphors of Ezek. 16 and 23. Is it possible that a later scribe made a similar connection and added it to the text to connect it to these metaphors in Ezekiel? This is no more farfetched than those who propose a later editor included the pericope to balance out the supposed teaching on the Decalogue in John 7–10—that is the theme of adultery was missing. On this latter theory, see Brooke, "Christ and the Law in John 7–10," 107. For a discussion on the pericope of John 7:53—8:11, see Peter M. Phillips, "The Adulterous Woman: Nameless, Partnerless, Defenseless," in *Character Studies in the Fourth Gospel: Narrative Approaches to Seventy Figures in John*, ed. Steven A. Hunt, D. Francois Tolmie, and Ruben Zimmermann, WUNT 314 (Tübingen: Mohr Siebeck, 2013), 407–20; and J. Martin C. Scott, "On the Trail of a Good Story: John 7.53—8.11 in the Gospel Tradition," in *Ciphers in the Sand: Interpretations of the Woman Taken in Adultery (John 7.53—8.11)*, ed. Larry J. Kreitzer and Deborah W. Rooke (Sheffield: Sheffield Academic, 2000), 53–82. See especially Scott (72–80) for a series of theories as to why the text may have been excluded and then later included in John. For a discussion on the Johannine/non-Johannine legitimacy of the text, see Bart D. Ehrman, "Jesus and the Adulteress," *NTS* 34, no. 1 (1988): 24–44; John Paul Heil, "The Story of Jesus and the Adulteress (John 7,53—8,11) Reconsidered," *Bib* 72, no. 2 (1991): 182–91; and the refutation of that article by Daniel Wallace, "Reconsidering 'The Story of Jesus and the Adulteress Reconsidered'," *NTS* 39, no. 2 (1993): 290–96. For Heil's response to Wallace, see John Paul Heil, "A Rejoinder to 'Reconsidering The Story of Jesus and the Adulteress Reconsidered' (John 7:53—8:11)," *EgT* 25, no. 3 (1994): 361–66. See also Chris Keith, *The Pericope Adulterae, the Gospel of John, and the Literacy of Jesus* (Leiden: Brill, 2009), esp. 119–40, for an argument in favor of the location of the pericope in its present position based on the earliest manuscript evidence in Codex D Bezae c. 400 C.E. Keith (256) concludes that the pericope may have entered the Johannine tradition/text c. the mid-second century or as late as the early- to mid-fourth century; however he opts for the third century as a "cautious estimate."

are addressed in the last portions of John known as the Farewell Discourses and the post-resurrection scene (John 13–21).

Beyond these visionary sequences John also utilized the concept of Ezekiel's sign acts and his rhetorical use of coming to the knowledge of Yahweh.[45] The former finds striking parallels with the signs of Jesus that John used to vindicate Jesus' message and divinity. The latter, closely linked to the first, is the use of Jesus' signs and "I Am" Sayings to bring about belief/knowledge of who Jesus was (John 20:31). In Ezekiel, the phrase "then you/they will know that I am Yahweh" appears no less than sixty-three times,[46] and is closely linked to the covenant (see more in chapter 5 below).[47] These motifs along with a number of other parallels inform our understanding of the Fourth Gospel and will hopefully help us understand why John is so different from the Synoptics.

Therefore, in this work I will examine several of the unique features of the Gospel of John in light of Ezekiel's work. These include: 1) the Johannine Prologue of chapter 1; 2) John's use of signs to vindicate Jesus' divinity (John 2–12); 3) the early temple cleansing; 4) the "I Am" Sayings of Jesus; 5) the prayer of unity (John 17); 6) the insufflation of chapter 20, which effected the new covenant of "peace"; and 7) Jesus' return to Jerusalem as a triumphant king. By looking at these literary features with a view to Ezekiel's prophecy, several interesting connections will emerge. Finally, I must stress

---

45. As will be demonstrated in chapter 5, Ezekiel uses the "recognition formula" (i.e., "then they/you will know that I am Yahweh") more than any other author in the Hebrew Bible. One of the key rhetorical features of Ezekiel is his desire that the exiles would come to a knowledge of Yahweh as their covenant God. Indeed, John appears to have a similar rhetorical agenda for Jesus when he uses the signs to highlight the work of Jesus.
46. There are several variations of this form in Ezekiel. For example, "To make myself known to them" (20:5, 19); "I am the Lord your God" (20:7, 19); they will "know the Lord has spoken" (5:13; 17:21; 37:14); they will "know the Lord does the smiting" (7:9; 21:2; 22:22); they will "know I have not done this in vain" (14:23); they will "know the Lord is with them" (34:30); they will know "the Lord has heard" (35:12); and the nations will know "that the Lord has rebuilt the ruined places" (36:36).
47. See also Peterson, *Ezekiel in Context*, 257–60.

from the outset that I am not trying to explain every unique feature of the Gospel, but rather only some of the more pronounced ones. Even though John may have used key motifs and structural patterns from Ezekiel, he still had his own message to present. Moreover, to restrict John only to Ezekielian parallels would be to remove his literary license to present his message.

Authorial Presuppositions

Before I begin my discussion on the parallels between the Gospel of John and the book of Ezekiel, it seems only appropriate to state from the outset a few of my presuppositions regarding proposed audience, authorship, and date.[48]

To begin, the exact audience of the Gospel continues to be an area of debate.[49] Suffice it to say that if the parallels that I am suggesting here obtain, then the most likely audience would be Jewish—whether Diaspora, proselytes, or other need not matter.[50] While one cannot exclude with certainty a non-Jewish Christian audience,[51] a Jewish audience would have been more apt to recognize the structural and thematic connections to Ezekiel not to mention the key motifs.[52]

---

48. For an excellent discussion on the setting for the Fourth Gospel, see Andreas J. Köstenberger, "The Destruction of the Second Temple and the Composition of the Fourth Gospel," in *Challenging Perspectives on the Gospel of John*, ed. John Lierman, WUNT 2.219 (Tübingen: Mohr Siebeck, 2006), 69–108.
49. For a brief discussion, see Paul S. Minear, "The Audience of the Fourth Evangelist," in *Interpreting the Gospels*, ed. James Luther Mays (Philadelphia: Fortress Press, 1981), 247–64.
50. Andreas J. Köstenberger, *Studies on John and Gender: A Decade of Scholarship*, SBLit 38 (New York: Peter Lang, 2001), 115n41, draws the same conclusion. So too Craig A. Evans, *Word and Glory: On the Exegetical and Theological Background of John's Prologue*, JSNTSup 89 (Sheffield: JSOT, 1993), 172. The audience may be Jewish believers who needed their faith deepened. On this see Eric Plumer, "The Absence of Exorcisms in the Fourth Gospel," *Bib* 78, no. 3 (1997): 350–68 (354).
51. Richard Bauckham, "John for Readers of Mark," in *The Gospels for All Christians: Rethinking the Gospel Audiences*, ed. Richard Bauckham (Grand Rapids: Eerdmans, 1998), 148, notes that John was written to circulate to the churches in general.
52. For examples of the types of debates related to audience, see David Wenham, "The Enigma of the Fourth Gospel: Another Look," in *Understanding, Studying and Reading: New Testament Essays in Honour of John Ashton*, ed. Christopher Rowland and Crispin H. T. Fletcher-Louis,

Thus, I will move forward under the assumption that the audience is most likely a Jewish audience well versed in the Hebrew Bible.

Second, while a number of possibilities for the authorship of John have been given (e.g., John the Elder,[53] Lazarus,[54] the owner of the upper room, an unnamed Judean disciple not of the twelve,[55] John's "pupils,"[56] all believers,[57] John himself etc.),[58] the conclusions of B. F. Westcott and others that John the apostle was the author seems still to hold validity,[59] even though this authorial conclusion does not detract from my working thesis. However, once again, it is important to realize that whoever it was that authored the Fourth Gospel that person was steeped in Hebrew Bible traditions and specifically the book of Ezekiel. It is also noteworthy that the "John" who authored

---

JSNTSup 153 (Sheffield: Sheffield Academic, 1998), 102–28. Wenham (127) concludes that the Gospel was written to settle arguments between followers of John the Baptist and followers of Jesus as to who was the greatest thus explaining why the Gospel is so heavily Christological.

53. Richard Bauckham, *The Testimony of the Beloved Disciple* (Grand Rapids: Baker, 2008), 73–91.
54. Note the commentary by Kenneth K. Maahs, *The John You Never Knew*, 141–42.
55. Oscar Cullmann, *The Johannine Circle* (London: SCM, 1975), 84. For a detailed discussion on the different options for authorship, see ibid., 63–85.
56. Hengel, "Old Testament in the Fourth Gospel," 23.
57. Sandra M. Schneiders, *Written That You May Believe* (New York: Crossroad, 1999), 228.
58. For an excellent overview of authorship theories, see Blomberg, *The Historical Reliability of John's Gospel*, 22–41; Rudolf Schnackenburg, *The Gospel according to St. John Vol. I: Introduction and Commentary on Chapters 1–4*, HTCNT, trans. Kevin Smyth (New York: Herder and Herder, 1968), 75–104; and Craig S. Keener, *The Gospel of John: A Commentary*, 2 vols (Peabody, MA: Hendrickson, 2003; repr., Grand Rapids: Baker, 2012), 1:81–139. See also Barnabas Lindars, "Traditions behind the Fourth Gospel," in *L'Évangile de Jean, Sources, Rédaction, Théologie*, ed. M. De Jonge (Leuven: Gembloux and Leuven University Press, 1977), 105–24. Lindars (124) concludes that the evangelist and the final editor are one and the same person. D. E. H. Whitely, "Was John Written by a Sadducee?," *ANRW* II.25.3 (Berlin/New York: de Gruyter, 1985), 2481–2505 (2482–83). Whitely suggests that John the apostle influenced a "school" through memoirs and/or oral accounts from which they formulated the final form. For a detailed discussion on the theory of a "Johannine school," see R. Alan Culpepper, *The Johannine School*, SBLDS 26 (Missoula, MT: Scholars Press, 1975).
59. So too the conclusion of Blomberg, *Historical Reliability of John's Gospel*, 40. See B. F. Westcott, *The Gospel according to St. John* (London: John Murray, 1892), v–xxv, esp. xxi–xxxv, for an argument in favor of John the son of Zebedee. For a brief history of the challenge to Johannine authorship since the eighteenth century, see Köstenberger, *Studies on John and Gender*, 17–47. Köstenberger concludes that there is no good reason not to accept that the apostle John is in fact the author. See a similar conclusion by Maahs, *The John You Never Knew*, 142.

the book of Revelation also relied heavily on the Hebrew Bible prophets, and specifically Ezekiel (e.g., four living creatures: Ezek. 1–3; 10//Rev. 4:6, 8, 9; 5:6, 8, 11, 14; 6:1, 6; 7:11; 14:3; 15:7; 19:4; swallowing of the scroll: Ezek. 3:1-3//Rev. 6:14; the Gog and Magog oracles: Ezek. 38–39//Rev. 20:8; river imagery: Ezek. 47:1-6//Rev. 22:1-2; the tree of life: Ezek. 47:12//Rev. 22:2). Such similarities may cause one to reconsider the possibility that the same John who authored the Gospel also authored Revelation.[60]

Finally, I will follow the general scholarly consensus on the dating of the Fourth Gospel: a period post-70 C.E. or c. 85 C.E.[61] This late date fits well with my working theory of why John may have chosen to emulate the book of Ezekiel. It is to this I now turn.

Why Did John Choose the Book of Ezekiel?

On the one hand, it is possible that John's decision to write his gospel in the literary and structural shadow of Ezekiel's prophecy may simply be attributed to preference. John may have liked the writing style and general message of Ezekiel, a priestly prophet, something that finds validity if John was related to the priestly class (John 18:15). In this vein, while John may have seen himself as somewhat of a first-century prophet delivering "oracles"/a "word" from God,[62] it might better be said that he saw a parallel between Jesus and Ezekiel

---

60. Keener, *Gospel of John*, 1:139, suggests that it is possible that the same author wrote both books.
61. Robert Fortna, "The Gospel of John and the Signs Gospel," in *What We Have Heard from the Beginning: The Past, Present, and Future of Johannine Studies*, ed. Tom Thatcher (Waco, TX: Baylor University Press, 2007), 149–58. Fortna (154) proposes a date of 85 C.E. Köstenberger, "Destruction of the Second Temple," 78–79, also places it between 80 and 90 C.E. O'Day, "Gospel of John," 9:505, suggests 75–80 C.E. These earlier dates have served to undermine the theories of those, who in an earlier era, propounded a mid-to-late second-century date. See for example Edwyn Hoskyns, *The Fourth Gospel Vol. 1* (London: Faber and Faber Limited, 1940), 105.
62. That is, if John may be connected to the prophetic aspects of Revelation (Rev. 1:3; 22:7, 10, 18, 19). Keener, *The Gospel of John*, 1:139, suggests that both books came from the same "community" and could possibly "share the same authorship."

in this regard.⁶³ Ezekiel was a prophet and a priest whose ministry was marked by signs, visions, and metaphors. At the end of that ministry few believed his message. Similarly, Jesus was the prophet and priest *par excellence*, whose ministry John highlighted by signs and metaphors (see more below).⁶⁴ At the end of Jesus' ministry, few believed his message.

On the other hand, John may have had a personal rhetorical agenda that meshed with the rhetoric and agenda of the sixth-century prophet. In this regard, there are no less than three levels of continuity between Ezekiel's and John's lives and experience: 1) historical/geo-political, 2) socio-religious, and 3) personal. To begin, John may have seen in the historical setting of Ezekiel a similar historical picture present in the first century. This is presented clearest in the two watershed moments in Israel's history experienced by both the prophet Ezekiel and John, both involving the destruction of Israel's temple and Yahweh's abode (586 B.C.E. and 70 C.E.).⁶⁵ In both cases, these authors had lived before, during, and in the aftermath of these watershed moments. Furthermore, both Ezekiel and John experienced the oppression of a foreign power (Babylon and Rome respectively), and both nation's rulers were responsible for sending each author into exile.⁶⁶ What is more, if John the Revelator is the same person who wrote the Fourth Gospel, then even the exile to a foreign land followed by the spiritual experience of seeing prophetic visions would have resonated with John.

---

63. So too Bullock, "Ezekiel: Bridge between the Testaments," 29.
64. The metaphors include Jesus as the "Light," "Bread of life," the "Good Shepherd," etc.
65. So too the conclusion of Köstenberger, "The Destruction of the Second Temple," esp. 78–82, 92–93.
66. According to tradition, John clearly left Jerusalem at some point and ended up in Ephesus. This may have been a self-imposed exile to avoid the destruction of Jerusalem. It is also possible that if the apostle John is the same person who wrote Revelation then he literally ended up in exile on Patmos. Thus both men, John and Ezekiel, experienced exile at the hands of their oppressors.

Second, the socio-religious setting is similar as well. Both periods of Israel's history reflected a time when, at least according to the literary perspective of John and Ezekiel, people paid only lip service to God. As Jeremiah noted, they were trusting in the temple (cf. Jer. 7:4; John 2:20; Mark 13:1-2; Luke 21:5-6) while their hearts were far from God (Ezek. 6:9; 8; 11:21; 14:3, 5; John 2:13-22; 8:44). In Ezekiel's era, Yahweh had "visited" Jerusalem and had brought a message of warning and ultimate destruction; yet had also offered hope for those who would listen to Yahweh's voice through the prophet (Ezek. 11:14-21; 16:42, 51-63; 17:22-24; 18:14-23; and 20:39-44). In the Gospel of John, Jesus' message is shown to have echoed the same sentiments (judgment: John 3:18; 12:47-48; and hope: John 1:7, 12; 3:16; 4:41).

Finally, on the personal level, apart from the numerous personal connections associated with our discussion above for points 1 and 2, if the traditional stance that John the apostle is the author is correct, then John, as perhaps the only surviving apostle (John 21:21-24), may have been able to commiserate with Ezekiel who also experienced the lonely life as the solitary voice for Yahweh in exile, especially after Ezekiel lost his wife (Ezek. 24:16-18).[67]

These similar circumstances, among others, may account for the close parallels between the two books. In Ezekiel's day, the prophet had warned of coming judgment because the nation, in the prophet's mind, had failed to adhere to the words and warnings of Yahweh's mouthpiece, Ezekiel. In John's day, from the view of the Gospel writer, Israel again had failed to listen to Yahweh's mouthpiece *par excellence*: Jesus. As a result of that rejection, both John and Ezekiel had lived through the destruction of the city and temple and now were living in exile.

---

67. Apart from the debate of the dating of the book, Daniel may fit into this period, but he does not fit the classical prophetic mold. He is more of a prophetic "wise man."

John's Gospel and the Book of Ezekiel as a Lawsuit

Before moving on to our actual comparisons in the chapters that follow, it needs to be noted that there is a close association between the word of the prophet as a covenant enforcer and the covenant lawsuit genre (also known as the רִיב *rîḇ* formula).[68] A number of scholars are now beginning to look at the possibility that the Fourth Gospel may in fact be formulated in ways that parallel the Old Testament prophetic lawsuit, although perhaps not with the extreme rigidity of the formula as proposed by Herbert Huffmon and Julien Harvey.[69] Recently, Cornelius Bennema has suggested that,

> The concept of witness in the Fourth Gospel has a forensic dimension in that the author narrates his story of Jesus within the framework of a cosmic trial or lawsuit. In this trial, "the Jews" prosecute Jesus for his divine claims to provide eternal life, to work on God's behalf, and to have a unique relationship with him (e.g. 5:16-18, 40; 9:16; 10:30-39; 19:7). As in any trial, it is crucial to have credible witnesses and to sustain their testimony lest the case be lost. In this context, Jesus calls up various witnesses, including John (5:31-38). The Fourth Gospel gives special

---

68. Anthony Ernest Harvey, *Jesus on Trial: A Study in the Fourth Gospel* (London: SPCK, 1976), 96–100, notes the legal nuances of many of Jesus' activities.
69. See for example, Ernst Würthwein, "Der Ursprung der prophetischen Gerichtsrede," *ZAW* 49, no. 1 (1952): 1–16; George E. Mendenhall, "Covenant Form in Israelite Tradition," *BA* 17, no. 3 (1954): 50–76; idem, *Law and Covenant in Israel and the Ancient Near East* (Pittsburgh, PA: Biblical Colloquium, 1955); Herbert B. Huffmon, "The Covenant Lawsuit in the Prophets," *JBL* 78, no. 4 (1959): 285–95; Julien Harvey, "Le RÎB-Pattern: Réquisitoire Prophétique sur la Rupture de l'alliance," *Bib* 43, no. 2 (1962): 172–96; idem, *Le Plaidoyer Prophétique contra Israël Après la Rupture de l'alliance*, Studia 22 (Montreal: Les Éditions Bellarmin, 1967); Hans Jochen Boecker, *Redeformen des Rechtslebens im Alten Testament*, 2 erweiterte Auflage (Neukirchen-Vluyn: Verlag des Erziehungsvereins, 1970); James Limburg, "The Root רִיב and the Prophetic Lawsuit Speeches," *JBL* 88, no. 3 (1969): 291–304; G. Ernest Wright, "The Lawsuit of God: A Form-Critical Study of Deuteronomy 32," in *Israel's Prophetic Heritage: Essays in Honor of James Muilenburg*, ed. Bernhard Anderson and Walter Harrelson (New York: Harper, 1962), 26–67, esp. 34–36, 41–49; M. O'Rourke Boyle, "The Covenant Lawsuit of the Prophet Amos: III 1–IV 13," *VT* 21, no. 3 (1971): 338–62; Claus Westermann, *Basic Forms of Prophetic Speech*, trans. Hugh Clayton White (Philadelphia: Westminster Press, 1967), 199–200; and B. Gemser, "The rîḇ–or Controversy–Pattern in Hebrew Mentality," in *Wisdom in Israel and in the Ancient Near East: Presented to H. H. Rowley*, ed. M. Noth and D. Winston Thomas, VTSup 3 (Leiden: Brill, 1955), 120–37.

attention to eyewitnesses—those who have seen and heard Jesus and can give a first-hand testimony. John is one such eyewitness but there are others: the Samaritan woman testifies to her kinfolk (4:28-29); the man born blind testifies before the hostile Jewish authorities (9:13-17, 24-34); Mary Magdalene, the first eyewitness to Jesus' resurrection, testifies to the disciples (20:11-18); the disciples are appointed to testify before the hostile world because they have been eyewitnesses from the beginning (15:18-27); finally, the Fourth Gospel is commended to the reader as a trustworthy account of Jesus' life since it is based on the eyewitness testimony of the beloved disciple (19:35; 21:24). It is important that a witness testifies about Jesus and does not remain silent. The Fourth Gospel mentions the "fear of the Jews" as a major factor that prevents people from testifying (7:13; 9:22; 12:42; 19:38; 20:19).[70]

The parallels of the court setting in John with the larger rhetorical purposes of Ezekiel are striking. While the book of Ezekiel does not have the rigid prophetic lawsuit formula such as Isa. 1:2-20; 3:13-15; Jer. 2:2-37; Micah 6:1-8; and Amos 3:1—4:13 (cf. also Deut. 32:1-25, Ps. 50), the prophet does, nonetheless, serve as a covenant enforcer who calls Judah to task for their covenant violations. Thus, Ezekiel is called as a witness of sorts against the rebellious exiles (Ezek. 2:3-7; 3) in their rejection and breaking of the covenant. Ezekiel's sign acts serve as vindication of his message and as a witness against the wayward people in the same way Jesus' signs serve to vindicate him in the face of unbelief in the Gospel of John. Moreover, the witnesses noted by Bennema above, serve in concert with the signs as a testimony of who Jesus is. While Ezekiel records no other testimonies per se as a witness to Yahweh's works, the prophet himself uses the god-demanded sign acts in tandem with the prophetic declaration to testify to the truthfulness of Yahweh's

---

70. Cornelius Bennema, "The Character of John in the Fourth Gospel," *JETS* 52, no. 2 (2009): 271–84 (272). See further Anthony Ernest Harvey, *Jesus on Trial*; Andrew T. Lincoln, *Truth on Trial: The Lawsuit Motif in the Fourth Gospel* (Peabody, MA: Hendrickson, 2000), esp. 36–56; and Allison A. Trites, *The New Testament Concept of Witness*, SNTSMS 31 (Cambridge: Cambridge University Press, 1977), 78–127. These last three are noted by Bennema, 272n5.

coming judgment. In both books the verbal and visual witnesses serve to vindicate the messenger (i.e., Ezekiel and Jesus), and convict the people of unbelief and the breaking of the covenant. It is possible that John picked up on these lawsuit cues in Ezekiel and the other prophets and adopted them for a first-century audience. Indeed, John was not the only New Testament author to adopt lawsuit language from the Hebrew Bible in order to convict a Messiah-rejecting audience. Luke's presentation of Stephen's defense in Acts 7 in effect is fashioned after an extended and modified lawsuit format.[71]

Into this setting of the lawsuit, a harmonious chord is struck between the judgment for the people's rejection of the message of Ezekiel, and later, Jesus. The theme of judgment is the hallmark of Ezek. 1–3 and 8–11. Indeed, Ezekiel depicts Yahweh himself as the presiding judge over the destruction of Jerusalem (Ezek. 11:23; 21:19-23). This motif finds affinity in John. As a matter of fact, John spends more time focusing on Jesus' judgment on the world than any other gospel (John 3:19; 5:22, 24, 27, 29, 30; 7:24; 8:15-16, 26; 9:39; 12:31; 16:8, 11).[72] At the same time, John tempers the harshness of complete judgment without mercy by noting that Jesus did not come into the world to judge the world (John 3:17; 12:47). This disclaimer, however, must be understood in the context of the present age/First Coming of Jesus' ministry. It is only at a later period, that is Jesus' Second Coming, that Jesus will be the final judge of all humanity (John 12:48; cf. Rev. 6; 14:7; 16:5, 7; 18:8, 10, 20; 19:2,

---

71. Brian Neil Peterson, "Stephen's Speech as a Modified Rib Formula," *JETS* 57, no. 2 (2014): 351–69.
72. The term used throughout John is κρίσις (*krisis* "judgment"). In Ezekiel the dominant term is κρίμα (*krima* "judgment," "verdict," or "lawsuit"), which can have a legal/lawsuit nuance. In the Synoptic Gospels κρίσις (*krisis*) is used, which is the same term as used in John, but the focus in the former is on the judgment of nations (e.g., Matt. 10:15; 11:22, 24; 12:41-42; Luke 10:14; 11:31-32). For a brief discussion of the apparent conflicts between the statements of whether Jesus did not come to judge or vice versa (John 5:22, 27; 3:17; 12:47), cf. Teeple, "Methodology in Source Analysis," 284.

11). Again, Ezekiel, the "son of man," also plays the role of judge for his community (Ezek. 20:4; 22:2; 23:36) as does Jesus, who is given the same authority according to John 5:27 because he is *the* "Son of man."[73] Interestingly on this titular phrase, Bullock notes that "[i]t may be worth mentioning that John does not use there the usual *ho huios tou anthrōpou* but *huios anthrōpou*, which is comparable to Ezekiel's *ben-'ādām*."[74] Linguistic clues and parallels such as these appear throughout the texts of Ezekiel and John. A close examination of the opening chapters of the books of both Ezekiel and John betray some of the clearest connections. It is to these opening chapters that we now turn to begin our analysis.

---

73. Bullock, "Ezekiel," 28.
74. Ibid., 28. So too Bruce Vawter, "Ezekiel and John," *CBQ* 26, no. 4 (1964): 454.

2

John 1 and Ezekiel 1–3 Juxtaposed

> The Prologue is the most influential christological text in the New Testament. It leads us into Johannine Christology and cannot be separated from it. Moreover, it showed the early church the way to christological truth.[1]

Martin Hengel's assessment of the value of the Johannine Prologue cannot be overstated.[2] What John does in the opening lines of his Gospel is unlike anything the other Synoptic writers attempt to do. This introductory pericope is also "fundamental to the narrative structure of the Gospel.... The subsequent narrative 'shows' what the Prologue 'tells.'"[3] In other words, the opening pericope sets the tone for all that is to follow. The opening chapters of Ezekiel are no

---

1. Martin Hengel, "The Prologue of the Gospel of John as the Gateway to Christological Truth," in *The Gospel of John and Christian Theology*, ed. Richard Bauckham and Carl Mosser (Grand Rapids: Eerdmans, 2008), 265–94 (289).
2. The history of research on John 1, or its parts, is legion and will not be discussed here. For an annotated bibliography on this topic as of 2013, see Stanley E. Porter and Andrew K. Gabriel, *Johannine Writings and Apocalyptic* (Leiden: Brill, 2013), 171–77.
3. Sherri Brown, "John the Baptist: Witness and Embodiment of the Prologue in the Gospel of John," in *Characters and Characterization in the Gospel of John*, ed. Christopher W. Skinner, LNTS 461 (London: T & T Clark, 2013), 147–64 (148).

less important to the overall tenor of Ezekiel's prophecies.[4] Indeed, it could just as easily be said of Ezekiel that "the subsequent narrative 'shows' what the opening vision 'tells.'"

However, before we begin our discussion on the John-Ezekiel parallels, a word of caution is in order when it comes to using terms like "Prologue" and "appendix" (on the latter see more below). New evidence shows that John's "Prologue" (John 1:1-18)[5] should no longer be labeled as such.[6] Instead we should perhaps look at the text of the first chapter holistically even though the chapter may have been divided into smaller units for liturgical readings and the like at a later date (e.g., 1:1-5; 1:6-25 etc.). As such, for the discussion that follows, I will use the term "Prologue" to refer to the larger literary block of 1:1-51 as a unit. What is most important to my discussion is how John 1 compares to Ezek. 1–3.[7] Therefore, in this chapter I will juxtapose the opening chapter of John with the opening vision of Ezek. 1–3, which is the first "peak" in my proposed structure of Ezekiel (see chart in chapter 1).

---

4. Note that the same throne vision appears in three places: Ezek. 1–3; 8–11; and 40–43.
5. Entire monographs have been written on these opening eighteen verses. E.g., Craig A. Evans, *Word and Glory: On the Exegetical and Theological Background of John's Prologue*, JSNTSup 89 (Sheffield: JSOT, 1993); and Peter M. Phillips, *The Prologue of the Fourth Gospel: A Sequential Reading*, LNTS 294 (London: T & T Clark, 2006).
6. Peter J. Williams, "Not the Prologue of John," *JSNT* 33, no. 4 (2011): 375–86. For earlier attempts at formulating a structure for the putative Prologue, see for example, R. Alan Culpepper, "The Pivot of John's Prologue," *NTS* 27, no. 1 (1980): 1–31; Mary Coloe, "The Structure of the Johannine Prologue and Genesis 1," *ABR* 45 (1997): 40–55; Charles Giblin, "Two Complementary Literary Structures in John 1:1-18," *JBL* 104, no. 1 (1985): 87–103; and Jean Irigoin, "La composition rythmique du prologue de Jean (I, 1-18)," *RB* 78, no. 4 (1971): 501–14. These last four entries are noted by Brown, "John the Baptist," 149n7.
7. The prominent scholarly perspective is that good portions of John 1 were originally associated with a hymn or a sermon. On the former, see Wilson Paroschi, *Incarnation and Covenant in the Prologue to the Fourth Gospel (John 1:1-18)* (Frankfurt am Main: Peter Lang, 2006), 190, who cautions that "There is nothing in the Prologue, either in its present form or in any assumed reconstruction that necessarily requires it to be classified as a hymn, or even as a poem." For the sermon theory see, Barnabas Lindars, *John*, NTG 4, fourth ed. (Sheffield: Sheffield Academic, 1998), 35–36.

John 1 Compared to Ezekiel 1–3

> For every alleged parallel idea between John and gnosticism or Hellenism, there is a more sensible one in Judaism in its own conceptual context—the Jewish Bible. If there are shared conceptual similarities between John and Qumran, these similarities do not go any further than the same pool into which they both reached for their ideas—Israel's Scriptures.[8]

Saeed Hamid-Khani's assertion is indeed correct when it comes to looking for influences on the Fourth Gospel. And I would argue that Ezekiel seems to be a good place to start when it comes to influences on John 1. Apart from the larger motifs mentioned in the opening paragraph of this chapter, there are no less than eighteen literary, thematic, and motif parallels between John 1 and Ezekiel 1–3. While one may argue that some of these are only tangential, when placed together the evidence seems overwhelming that John has the book of Ezekiel in mind when he is fashioning his Gospel. In the remainder of this chapter I will systematically work through these parallels. Some of the parallels will need only minor comments whereas others will require extended discussion. Where needed, the Greek text will be included.

The Divinity of Jesus and Yahweh Compared

In the opening verses of chapter 1 (1:1, 15), Jesus' omnipotence, eternality, and majesty are presented in a similar fashion as Ezekiel's depiction of Yahweh in his opening vision. The opening verse reads: Ἐν ἀρχῇ ἦν ὁ λόγος καὶ ὁ λόγος ἦν πρὸς τὸν θεόν καὶ θεὸς ἦν

---

8. Saeed Hamid-Khani, *Revelation and Concealment of Christ: A Theological Inquiry into the Elusive Language of the Fourth Gospel*, WUNT 120 (Tübingen: Mohr Siebeck, 2000), 135. So too the conclusion of Marianne Meye Thompson, "'Every Picture Tells a Story': Imagery for God in the Gospel of John," in *Imagery in the Gospel of John: Terms, Forms, Themes, and Theology of Johannine Figurative Language*, ed. Jörg Frey, Jan G. van der Watt, and Ruben Zimmermann, WUNT 200 (Tübingen: Mohr Siebeck, 2006), 259–77 (269).

ὁ λόγος ("In the beginning was the Word and the Word was with God and the Word was God"). Of the sixty-six books in the Bible, only two begin with sustained exalted language for God: Ezekiel and John.[9] In both cases we see a theophanic revelation of God in a terrestrial setting. For John it is the eternal λόγος (*logos*/Word) embodied in Jesus, whereas in Ezekiel his vision of the chariot-throne reveals the כבוד (*kāḇôḏ*/glory) of Yahweh.

Ezekiel's vision gives an exalted presentation of Yahweh as divine Suzerain and Sovereign over Israel, the nations, and all of creation. Yahweh's appearance in Babylon is wrapped in theophanic and creation imagery as Yahweh is borne along by the four four-faced living beings. Many interpreters as well as rabbinic exegetes (e.g., *Exodus Rabbah* 23:13) suggest that the symbolism of the four faces of the four creatures represent the four domains of creation: the lion = the king of the beasts; the ox = the king of the domesticated animals; the eagle the king of the air; and human figure = the one with dominion over the animals (Gen. 1:28).[10] At the same time, there appears to be a double entendre at work as the four faces may also represent the four gods of the Babylonian pantheon (Nergal, Marduk, Ninib, and Nabu respectively).[11] Babylon, represented by its gods,

---

9. The book of Hebrews and 1 John comes close, but in both cases these chapters are much shorter. Also, when chapter and verse dividers are removed, Ezekiel's first vision extends to 3:14 (a total of 52 verses, similar in length to John's 51 verses; Ezekiel is roughly 1130 words in the LXX and John has 880).
10. E.g., Douglas Stuart, *Ezekiel*, TCC 18 (Dallas, TX: Word, 1989), 32; and Moshe Greenberg, "Ezekiel's Vision: Literary and Iconographic Aspects," in *History, Historiography and Interpretation*, ed. H. Tadmor and M. Weinfeld (Jerusalem: Magnes, 1983), 159–68 (164–65); Charles Walmesley, "Ezechiel's Vision Explained: Or the Explication of the Vision Exhibited to Ezechiel the Prophet, and Described in the first Chapter of His Prophecy by Sig. Pasturini," in *Religion and Philosophy* (London: J. P. Coghlan, 1778): 3–73 (26–30).
11. Isaac G. Matthews, *Ezekiel* (Philadelphia, PA: The American Baptist Publication Society, 1939), 5; and Brian Neil Peterson, *Ezekiel in Context: Ezekiel's Message Understood in its Historical Setting of Covenant Curses and Ancient Near Eastern Mythological Motifs*, PTMS 182 (Eugene, OR: Pickwick Publications, 2012), 115–24. By the time of the first century, the geo-political symbolism of the faces had lost its importance and was reworked with a more scripturally-based interpretation. This is not surprising seeing how the early church fathers interpreted these

ruled the world in Ezekiel's day (cf. Daniel 2, 7). In Ezekiel's vision, Yahweh is seen in a position over these creatures/representations of Babylon and in turn, the world. Thus, Ezekiel utilizes imagery that presents Yahweh as both sovereign over all creation and the nations of the world.

John's opening depiction of Jesus mirrors both the creation imagery of Ezek. 1 (John 1:3) and the exalted nature of Ezekiel's presentation of Yahweh. John's high Christological stance can be seen in the opening lines of John 1 whereby Jesus is presented as deity whose "beginning" pre-dates the creation event of Genesis 1.[12] What is more, Jesus is responsible for creating all things (John 1:3)! The opening words ἐν ἀρχῇ (*en archēi*/"in the beginning") parallel those in the LXX version of Gen. 1:1 and situate the reader at the very beginning of Israel's "sacred narrative history."[13] Indeed, Sharon Ringe rightly notes that the opening lines of John 1 "sets the stage for a story of the continued engagement of the divine Creator with the creation."[14] Conversely, Matthew and Luke open their gospels with the physical birth of Jesus in Bethlehem thus creating the possibility of confusion for later readers that Jesus was not fully God. John, however, removes all possibility for doubt by connecting Jesus directly to the Creator God of Genesis. As Martin Hengel notes, "So with complete consistency it is said καὶ θεὸς ἦν ὁ λόγος—the eternal Word is of one being with God . . . John 1:1

---

faces as representative of the four gospels (cf. Irenaeus, *Adversus Haereses* 3.11.8; Augustine, *De consensu evangelistarum* 1.6.9). Even Ezekiel himself reinterpreted his earlier vision in its second appearance (see Peterson, *Ezekiel in Context*, 123–24).

12. Many have noted that the language here shows the existence of Jesus before creation. See for example, Andreas J. Köstenberger, *John*, BECNT (Grand Rapids: Baker, 2004), 25. For a discussion of John's use of Genesis, see John Painter, "Earth Made Whole: John's Rereading of Genesis," in *Word, Theology, and Community in John*, ed. John Painter, R. Alan Culpepper, and Fernando F. Segovia (St. Louis: Chalice, 2002), 65–84.
13. Brown, "John the Baptist," 150.
14. Sharon H. Ringe, *Wisdom's Friends: Community and Christology in the Fourth Gospel* (Louisville: Westminster John Knox, 1999), 49.

corresponds to the key statement in the Gospel, 'I and the Father are one,' 10:30."[15]

Yet, it must be made clear from the outset, that although the parallels between Jesus and the Father are numerous, I am not suggesting that John is saying specifically that Jesus = God (Yahweh).[16] On the contrary, what John is doing is comparing the glory and works of Yahweh with Jesus (John 1:14, 18; 3:35; 4:21, 23; 5:17) thus drawing a connection between the divinity of each (John 5:18; 10:30; 14:9).[17] For, as Warren Carter rightly notes concerning John's presentation, "To honor/love/know the Son is to honor/love/know the Father. Not to honor/know/love Jesus is not to honor/know/love the Father. To hate Jesus is to hate the Father. . . ."[18]

Next, the use of λόγος (*logos*/word) in this opening verse has generated numerous debates related to John's possible utilization of Gnostic imagery and/or lady wisdom paralleled with Jesus.[19] In the latter case, some suggest that the reason John uses λόγος instead of σοφία (*sophia*/wisdom) may have to do with the negative connotations of the feminine attributes associated with σοφία, especially those proposed by Philo, namely, that the feminine was associated with that which is "transient, imperfect, physical, and

---

15. Hengel, "The Prologue of the Gospel of John," 272.
16. For more on this distinction between God the Father and Jesus, see Thompson, "'Every Picture," 262.
17. So too the conclusion of Gary T. Manning, *Echoes of a Prophet: The Use of Ezekiel in the Gospel of John and in Literature of the Second Temple Period* (London: T & T Clark, 2004), 153. On the role of God the Father in John, see Paul W. Meyer, "'The Father': The Presentation of God in the Fourth Gospel," in *Exploring the Gospel of John: In Honor of D. Moody Smith*, ed. R. Alan Culpepper and C. Clifton Black (Louisville: Westminster John Knox, 1996), 255–73; Warren Carter, *John and Empire: Initial Explorations* (New York: T & T Clark, 2008), 235–55; and Stan Harstine, "The Fourth Gospel's Characterization of God: A Rhetorical Perspective," in *Characters and Characterization in the Gospel of John*, ed. Christopher W. Skinner, LNTS 461 (London: T & T Clark, 2013), 131–46.
18. Carter, *John and Empire*, 249.
19. For a brief overview of this see Colleen M. Conway, "Gospel of John," *NIDB* 3:356–70 (366–67). However, note the warnings in relying on non-biblical sources as influencing John, by Hamid-Khani, *Revelation and Concealment of Christ*, 135.

earthly."[20] This solution is not that satisfying seeing how it is rooted heavily in Platonic, Stoic, Hellenistic, and/or allegorical thought.[21] If John wanted to connect Jesus merely to creation imagery by using the term σοφία, he certainly had biblical precedent for doing so. In Proverbs 8, σοφία is used for this very thing—creation activity (cf. also Ben Sirach and the Wisdom of Solomon).[22] Furthermore, feminine ideas and words are often used in the Old Testament to depict God's actions (Deut. 32:11-12, 18; Isa. 42:14; 49:15; 66:13; Pss. 91:4; 131:2; Hos. 11:3-4; 13:8), not to mention the fact that other Gospel writers record that Jesus likens himself to a mother hen (Matt. 23:37; Luke 13:34)! Thus, these speculative theories are simply not convincing.

It is more likely that the reason for John's use of λόγος as opposed to σοφία is directly connected to the use of λόγος in the LXX to translate the Hebrew term for "word" (דבר; *dābār*).[23] In this case, דבר not only connects Jesus to the Hebrew Bible tradition but דבר is actually masculine in gender; if gender of a given word was in fact a concern to John, which I doubt.[24] While it is true that Yahweh

---

20. Ringe, *Wisdom's Friends*, 43. Cf. Sheri D. Kling, "Wisdom Became Flesh: An Analysis of the Prologue to the Gospel of John," *CTM* 40, no. 3 (2013): 184–87. That is not to say that wisdom connections are absent from John, especially in chapter 1, but rather that the use of the logos/creation motif appears to be used more for the purpose of drawing links between Yahweh and Jesus and his deity. The logos motif also allows Jesus to become the incarnate Word of God in place of the prophets. See Elizabeth A. Johnson, *She Who Is: The Mystery of God in Feminist Theological Discourse*, tenth ed. (New York: Crossroads, 2002), 96–98, for a connection of Wisdom and Word in the Wisdom of Solomon. See also the comments by Painter, "Earth Made Whole," 75.
21. So too Phillips, *The Prologue of the Fourth Gospel*, 107–114. Phillips (107) notes that Philo uses the lexeme λόγος over fourteen hundred times. See also the cautions by Mark A. Matson, "The Contribution of the Temple Cleansing by the Fourth Gospel," SBLSP 31 (Atlanta: Scholars, 1992), 489–506 (491–92), concerning unfounded links between John and Greek thought.
22. See more on this in M. Scott, *Sophia and the Johannine Jesus*, JSNTSup 71 (Sheffield: Sheffield Academic, 1992); and Ringe, *Wisdom's Friends*, 33–37.
23. Köstenberger, *John*, 27, rightly notes the connection of λόγος to the Word of God in the Old Testament. See also similar comments by Phillips, *Prologue of the Fourth Gospel*, 114.
24. Contra Johnson, *She Who Is*, 98, and those she notes in footnote 48 (e.g., Edward Schweizer, F. Braun, and W. Knox). And contra idem, "Wisdom was made Flesh and Pitched Her Tent

creates by his דבר (Gen. 1:6, 9, 14, 20, 24, 26, 28),[25] it is also true that it is the דבר of Yahweh that comes expressly to the prophets (Ezek. 1:3; 3:16; Jer. 1:2; 11:1; Isa. 1:10; Hos. 1:1; Joel 1:1; Jonah 1:1; Micah 1:1). Interestingly, the phrase "the word[26] of the Lord came" (ויהי דבר־יהוה)[27] appears fifty times in Ezekiel; the next closest in frequency among the prophets is Jeremiah with twenty-one appearances.[28] It is therefore the book of Ezekiel that has the most directly expressed revelation of Yahweh's word to the people. In the context of John, Jesus becomes the "Prophet" *par excellence* not only delivering the words of God, but becoming the Word of God incarnate.[29] Concerning the role of Jesus as Prophet, Francis J. Moloney notes, "The narrative and discourse material throughout the Gospel claim, in various ways, that Jesus 'utters the words of God' (3:34; see 8:17-18; 12:44-45, 50; 15:15)."[30] John's use of this language becomes clear when this understanding of the use of λόγος is combined with the visionary links in the book of Ezekiel that I am advocating here.

Therefore, in this opening verse John has made connections in three ways to the book of Ezekiel: 1) by using sustained exalted language to depict Jesus; 2) by using Genesis creation imagery found also in Ezek. 1; and 3) by the use of λόγος to connect Jesus to the

---

Among Us," in *Reconstructing the Christ Symbol: Essays in Feminist Christology*, ed. Maryanne Stevens (New York: Paulist, 1993), 95–117 (105), where Johnson propounds that the switching was done by a later editor. Of course there is absolutely no textual evidence that this is so.

25. Jeannine K. Brown, "Creation's Renewal in the Gospel of John," *CBQ* 72, no. 2 (2010): 276–90 (277).
26. The LXX here is λόγος.
27. Variations of the Perfect and Imperfect verb of היה (*hāyâ*/to be) appear.
28. Ezek. 1:3; 3:16; 6:1; 7:1; 11:14; 12:1, 8, 17, 21, 26; 13:1; 14:2, 12; 15:1; 16:1; 17:1, 11; 18:1; 20:1, 45; 21:1, 8, 18; 22:1, 17, 23; 23:1; 24:1, 15, 20; 25:1; 26:1; 27:1; 28:1, 11, 20; 29:1, 17; 30:1, 20; 31:1; 32:1, 17; 33:1, 23; 34:1; 35:1; 36:1, 16; 37:15; 38:1. These do not include variations of the phrase which would increase the number.
29. Ringe, *Wisdom's Friends*, 53, rightly points up the fact that the term λόγος as a title never appears again in John. This makes perfect sense in that Jesus now becomes the living Word, and by his very life and actions, he delivers the Word of God to humanity.
30. Francis J. Moloney, *The Gospel of John Text and Context*, BIS 72 (Boston: Brill, 2005), 341.

revelation of God's plan through the prophetic/spoken and revealed word. Not surprisingly, Jesus himself notes that he is the revelation of all the Scriptures (John 5:39).[31]

Light Imagery

In John 1:4-9 and Ezek. 1:4, 13-14, 27-28, light imagery is a common motif used to portray the glory of Jesus and Yahweh respectively. Now while I will be dealing more with the concept of light in the context of the "I Am" Sayings in chapter 5 below, it is important to note that the radiant presence of Yahweh is nowhere more clearly depicted than in the vision of Ezekiel in chapters 1–3 (Ezek. 1:27-28).[32] Now that is not to say that Yahweh is never depicted in luminescent terms in other biblical books (cf. Exod. 13:21; 14:20; Pss. 27:1; 43:3; 44:3; Isa. 2:5; 9:2; 10:17; 42:6; 49:6), but rather, that the light/brightness imagery in Ezekiel's theophany does not find parallels elsewhere (cf. Ezek. 43:2).[33] Juxtaposed with this revelatory context, later in his second vision, Ezekiel sees the wicked deeds of the people being performed in the "dark" (חשך/ḥōšek; Ezek. 8:12a). The people did not comprehend Yahweh's presence or the repercussions of their sin. Nevertheless, Yahweh's efflorescent appearance will dispel the nation's notion that Yahweh does not see their deeds (Ezek. 8:12b); Yahweh will cast metaphorical light on them and bring upon them Yahweh's righteous judgment. Thus it is fitting that in John's introduction of Jesus as God he too stresses that the world, in their sin, did not comprehend the metaphorical light of Jesus (John 1:5).[34]

---

31. See also ibid., 339.
32. On the concept of light imagery associated with deity in Ezekiel and the ANE, see Peterson, *Ezekiel in Context*, 127–29.
33. The Hebrew term for "light" in this context is נגה (*nōgah*) meaning "brightness" or "radiance." The LXX uses φέγγος (*pheggos*) meaning "light."
34. Köstenberger, *John*, 30, points out that, much like in Genesis 1, light brings life.

Introductions of Ezekiel and John the Baptist

John 1 gives an introduction to the prophet (John 1:6-36), John the Baptist, which parallels the introduction of Ezekiel (Ezek. 1:3).[35] The strategic placement of John the Baptist's introduction in chapter 1 as the "witness" (μαρτυρέω/*martureō*) to the light and divinity of Jesus finds parallels with the introduction and call of Ezekiel who served as the witness and spokesperson for Yahweh (cf. John 1:7, 8, 15, 19, 32, 34; 3:27-36; 5:33-36; 10:41; Ezek. 1:3; 2:1-3:11). Like the Old Testament prophets in a given era, the author presents John the Baptist as the paradigmatic witness perhaps with the desire to draw a connection to the Old Testament prophets.[36] This resonates with Ezekiel's calling to go before the people and declare the awesome splendor and fearful judgment of Yahweh, a message that was rejected by the people (Ezek. 2:7; 3:7, 11, 27). John the Baptist falls into that same category, and suffered the same fate as many of the prophets of God (cf. Matt. 14:10; Mark 6:27; Luke 9:9).

Furthermore, the presence of John the Baptist in these opening lines is purposeful in light of the connections to Ezekiel. In Ezek. 1, the introduction of Ezekiel is overshadowed by the heavenly vision of Yahweh. In a parenthetical aside in Ezek. 1:2-3, the prophet Ezekiel is quickly introduced as a witness of Yahweh's glory (*kābôd*). After this, the vision quickly resumes with a description of the awesome splendor of Yahweh. The interweaving of the prophetic introduction with the revelation of the divine is mirrored in both books' introductory chapters. Ezekiel and John the Baptist are secondary figures in light of the divine presence, but still serve as important witnesses to this very revelation.

---

35. Charles K. Barrett, "The Old Testament in the Fourth Gospel," *JTS* 48, no. 2 (1947): 165–66, rightly notes the parallels between John the Baptist and the Old Testament prophets.
36. So too Köstenberger, *John*, 45, 64.

While the title of "prophet" is rejected by John the Baptist himself, he nonetheless served in that role and was recognized as such (Matt. 11:9-11; 14:5; 21:26; Mark 11:32; Luke 7:26; 20:6; cf. John 1:21-25). Similarly, Ezekiel never identifies himself as a prophet but he is declared to be one by Yahweh (Ezek. 2:5; 33:33) just as John the Baptist was so identified by Jesus (Matt. 11:9; Luke 7:26). Further, Yahweh's direct testimony and vindication of the prophetic calling of Ezekiel—epitomized in the phrase, "then they will know that a prophet has been among them"—serves as bookends for Ezekiel's ministry prior to the fall of Jerusalem (Ezek. 2:5; 33:33). In the Fourth Gospel, John the Baptist's ministry is vindicated by the author/people (John 1:7, 34; 10:41) as is Jesus' (John 5:33). However, once John the Baptist's work is done, Jesus steps into the role as prophet. And, similar to Ezekiel, Jesus' ministry is bookended by God's approbation (John 5:37; 8:18; 12:28).[37] It is noteworthy that Ezekiel is the only Old Testament prophet to receive a double attribution and vindication from Yahweh concerning his calling and ministry, a striking anomaly that is mirrored in Jesus' and the author's praise for John the Baptist (John 1:7; 5:33; 10:41) and God's vindication of Jesus (John 5:37; 8:18; 12:28).

Finally, both John and Ezekiel were sought out by religious leaders for a word from God (John 1:19; 3:26; Ezek. 8:1; 14:1; 20:1). Of course Jeremiah also comes to mind in his relationship with Zedekiah (Jeremiah 21). However, it is Ezekiel and John who are sought out by the religious elite/elders in order to get clarity on a present condition, John concerning his possible role as "the Prophet" and Ezekiel for spiritual direction (John 1:21; Ezek. 14:1; 20:1).

Much like the Synoptic writers, John encapsulates John the Baptist's ministry in this opening chapter; by chapter 3 of the Gospel, John the Baptist all but disappears from the scene. Into this void,

---

37. So too ibid., 33.

Jesus becomes the living Word of God who bears witness through his signs, going beyond the testimony of John the Baptist (John 4:1; 5:36). John the Baptist himself makes the statement, "He must increase but I must decrease" (John 3:30). At this point Jesus takes over the role as spokesperson for the Father (John 4:19; 6:14; 7:40; 9:17). Jesus now becomes the prophet *par excellence* superseding even John the Baptist (John 1:26-27) and drawing to a close the salvific work begun at creation and continued through the prophets (John 4:34; 5:36).[38] From John 2 and onward, Jesus begins to perform signs, a parallel with Ezekiel's sign acts (see chapter 4 below). It is clear that Jesus in fact saw himself functioning in the office of the prophet, replete with the common rejection motif so prevalent in the Old Testament prophetic texts (John 4:44). It is this rejection motif that serves as our next point of interest.

The Presence of a Rejection Motif

In both books, the motif of rejection marks the opening portions. Jesus was rejected by his own people (John 1:11) similar to the rejection of Yahweh and Ezekiel by their nation (Ezek. 2; 3). As previously noted, John 1 sets the tone for the rest of the Fourth Gospel. This is exemplified in John 1:11 by the rejection of Jesus despite his numerous signs (cf. John 4:44; Matt. 13:57; Mark 6:1-6; Luke 4:24). This motif of rejection serves as an inclusio to Jesus' public ministry (John 1:11; 12:37). He was threatened with stoning and finally crucified (John 8:59; 10:31; 19:1-30). Ezekiel's ministry was also marked with rejection (Ezek. 2–3; 33:32). The oft-repeated phrase "rebellious house" (בית מרי *bêṯ merî*) assigned to Israel—connoting rejection of the prophet's words—also serves as an

---

38. Brown, "Creation's Renewal," 277. While Brown (285) sees this as an allusion to the completion of the creation account of Genesis 1 and 2—specifically the Sabbath rest—a better understanding may be the work/promise of salvation (Gen. 3:15).

inclusio to the oracles of doom and the prophet's public ministry to the exiles.[39] After the city of Jerusalem falls in chapter 33 (chapters 25–32 consisting of oracles against the nations), Ezekiel's message switches to one of hope—a similar shift after the crucifixion of Jesus (John 20–21).

The Divine Presence Dwelling with Humanity

John's use of the phrase, καὶ ὁ λόγος σὰρξ ἐγένετο καὶ ἐσκήνωσεν ἐν ἡμῖν ("And the Word became flesh and "tabernacled" among us"; John 1:14a) draws the reader's attention to the Hebrew Bible. Indeed, Sheri Kling correctly notes that the verb used in John 1:14 σκηνόω (skēnoō/dwelled) smacks of Hebrew Bible allusions to Yahweh's dwelling in a "tent" (σκηνή skēnē) among the Israelites (cf. Exod. 33:9; 40:34; cf. Rev. 7:15; 12:12; 13:6; 21:3).[40] However, unlike the Hebrew Bible presentation of God dwelling in the midst of Israel, Jesus' dwelling among the people changes dramatically in the Fourth Gospel in that Jesus takes on flesh and blood form as opposed to a theophanic representation. Jesus not only shares in his identity with God, he becomes God's Word in flesh![41]

More importantly, the phrase "he became flesh and tabernacled among the people" recalls the statement by the prophet Ezekiel that Yahweh became a "sanctuary" (מִקְדָּשׁ *miqdāš*) in their midst in a foreign land for a short time (Ezek. 11:16).[42] This brief dwelling is balanced by the eschatological hope in Ezekiel that Yahweh will set his sanctuary in their midst forever (Ezek. 37:26 and 28; cf. Ezek.

---

39. See Peterson, *Ezekiel in Context*, 178–80.
40. Kling, "Wisdom Became Flesh," 179–87 (183). The fact that the only other place where this term is used in the New Testament is in Revelation may, once again, reflect similar authorship.
41. Gail R. O'Day, "The Gospel of John: Introduction, Commentary and Reflections," in *New Interpreter's Bible: A Commentary in Twelve Volumes*, ed. Neil Alexander (Nashville: Abingdon, 1995), 9:495.
42. So too the connection of Daniel Block, *The Book of Ezekiel: Chapters 1–24*, NICOT (Grand Rapids: Eerdmans, 1998), 349.

40–48). In the LXX, the word used in the Ezekielian passage to speak of Yahweh's "tabernacling" among the exiles for a "little while" is μικρός (*mikros*). Interestingly, of all the Gospels, it is only the Fourth Gospel that uses this same Greek term, also translated as "a little while," to describe the brevity of Jesus' earthly stay in a "foreign" land (i.e., the earth; cf. John 7:33; 12:35; 13:33; 14:19; 16:16 [2x], 17 [2x], 18, 19 [2x]). And the hope of Yahweh's eternal dwelling among his people (Ezek. 40–43) finds a fitting parallel with Jesus' promise to his followers of a future reunion (John 14:2-3; 21:23). Of course the "sanctuary" (i.e., Yahweh's dwelling place) is Jesus himself—a spiritual temple. This is further bolstered by the reality that Jesus goes on to tell the woman at the well that those who come to God must worship God in spirit and in truth (John 4:23-24), not in an earthly temple (John 4:21).[43]

The Glory of Yahweh and Jesus

In the opening chapters of each book, the heavenly glory connected to divine revelation plays a central role (cf. John 1:14b; Ezek. 1:28; 3:12, 23). What is more, Yahweh's and Jesus' revealed glory serves as a unifying motif throughout both books (John 1:14 [2x]; 2:11; 11:40; 12:41; 17:5, 22, 24; Ezek. 1:28; 3:12, 23; 10:4 [2x], 18; 11:23; 43:4, 5; 44:4).[44] Rudolf Schnackenburg rightly notes that, "the underlying concept of *doxa* [in the Fourth Gospel] draws on the Old Testament idea of God's *kabod*, in which God reveals himself in theophanies as mighty to save . . ."[45] and, I would add, to judge.[46] Similarly Ernst

---

43. So too, Barrett, The Old Testament in the Fourth Gospel," 160–61. See also Andreas J. Köstenberger, "The Destruction of the Second Temple and the Composition of the Fourth Gospel," in *Challenging Perspectives on the Gospel of John*, ed. John Lierman, WUNT 2.219 (Tübingen: Mohr Siebeck, 2006), 101–102.
44. Here in Ezekiel I have limited my search to the phrase the "glory of the Lord." This also appears in Isa. 35:2; 40:5; 58:8; 60:1. For an excellent discussion on Jesus' glory as God, see Ernst Käsemann, *The Testament of Jesus: A Study of the Gospel of John in Light of Chapter 17*, trans. Gerhard Krodel (London: SCM, 1968), 1–26.

Käsemann elevates the motif of the revealed glory of Jesus so highly in the Fourth Gospel that he sees "the earthly life of Jesus merely as a backdrop for the Son of God proceeding through the world of man and as the scene of the inbreaking of the heavenly glory."[47]

As with our first main point above (*The Divinity of Jesus and Yahweh Compared*), the theophanic imagery in Ezekiel finds close affinity with the picture in John 1. The revelation of both Yahweh and Jesus in their respective books was an in-breaking of God into the realm of humanity that appealed to the senses and changed those who came in contact with the divine. Within the very first verse of Ezekiel, the prophet caught a glimpse of Yahweh with the mind's eye through his visionary experience (i.e., through his sight). The Greek word ὁράω (*horaō*; "to see") is used in the LXX to connect the event to the senses: Ezekiel is beholding the glory (כבוד/*kābôd* in the LXX δόξα/*doxa*) of Yahweh![48] John takes this one step further by depicting both the glory (δόξα/*doxa*; John 1:14; 2:11) and the tangible presence of God. Jesus was the δόξα (i.e., the Old Testament *kābôd*) of God incarnate.

In this regard, the revelation of God's glory to mere flesh and blood, at any time, can cause a sensory overload. For example, seeing the glory of Yahweh caused Ezekiel to be dumbfounded for seven days (Ezek. 3:15; cf. Dan. 8:27). The comparison suggests that one cannot handle the topic of the revelation of Jesus'/Yahweh's glory without handling the effect it has on the senses.

---

45. Rudolf Schnackenburg, *The Gospel according to St. John Vol. II: Commentary on Chapters 5–12*, HTCNT, trans. Cecily Hastings, Francis McDonagh, David Smith and Richard Foley (London: Burns & Oates, 1980), 402. On the other hand, Nijay K. Gupta, "Gloria in Profundis: Comparing the Glory of Moses in Sirach to Jesus in the Fourth Gospel," *HBT* 36, no. 1 (2014): 60–78, posits that John had Ben Sira's exalted praise and glory of Moses in view (Sirach 45:1-5).
46. So too Peter Riga, "Signs of Glory: The Use of Semeion in John's Gospel," *Int* 17, no. 4 (1963): 402–24, esp. 419–20.
47. Käsemann, *Testament of Jesus*, 13.
48. For a brief discussion on "seeing and hearing is believing," see Robert Kysar, *John the Maverick Gospel*, rev. ed. (Louisville: Westminster John Knox, 1993), 86–90.

Dorothy Lee has written an insightful article dealing with the role of the senses and experiencing the revelation of God's/Jesus' glory in John. She comments,

> It is not surprising, therefore, that the most significant Johannine image based on the senses is that of sight, mostly found in the verbal form "to see." While there is a more mundane meaning, there is also a metaphorical sense for this verb in the Gospel—or, rather, cluster of verbs. The pronoun "we" in 1:14 (ἐθεασάμεθα, "we beheld") makes clear that we are speaking, from the start, of more than physical sight. In the Fourth Gospel, many see Jesus with physical eyes, but only believers truly see him—so much so that '[t]he believers' seeing [of] the δόξα ["glory"] of the incarnate Logos ... forms a high point of the prologue.[49]

As just noted, in the book of Ezekiel, the visionary medium also plays the dominant role in how Yahweh reveals Yahweh's glory and plans to the prophet. In this vein, the sign acts (and metaphors of Ezek. 16 and 23) also serve as a stimulating visual image of the prophet's message. Yet, the metaphorical sense of seeing, as Lee suggests for the Johannine audience, was also vital for belief in Ezekiel's day. Ezekiel's audience failed to truly see/grasp with their spiritual eyes the message of the prophet (Ezek. 12:2). Ezekiel stood alone in this regard.

On a side note, it is also noteworthy that beyond the sense of sight in experiencing the glory of God, the remaining four senses also appear in these opening chapters and throughout John as vital mediums of experiencing God. In this regard, Lee continues her analysis by pointing to the role of hearing (John 8:26, 40; 12:29; 16:13 etc.), taste (John 2:1-11; 4:10-14; 7:37-39 etc.), touch (John 10:28-29;

---

49. Dorothy Lee, "The Gospel of John and the Five Senses," *JBL* 129, no. 1 (2010): 115–27 (117). The latter portion of Lee's quotation is from Udo Schnelle, *Antidocetic Christology in the Gospel of John: An Investigation of the Place of the Fourth Gospel in the Johannine School* (Minneapolis: Fortress Press, 1992), 223. Lee notes (223n9) that "There is no single word for "see/sight" in the Greek of John's Gospel. Several synonymous verbs are used (ὁρᾶν, θεωρεῖν, θεᾶσθαι, βλέπειν, ἐμβλέπειν; also ἀναβλέπειν) with meanings that, in most cases, can be distinguished only in their specific linguistic context. Verbs associated with vision occur more than 130 times in the Fourth Gospel. The noun εἶδος also appears (5:37)."

7:30, 44; 10:39; 18:22-23; 19:3; 20:17 etc.), and smell (John 11:39; 12:3; 19:38-40). Again, one can find parallels in Ezekiel especially in the opening chapters (hearing: Ezek. 1:24, 28; 2:2; 3:12, 13, 17, 27; etc.; tasting: 3:3; 4:12; 12:18-19; 18:2; touching: 1:28; 2:2, 6; 3:12, 14, 22, 24; smell: 3:3; 4:12 [taste and smell go hand-in-hand although the smell of human or animal dung while cooking would be repugnant; cf. Ezek. 4:12, 15]). Not surprisingly, many of these sensory references find connections between the sign acts of Ezekiel and the signs of John (e.g., taste/eating; cf. Ezek. 4:12; 12:18-19//John 2:1-11; 6:1-15).

Allusions to the Hebrew Bible

John draws attention to the Law and the Prophets throughout his opening chapter thus focusing the reader's attention on the Old Testament (1:17, 21, 23, 45 note especially John 1:23//Isa. 40:3; Isa. 11:2//John 1:32-33). As noted in my opening chapter, even though John does not quote Ezekiel directly, he does, nonetheless, appear to be making allusions to the prophet's work throughout. However, John does not limit his references to one Old Testament book. On the contrary, he places quotations at key junctures to draw the reader's attention to his frame of reference. By noting the Law of Moses, the prophet Elijah, and by quoting Isaiah (John 1:17, 21, 23 respectively; cf. John 1:44) John situates his reader in his literary milieu.[50] It seems telling of this desire to connect the reader to the Jewish Scriptures when John starts his Gospel with the opening phrase of the Hebrew Bible: "In the beginning" (see above).

---

50. So too Phillips, *Prologue of the Fourth Gospel*, 147.

Jerusalem Plays a Central Role

It goes without saying that Jerusalem plays a central role in both the Old and New Testaments. Here in John 1:19, Jerusalem is connected with John the Baptist's ministry. Although Jerusalem does not appear in the book of Ezekiel until chapter 4, the basic thrust of the oracles up until chapter 24 is directed at the city and its inhabitants. In the Fourth Gospel, John emphasizes Jesus' travels to and from the city by going up to three different Passover feasts (John 2:13; 6:4; 11:55). I will return to this below.

References to Priests

In both books, the opening chapter(s) reference priests and/or priestly roles in the Jerusalem temple (Ezek. 1:1//John 1:19-27). The introduction of priests and Levites from Jerusalem coming to question John the Baptist about his spiritual role is unique to John.[51] Jerusalem appears numerous times in the New Testament, but not with this connection to priests *and* Levites. Here the interlocutors inquire as to whether John is the "Prophet" to come, no doubt in an attempt to see if the city and nation would be delivered by the Messiah (i.e., John the Baptist) from the Roman oppression. John the Baptist confirms that he is not the Messiah and refuses even to acknowledge his role as the "Elijah" figure (John 1:21). With the destruction of the temple and city in 70 C.E., the priests and Levites lost their priestly occupations, something John the Baptist intimated in his interaction with them (cf. Matt. 3:7; Luke 3:7).

The religious-historical context finds a parallel with the setting of Ezekiel's first vision in his thirtieth year.[52] This would have been the

---

51. The term "Levite" does appear in Luke 10:32; Acts 4:36.
52. On the interpretation of the thirtieth year, see Margaret S. Odell, "You Are What You Eat: Ezekiel and the Scroll," *JBL* 117, no. 2 (1998): 229–48, esp. 238–41; Terry J. Betts, *Ezekiel the*

time when Ezekiel would have begun his ministry in the temple as a priest. The judgment of Yahweh had caused many to go into exile between 604 and 597 B.C.E.—Ezekiel included—thus causing a loss of his priestly occupation. Ezekiel's prophetic message would ultimately be one that would preface the end of the occupation of priests and Levites in Jerusalem c. 586 B.C.E.

Moreover, in both eras, the religious elite sought out the prophets/Jesus for a word from God, as they did with John the Baptist (John 1:19-27). In John 3, Nicodemus comes to Jesus for spiritual insights, something paralleled in Ezekiel when the prophet is approached by the elders (Ezek. 8:1; 14:1; 20:1 cf. 7:26). In both cases, the rulers and elders of the people had failed to see the importance of true devotion to God (John 1:21; 3:4//Ezek. 20:3), or even to grasp the importance of the prophetic word (Ezek. 8–10; 14; John 3:10). In a world of spiritual darkness they could not comprehend the Light (John 1:5).

Ministry Outside of Judea/Judah

John situates the ministry of John the Baptist in Bethany, which is part of the tetrarchy of Perea outside of Judea proper (John 1:28). None of the Synoptic writers locate John the Baptist in this region specifically (cf. Matt. 3:1-17; Mark 1:3-8; Luke 3:2-20).[53] People came to John the Baptist by the Jordan to be baptized and to be ministered to (e.g., John 1:19). Three points of comparison stand out as important when compared to the opening chapters of Ezekiel: 1) as with John the Baptist, we find the prophet Ezekiel living/ministering beside a river (i.e., the river Chebar) in Babylon outside of Judah (Ezek. 1:1, 3; 3:15, 23);[54] 2) as with John the Baptist, people came to Ezekiel to inquire of Yahweh and to be ministered to (Ezek. 8:1; 14:1;

Priest: A Custodian of the Tôrâ, SBLit 74 (New York: Peter Lang, 2005), 50–53; and J. E. Miller, "The Thirtieth Year of Ezekiel 1:1," *RB* 99, no. 3 (1992): 499–503.

53. Luke only notes that he was ministering in "all the district around the Jordan" (Luke 3:3).

20:1), and in both cases the religious elite are met with the proverbial cold shoulder (Ezek. 7:26; 20:1-4); and 3) just as Jesus came to John at his place of ministry in Perea, so too Yahweh appeared before Ezekiel in his place of ministry in Babylon (Ezek. 1:4; 3:23).

Concerning this last point, whereas the ancients felt that gods were localized (e.g., 1 Kgs. 20:23-28; 2 Kgs. 5:17), in Ezekiel Yahweh makes it clear by his appearance and calling of Ezekiel in Babylon that God is not bound by borders.[55] Interestingly, this same motif is picked up in John 4 with Jesus' conversation with the woman at the well. When asked by the woman concerning the correct mountain on which to worship God, Jesus makes it clear that those who worship God must do so in spirit and in truth, for God does not dwell in Jerusalem or on Mt. Gerizim (John 4:21-24).

The Removal of Sin by God

It goes without saying that Jesus came to take away the sins if the world as noted in John 1:29. In Ezekiel, Yahweh came in visionary form to take away/purge the "sin" of Israel (Ezek. 1-3; 9-10). As such, it is safe to say that as a part of the overall motif of theophany and revelation of the divine, a key purpose of both Ezekiel and John is to show how God removes/purges sin from Israel/the world. It is only in the Fourth Gospel that this declaration is found on the lips of John the Baptist once again showing specific rhetorical intent. John's statement concerning Jesus' purpose for coming to earth could not be any closer to the purpose for Yahweh's appearance to Ezekiel in Babylon (Ezek. 1-3). Pregnant with covenant symbolism, Yahweh, the Suzerain of Israel, appears in a theophany before Ezekiel with

---

54. While it is obvious that there is a vast difference in distance between Bethany and Babylon, the important feature is that John makes a point to note that John the Baptist is ministering outside of Judea and by extension outside Jerusalem, the holy city.
55. On the concept of Israel's perspective about the land, see Block, *Ezekiel: Chapters 1–24*, 163.

the purpose of purging Yahweh's wayward vassal, Judah, of her sin.[56] This would be done by either repentance or judgment (Ezek. 11:21; 18; cf. Jer. 5:3; 15:7; 17:24-27; 18:1-10; 26:3-6; 27:17; 38:17, 23). Of course the nation chose the latter and suffered the departure of Yahweh from the temple (Ezek. 11:22-23), the destruction of the city and temple (Ezek. 33:21), and exile at the hands of the Babylonians (Ezek. 33). In the same regard, Jesus came to take away the sin of the world but his own people did not receive him (John 1:11). Even with all of his revelatory signs, the people rejected the message of the Prophet, and as a result of their sin, suffered devastating loss at the hands of the Romans in 70 C.E.

The Role of the Spirit

In the opening of both books, we see similarities in how the Spirit equips the prophet and Jesus for their respective ministries. John the Baptist had said that the one who has the Spirit descending upon them and remaining, he is the one who baptizes with the Holy Spirit (John 1:33). Of course, in the context we see the Spirit descending on Jesus (John 1:32) and Jesus being identified as the "Lamb of God" (John 1:36). In the book of Ezekiel, the prophet's call is initiated by the Spirit coming to him (after the initial shock of the vision had set in) and setting Ezekiel on his feet (Ezek. 2:2). The text begins though with Ezekiel saying that the Spirit "entered into me" (ותבא בי רוח). Hassell Bullock says it well when he notes,

> In no other OT prophetic call do we have the associations with the "spirit" as we do in Ezekiel's experience. Further, we have no other instance in the OT where the heavens are opened to permit divine revelation. If the experience of Jesus at his baptism is viewed as the inaugural experience of his prophetic work, then the precedent for the attendant circumstances can be found in the inaugural vision of

---

56. See Peterson, *Ezekiel in Context*, 103–15.

the prophet Ezekiel. While we may write off these affinities as mere coincidence, the intent of the gospels to demonstrate the prophetic function of Jesus cannot be dismissed so easily.[57]

While Bullock's comments take into account the gospels in general, on the latter point regarding Jesus' prophetic role, I could not agree more. And, as we will see, numerous other parallels are evident, especially in the Fourth Gospel.[58]

Avian Imagery

In both Ezekiel and John avian imagery is used in conjunction with the Spirit of God. What is more, this imagery is depicted as descending from heaven. In the Fourth Gospel, the Spirit of God descends from heaven as a dove (John 1:32). John the Baptist does not make a direct statement saying that he saw a dove, but rather, that the Spirit was "like" (ὡς) a dove that remained on Jesus. Similarly in Ezekiel, the prophet uses the idea of "likeness" or the comparison (ὡς in the LXX) throughout chapter 1 to describe the theophany that he is seeing (Ezek. 1:4, 5, 7, 13 [2x], 16, 22, 24, 26 [2x], 27 [2x], 28; cf. John 1:14, 32). The four living creatures are composite beings with wings like a bird descending from heaven under the administration of Yahweh. What is more, the Spirit in Ezekiel is closely associated with the avian-like living beings (Ezek. 1:20, 21; 10:17). In this vein, the Spirit's omniscience, reflected in the symbolic ubiquitous eyes of the living beings, finds affinity with the omniscience of the Spirit both in the life of Jesus and in the Church (Ezek. 1:18; 10:12; John 2:24-25; 4:29, 39; 6:64; 11:14; 13:21-26; on the role of the Spirit in the Church, cf. Acts 5:1-10; 10:19; 11:12, 28; 13:2, 4; 16:6, 7; 21:4, 11).[59] Finally, one cannot help but notice the avian imagery associated

---

57. Hassell Bullock, "Ezekiel: Bridge between the Testaments," *JETS* 25, no. 1 (1982): 23–31 (24).
58. Note also the connection to Jesus' thirtieth year (Luke 3:23//Ezek. 1:1).

with Yahweh's departure from the temple in Ezek. 10, something that finds affinity with similar ancient Near Eastern texts.[60]

The Inclusion of a Call Narrative

The calling of the apostles and Ezekiel appears in both accounts (John 1:37-51; Ezek. 2–3). While all the pericopae recording the calling of the disciples fall canonically early in the Synoptic Gospels, it is only Mark's and John's presentations where the calls appear in the very first chapter (cf. Matt. 4:18-22; Mark 1:16-20; Luke 6:13-16). However, it is only the Fourth Gospel that gives an extended presentation covering fifteen verses (John 1:37-51). This extended call narrative in the opening chapter of John matches the early call narrative in the Ezekielian narrative (Ezek. 2–3).[61] As with many of the other parallel motifs we have been examining, the Johannine call pericope appears within the clustering of motifs in chapter 1.

Closely associated with this concept of calling and witnessing is the motif of fear/intimidation, which plays a central role in both books. Both Ezekiel and those testifying of Jesus face persecution at the hands of a hard-hearted nation. In Ezekiel's call narrative he is given a mandate by God to speak and not to "fear" the "rebellious" people (in Ezek. 2:6 the verb φοβέομαι ["to fear"] is used three times). In John, the people are slow to testify of Jesus for "fear of the Jews" (John 7:13; 9:22; 12:42; 19:38; 20:19). The Synoptics do not record Jesus' followers fearing the Jews although the authorities fear the crowds (Mark 11:32; Luke 22:2). Interestingly, of all the call narratives of the

---

59. For a discussion on the symbolism behind the eyes in Ezekiel's vision, see Peterson, *Ezekiel in Context*, 130–36.
60. See ibid., 153–56, 159–69; and Donna Lee Petter, *The Book of Ezekiel and Mesopotamian City Laments*, OBO 246 (Göttingen: Vandenhoeck & Ruprecht, 2011), 18, 89.
61. Ezekiel's call comes roughly thirty verses into the book of Ezekiel (chapter 1 covers 28 of these verses).

Major Prophets, only Ezekiel is told by Yahweh not to fear those he ministers to.

Judgment from the North

Both Yahweh and Jesus are referenced as coming from a northerly direction/area (Ezek. 1:4; John 1:46). Nathaniel points out that Jesus came from Nazareth (in the north of Israel) from which "nothing good can come" (1:46). While some may see this allusion as tangential, it is interesting that Ezekiel's vision of Yahweh comes from the "north" (צפון ṣapôn; Ezek. 1:4; cf. 9:2). In the Jewish mindset, this directional motif carries negative connotations, especially for the city of Jerusalem. Destruction and judgment were the hallmark of attacks on the northern approaches to the city. Nebuchadnezzar, Pompey, and Titus all breached the city walls on the north.[62] The judgment of Yahweh also is depicted in Jeremiah as coming from the northerly direction (Jer. 1:13-15; 4:5-8, 13-22, 27-31; 6:1-8, 22-26; 8:14-17; 10:22; 25:9; 46:24).[63] It is very likely that John's inclusion of this quip by Nathaniel carried theological and prophetic import. This makes sense in light of Jesus' early judgment/cleansing of the temple (John 2:13-22; see chapter 4 below), and the prophetic foreboding of the destruction of Jerusalem in this symbolic act.

The Motif of Divine Kingship

The kingship of Yahweh/Jesus plays a key role not only in the opening chapter(s) of Ezekiel and John but also throughout the books as a whole. Because I will be dealing with this subject more in chapter

---

62. Cf. Peterson, *Ezekiel in Context*, 136–40; Samuel George Moule, *Notes on Ezekiel* (Tunbridge Wells, Great Britain: C. Baldwin, 1940), 8, and Bruce Vawter and Leslie J. Hoppe, *A New Heart: A Commentary on the Book of Ezekiel* (Grand Rapids: Eerdmans, 1991), 26.
63. See also comments by Petter, *The Book of Ezekiel*, 107.

6, I will only make a few summary statements here. First, only John makes the connection to Jesus' kingship over Israel and uses it as an inclusio for his public ministry (John 1:49; 12:13). Second, John places it in his very first chapter which in turn parallels Ezekiel's first vision where he seeks to present, through the imagery of his visionary experience, that Yahweh as the true King/Suzerain of Israel (Ezek. 1; 20:33; i.e., it is not Zedekiah).[64] Third, even though in both the Fourth Gospel and Ezekiel the people reject their heavenly King, the sovereign plan of God is not thwarted as both Yahweh and Jesus are depicted as the King of the nation regardless of the people's rejection (Ezek. 20:30; John 18:36-37; cf. Matt. 27:37; Mark 15:2; Luke 23:2).[65]

The Opened Heavens

The motif of the heavens (οὐρανός *ouranos*) being opened (ἀνοίγω *anoigō*) with the movement of angelic/heavenly beings associated with the divine figure obtains for both accounts. In John 1:51, Jesus declares to his disciples that they will see the heavens opened and angels ascending and descending on the Son of Man. The facile connection to the image depicted in Jesus' declaration is of course Jacob's night vision of the heavenly ladder (Gen. 28:12-22). However, in the context of Ezekielian motifs, one can easily draw the connection to Ezekiel where we see the heavens opened and the descending and ascending movement of heavenly beings[66] connected to Yahweh (Ezek. 1:5-23; 10:1-20).[67] This parallel is strengthened by

---

64. Peterson, *Ezekiel in Context*, 96.
65. Even though the Synoptic writers identify Jesus as the King of the Jews, it is on the lips of Pilate. Moreover, it is only John who uses the phrase "King of Israel." Also, none of the Synoptics record this attribution of "king" at the beginning of their gospels.
66. For an alternate position on the ascent-descent motif focused on the glorification of Jesus on the cross, see John W. Pryor, "The Johannine Son of Man and the Ascent-Descent Motif," *JETS* 34, no. 3 (1991): 341–51.
67. Gary T. Manning, *Echoes of a Prophet: The Use of Ezekiel in the Gospel of John and in Literature of the Second Temple Period* (London: T & T Clark, 2004), 155–60, correctly notes the numerous

linguistic connections. In 1:51, John uses the verb ἀνοίγω (*anoigō*) to denote the *opened* heavens (οὐρανός). Not surprisingly, this phrase is not used in the Genesis account but is used in Ezek. 1:1. What is more, the use of the verb ἀνοίγω with οὐρανός only appears four places in the Bible: Ezek. 1:1, John 1:51, Matt. 3:16, and Luke 3:21.[68] The Matthew and Luke texts are parallel to the Johannine text and thus do not detract from my point.[69] John may have had the Jacob account in view, but it also appears that he was completing this opening chapter of his Gospel with a connection once again back to the opening of Ezekiel's vision.[70] Where John draws a connection directly to Jesus and angelic beings, in Ezekiel, Yahweh has angelic/heavenly beings associated with him.

Also, in both pericopae it is divinity who initiates the interaction between God and humanity (John 1:6, 13//Ezek. 1:1 cf. Gen. 28:11-19).[71] However, for Ezekiel the initiation of divine-human interaction is for the purpose of judgment; in John it is for the hope of eternal life. Thus, John makes another connection to Yahweh's appearance in a foreign land found in Ezekiel with the purpose of delivering a warning with the possibility of hope if the nation listens. Further, chapter 1 of John comes full circle with a return to the heaven-centered imagery with which it started in verse 1. This is a

---

Second Temple texts that draw upon Ezek. 1. See for example, *Testament of Levi*, *1 Enoch*, and *Songs of the Sabbath Sacrifice*.
68. In Stephen's speech in Acts 7:56, the same phrase is used, but the verb is διανοίγω.
69. Luke uses an infinitival form of the verb whereas Matthew uses the same as Ezekiel (an aorist passive indicative). John rightly uses a perfect active participle in conjunction with the future middle form of ὁράω ("to see") to denote that they will see for themselves in the future that which has already begun. On the perfect translation of the verb ἀνοίγω, see Leon Morris, *The Gospel according to John*, NICNT, rev. ed. (Grand Rapids: Eerdmans, 1995), 150.
70. So too Craig S. Keener, *The Gospel of John: A Commentary*, 2 vols (Peabody, MA: Hendrickson, 2003; repr., Grand Rapids: Baker, 2012), 1:489; and Manning, *Echoes of a Prophet*, 150–55, esp. 151. In light of John 12:41, Manning also connects Isaiah 6 to John's overall theophanic thought process.
71. Cf. R. H. Lightfoot, "Unsolved New Testament Problems: The Cleansing of the Temple in St. John's Gospel," *ExpTim* 60, no. 3 (1948): 64–68 (65).

fitting conclusion as the Johannine terminology also brings us full circle with the Ezekielian references in Ezek. 1:1!

The Title: "Son of Man"

The title, "Son of Man," is used throughout John's Gospel in association with Jesus (John 1:51; 3:13, 14; 5:27; 6:27, 53, 62; 8:28; 9:35; 12:23, 34 [2x], 13:31) and ninety-three times in Ezekiel to identify the prophet.[72] Because the title "Son of Man" combines messianic and apocalyptic nuances, its use in the Fourth Gospel is most often linked to Daniel 7.[73] This is indeed a fitting connection in light of the messianic overtones in each context. Yet, one must keep in mind that many portions of Ezekiel, especially chapters 1–3, also fall into the category of apocalyptic.[74] As such, the frequency of the expression "son of man" in Ezekiel begs the question: Did John have Ezekiel in mind as well?[75] In keeping with the numerous parallel

---

72. The phrase appears twenty-six times in Luke; fourteen times in Mark, and thirty-one times in Matthew. For an extended bibliography up to 2008 on the Son of Man in John, see J. Harold Ellens, *The Son of Man in the Gospel of John*, NTM 28 (Sheffield: Sheffield Phoenix, 2010), 177–79.
73. Moloney, *The Gospel of John Text and Context*, 70. For a detailed treatment of this phrase, see idem, *The Johannine Son of Man*, BSR 14 (Rome: LAS, 1976); Frederick Dale Bruner, *The Gospel of John: A Commentary* (Grand Rapids: Eerdmans, 2012), 123; John Ashton, *Understanding the Fourth Gospel* (Oxford: Clarendon, 1991), 337–73; and Köstenberger, *John*, 85. Also see J. Coppens, "Les logia johanniques du fils de l'homme," in *L'Évangile de Jean, Sources, Rédaction, Théologie*, ed. M. De Jonge (Leuven: Gembloux and Leuven University Press, 1977), 311–15. Coppens concludes that Jesus is the antithesis of Adam in that Jesus functions as the "corporate personality" of humanity.
74. On the issue of Ezekiel as apocalyptic literature, see Peterson, *Ezekiel in Context*, 341–55. The author of Revelation had no problem adopting the imagery of Ezek. 1–3 for his apocalypse (cf. Revelation 4–7).
75. See also Peder Borgen, "Some Jewish Exegetical Traditions as the Background for the Son of Man Sayings in John's Gospel (John 3.14-44 and Context)," in *L'Évangile de Jean, Sources, Rédaction, Théologie*, ed. M. De Jonge (Leuven: Gembloux and Leuven University Press, 1977), 243–58. Ellens, *Son of Man*, 141–44, 174, rejects dependence on Ezekiel. However, he correctly notes that "Both Ezekiel and the Johannine Son of Man are called and commissioned to proclaim the impending arrival of God's reign on earth and the consequent reordering of earthly affairs" (143). Unfortunately, Ellens's criteria for dependence are too rigid. He suggests that because Ezekiel is not deity, there can be no interdependence. Due to this weakness, Ellens misses a number of other similarities that would lead one to make a stronger association. One

motifs that appear in John 1 and Ezek. 1–3 ("son of man" appears ten times in Ezek. 2–3 alone; cf. Ezek. 2:1, 3, 6, 8; 3:1, 3, 4, 10, 17, 25), the connection seems valid.[76] At the same time, the connection to Ezekiel as the prophet in a foreign land, along with the connection to humanity, is important.[77] In Ezekiel, it is only Yahweh who uses the phrase "son of man" to identify the prophet. The intent is to show the clear division between the earthly and the divine. Yahweh is otherness, and Ezekiel represents humanity and the earthly. Ezekiel's messenger role serves as the bridge between humanity and Yahweh. Of course John's use of "Son of Man" represents both the humanity of Jesus and Jesus' role as *the* messenger *par excellence* for his Father.[78] Gail O'Day states it well when she notes that the "Son of Man" designation in the Gospel "bridges the distance between heaven and earth."[79] Note, however, that it is Ezekiel who is lifted into the heavens on his visionary journeys and views angelic-like beings "bridging the distance between heaven and earth" (Ezek. 8:1-3; 37:1; 40:1), a fitting connection to John 1:51 and the ascending-descending angels (see immediately above).

of the most glaring connections is that both Jesus and Ezekiel bear the iniquity of their people (cf. Ezek. 4:4-6; John 1:29). Moreover, John could easily have used Ezekiel typologically as an archetype of Jesus without Ezekiel having to be a deity. And contra Ellens (144), Ezekiel *is* rhetorically asked to be a judge of Israel three times (cf. Ezek. 20:4; 22:2; 23:36).

76. Walter Wink, "'The Son of the Man' in the Gospel of John," in *Jesus in Johannine Tradition*, ed. Robert T. Fortna and Tom Thatcher (Louisville: Westminster John Knox, 2001), 117–23. Wink (117) makes a direct connection to Ezekiel, which he asserts, had "archetypal force" for John. He goes on to conclude that the language of Jewish mysticism in relation to Ezek. 1 is in view here (122). However, I do have a hard time accepting his connection of "Son of Man" with Yahweh. In Ezekiel, it is always spoken in reference to the prophet never Yahweh.

77. John W. Pryor, *John: Evangelist of the Covenant People: The Narrative and Themes of the Fourth Gospel* (Downers Grove, IL: InterVarsity, 1992), 14, sees these son of man references as only pointing to the exalted or heavenly connections of Jesus. However, this seems too restrictive. See also idem, "The Johannine Son of Man and the Descent-Ascent Motif," *JETS* 34, no. 3 (1991): 341–51.

78. See similar comments by Bullock, "Ezekiel," 28; and Dorothy A. Lee, "Martha and Mary: Levels of Characterization in Luke and John," in *Characters and Characterization in the Gospel of John*, ed. Christopher W. Skinner, LNTS 461 (London: T & T Clark, 2013), 197–220 (207).

79. O'Day, "The Gospel of John," 9:532. See also Gail R. O'Day and Susan E. Hylen, *John*, WBCom (Louisville: Westminster John Knox, 2006), 32–33.

Finally, Bruce Vawter summarizes well the importance of the role that Ezekiel as the "son of man" plays in influencing the Fourth Gospel:

> As respects the Johannine usage of Son of Man we may instance the following parallels . . . The Son of Man in Ezekiel is an exemplar of obedience to the divine will in the midst of a house of rebellion (2:8). He is filled with the word of God (3:1-4). He has a predilection for symbolic acts, signs, and is himself a sign for Israel (24:24). He is identified with the people of God, figuring their destiny in himself (4:4-15; 12:1-7, 17-20; 24:15-24). He is known as a speaker of parables (20:49). He is the judge of Israel (20:4ff.; 22:1ff.); moreover, he effects judgment by his words and works, a judgment which can be said to be coming and yet is here (21:12). He knows that there are those who cannot hear his word (3:27); he is spiritually stirred, distraught, he groans, his soul is troubled (3:14f.; 21:11). He stands in the presence of God whence he is sent to reveal the glory of Yahweh; the burden and refrain of his prophecy is "that they (you) may know *kî 'ănî Yhwh*; *egō eimi*." He offers mercy and forgiveness to Israel and resurrection to its dead bones through the spirit of God: *kai dōsō pneuma mou eis 'ymas kai zēsesthe* (37:14). He denounces the profanation of the temple, but looks forward to a covenant of peace when the divine dwelling *(kataskēnōsis mou)* will be among his people forever (37:26). He points to the true shepherd of the sheep of Israel. Other correspondences of this kind could be multiplied without difficulty.[80]

Concluding Observation

Before completing our study on John 1 and Ezek. 1–3, one further point needs to be made in relation to John's uniqueness vis-à-vis the Synoptics. Surprisingly, John is the only Gospel to omit the transfiguration of Jesus (Matt. 17:1-12; Mark 9:2-13; Luke 9:28-36). D. A. Carson outlines five of the most prominent scholarly explanations for this omission.[81] While these suggestions have a

---

80. Bruce Vawter, "Ezekiel and John," *CBQ* 26, no. 4 (1964): 450–58 (452–53).
81. D. A. Carson, *The Gospel according to John*, PNTC (Grand Rapids: Eerdmans, 1991), 93–95.

varying degree of plausibility, perhaps the reason for the lacuna is best explained in light of our discussion above. The reason for the absence of the transfiguration may have been due to the reality that John, following the motifs of Ezek. 1–3, had already portrayed Jesus as God here in chapter 1.[82] John does not need the transfiguration to further prove something that his audience has already been made aware of in the opening chapter.[83] From this point forward, the more important reality is that they come to recognize that Jesus is God in order that they may believe and be saved (John 20:31)!

Conclusion

The uniqueness of John's Prologue may be explained, to a large degree, by his desire to mirror motifs found in Ezekiel's inaugural vision, what I have also labeled as the first structural peak of the book of Ezekiel (see chart in chapter 1 above). We have found that the clustering of motifs in these fifty-one verses finds many thematic and linguistic parallels with Ezekiel's first three chapters. Whereas some may be more obvious than others (i.e., the λόγος/דבר parallels; the glory of Yahweh//Jesus; the introduction of a prophet; and the heavens being opened; the use of the phrase "Son of Man"), the remaining links begin to make more sense in light of these more glaring parallels and the sheer numbers. Nevertheless, if our theory is to obtain, then other structural and thematic clues between John and Ezekiel should be forthcoming as the text of the Fourth Gospel unfolds. Not surprisingly, this is exactly what we find when John records next Jesus' first sign in Cana, a parallel to Ezekiel's first signs

---

82. Keener, *The Gospel of John*, 1:489, suggests that 1:51 is analogous to the Synoptics' transfiguration.
83. Note also that the voice from heaven in John 12:28 has echoes of the transfiguration. Riga, "Signs of Glory," 414–16, suggests that the signs of Jesus reveal his glory and thus take the place of the transfiguration. While this is true, chapter 1 of John really is all that is needed to confirm Jesus' divinity.

in Ezek. 4–5. Furthermore, as we will see in chapter 4, the appearance of the temple cleansing early in the Gospel, as opposed to later, matches the second visionary "peak" of Ezekiel's structure. Thus, John appears to be following the visionary sequence of Ezekiel when he opts for the early placement of the temple-cleansing pericope. However, before we get to that discussion we must consider John's/Jesus' use of signs in light of the sign acts of Ezekiel. It is to this that we now turn.

3

John's Use of Signs and Ezekiel's Sign Acts

The special use of the Greek word σημεῖον in John is well known, but this study is intended to bring into focus several important aspects of 'signs' as a major contribution to the purpose for which the Gospel was written. It makes good sense to begin with John's own statement of purpose in xx. 30, 31. . . .[1]

Donald Guthrie's comments point up the central role that signs play in the Fourth Gospel in developing John's theological/Christological presentation. Even though John uses the term σημεῖον (*sēmeion*)[2] no less than seventeen times, John 20:31 makes it clear that particular signs were chosen from among many, which the writer, as some have hypothesized, drew from a "sign's source."[3] Craig Keener also notes

---

1. Donald Guthrie, "The Importance of Signs in the Fourth Gospel," *VE* 5 (1967): 72–83 (72).
2. John also uses the term ἔργον (*ergon*/work), which is almost exclusively spoken by Jesus (for two opposite cases, see 6:28-29 and 7:3).
3. While scholars have posited a theoretical "signs source" from which these signs were drawn, there is no reason not to believe that the signs were merely drawn from oral tradition stemming from first-hand experience or witnesses. For presentations of the sign source theory and/or its critique, see W. Nicol, *The Sēmeia in the Fourth Gospel*, NovTSup 32 (Leiden: Brill, 1972); W. D. Davies, "The Johannine 'Signs' of Jesus," in *A Companion to John: Readings in Johannine Theology (John's Gospel and Epistles)*, ed. Michael J. Taylor (New York: Alba, 1977), 91–115;

that the signs in John "point to a reality that must be interpreted."⁴ In this regard, it is clear that these signs were specifically chosen to help John's readers believe that Jesus is *the* Prophet (cf. Deut. 18:15-18) *and* the Son of God. The signs were performed in the midst of the people of Israel to effect this belief in Jesus' divinity. Interestingly, Ezekiel's sign acts were performed with a similar purpose in mind: belief in Yahweh as the sovereign God, and Ezekiel as Yahweh's prophet.⁵

The theological and pedagogical similarities between Jesus' signs and Ezekiel's sign acts are numerous. For example, the clear connection between the revelation of Jesus' glory and the signs he performed finds affinity with the revelation of Yahweh's glory and the sign acts of Ezekiel. Also, in Ezekiel's day, Ezekiel performed sign acts amongst his fellow exiles for the purpose of eliciting belief in his message and Yahweh.⁶ In many cases, due to the spiritual dullness of the people, Ezekiel had to "interpret" what the signs meant for the people (e.g., Ezek. 24:19; 37:18)—yet to no avail. According to

---

Guthrie, "Importance of Signs in the Fourth Gospel," 72–83; Marinus de Jonge, "Signs and Works in the Fourth Gospel," in *Miscellanea Neotestamentica* 2, ed. T. Baarda, A. F. J. Klijn and W. C. van Unnik, NovTSup 48 (Leiden: Brill, 1978), 107–25; Mark Kiley, "The Exegesis of God: Jesus' Signs in John 1–11," SBLSP 27 (Atlanta: GA: Scholars, 1988), 555–69 (Kiley argues that Psalm 23 and 27 are the governing factors behind John's use of the signs. Kiley [560] has to mix the motifs of Psalms 23 and 27 in order to make the parallels fit John's signs.); Peter Riga, "Signs of Glory: The Use of Semeion in John's Gospel," *Int* 17, no. 4 (1963): 402–24; Marianne Meye Thompson, "Signs and Faith in the Fourth Gospel," *BBR* 1 (1991): 89–108 esp. 89 nn1 and 2; idem, *The Humanity of Jesus in the Fourth Gospel* (Philadelphia: Fortress Press, 1988), 53–86; Gilbert Van Belle, *The Signs Source in the Fourth Gospel: Historical Survey and Critical Evaluation of the Semeia Hypothesis* (Leuven: Leuven University Press and Peeters, 1994); Robert T. Fortna, *The Gospel of Signs: A Reconstruction of the Narrative Source Underlying the Fourth Gospel*, SNTSMS 11 (Cambridge: Cambridge University Press, 1970); and Hans-Peter Heekerens, *Die Zeichen-Quelle der johanneischen Redaktion* (Stuttgart: Verlag Katholisches Bibelwerk, 1984). For a discussion on the development of the signs source theory within scholarship, see Tom Thatcher, "The Signs Gospel in Context," in *Jesus in Johannine Tradition*, ed. Robert T. Fortna and Tom Thatcher (Louisville: Westminster John Knox Press, 2001), 191–97.

4. Craig S. Keener, *The Gospel of John: A Commentary*, 2 vols (Peabody, MA: Hendrickson, 2003; repr., Grand Rapids: Baker, 2012), 1:276.
5. See similar comments by Riga, "Signs of Glory," 402–3.
6. See similar links to Ezekiel and comments by C. H. Dodd, *The Interpretation of the Fourth Gospel* (Cambridge: Cambridge University Press, 1953), 141.

the Fourth Gospel, a similar spiritual dullness was prevalent in Jesus' day, at least among the religious elite (e.g., John 5:18; 7:1, 20; 8:37; 11:53).[7]

This motif of unbelief, or should I say the attempt to overcome it, permeates both books. In ancient Israel, the prophetic word, sign acts, and miracles of the prophet were Yahweh's way of getting Israel's attention.[8] That is, the prophet was the mouthpiece of Yahweh. To reject Yahweh's prophet was to reject Yahweh (cf. 1 Sam. 8:7). Israel rejected Ezekiel's sign-act-laden message just as Israel later rejected Jesus' signs as exemplified in the remarks found in John 12:37. Not surprisingly, immediately following John 12:37, John quotes Isaiah 6:10, one of the clearest rejection passages among the Old Testament prophets. It reads: "Cause the heart of this people to be dull and their ears heavy/dull, and their eyes blind, lest they see with their eyes and hear with their ears and with their hearts they understand, and turn and be healed" (cf. Isa. 53:1). Therefore, according to the author of John when the people rejected the word/signs of Jesus, disaster, spiritual and physical, awaited them. In this regard, C. K. Barrett asserts that, with this quotation from Isaiah, "The public ministry of Jesus is at an end. Henceforth he will only speak privately with his disciples, and come forth in public to die. The story has been one of division, and the whole narrative turns upon the rejection of Israel—Israel's rejection of the truth, and God's rejection of Israel."[9] Here we see a perfect blending of prophetic pronouncement and New Testament Christology.

---

7. When I speak of the "spiritual dullness" and "unbelief" of the Jews, I am referring to how John portrays them in the Fourth Gospel. For clarification of how John depicts the Jews in his Gospel see the section "Is John Anti-Jewish" at the end of this chapter.
8. Hassell Bullock, "Ezekiel: Bridge between the Testaments," *JETS* 25, no. 1 (1982): 23–31 (25), rightly notes that in the other Gospels Jesus' preferred method of communication to the people was parables. Ezekiel was also a prophet who spoke in allegories/parables to his generation. In Ezek. 20:49, the prophet says of himself, "And I said, Alas O Lord Yahweh, they are saying of me, 'Is he not just speaking parables?'"
9. Charles K. Barrett, "The Old Testament in the Fourth Gospel," *JTS* 48, no. 2 (1947): 167.

Similarly in Ezekiel, even after the prophet had poured out his heart to the people they looked at him as nothing more than an entertainer. To this end, Yahweh says to Ezekiel, "And behold you are to them like a sensuous song; one who has a beautiful voice and who can play well on a stringed instrument; for they hear your words but none of them do them" (Ezek. 33:32). At the end of their public ministries, both Jesus and Ezekiel faced similar outcomes—only a remnant would listen. It is clear that John's quoting of prophetic texts like Isaiah, and his use of motifs like those in Ezekiel, prove that his message is thoroughly steeped in the Hebrew Bible.

In light of John's obvious reliance on the Old Testament prophets, and due to the tantalizing similarities between the use of signs and sign acts in each book, in this chapter I will analyze the possible connections between John's and Ezekiel's use of signs (σημεῖα/*sēmeia*) and sign acts (אות/'*ôt*; cf. Ezek. 4:3 and the LXX use of σημεῖα) to effect belief in Jesus and Yahweh, respectively.[10] However, before this can be undertaken we need to consider two further issues: 1) whether or not any other Old Testament passages may have influenced John's signs motif; and 2) what determined an actual sign/sign act. I will handle these topics seriatim.

What/Who Influenced John's Use of Signs?

Old Testament literary parallels to John's signs have been proposed based upon prophetic sign acts in general and/or the signs found in the Exodus event.[11] In the latter case, some try to see direct

---

10. The other dominant term used by Ezekiel is מופת (*môpēt*) which also means "sign" or "wonder."
11. See for example, Karl-Heinz Rengstorf, "σημεῖον," *TDNT* 7:191–261 (256–57), who sees Jesus as the "new Moses" (257); Raymond E. Brown, *The Gospel according to John I–XII*, AB 29 (New York: Doubleday, 1966), 527–29; Robert Houston Smith, "Exodus Typology in the Fourth Gospel," *JBL* 81, no. 4 (1962): 329–42 (Smith parallels John with Exodus 3–12); Wilson Paroschi, *Incarnation and Covenant in the Prologue to the Fourth Gospel (John 1:1–18)* (Frankfurt am Main: Peter Lang, 2006), 146–47; and Riga, "Signs of Glory," 402–403, 411.

typological connections between Jesus' signs and the signs Moses performed in Egypt (cf. Exod. 3:12; 4:8, 9, 17, 28, 30; 7:3, 9; 8:19; 10:1, 2; 11:9, 10; 12:13). A cursory reading of these connections indeed seems to betray evidence that would make for a strong case. The fact that the miraculous is involved finds harmony with what Jesus does in the Fourth Gospel and may have indeed served, in part, John's rhetorical purposes.[12] Nevertheless, there are a couple of problems with looking *only* to Moses' signs as a direct influence on John. First, the discrepancy in the number of signs creates a problem for this view (over a dozen compared to the six to eight in John).[13] Second, if John wanted to make such a strong connection to Moses, why did he not include something similar to Matthew's Sermon on the Mount (Matthew 5–7)?[14] Finally, Andreas Köstenberger has rightly noted that,

> It appears . . . that this is not where John's emphasis lies. This seems to be suggested by the fact that the phrase 'signs and wonders' which is characteristic for the types of signs performed during the exodus occurs only once in the Fourth Gospel, and there on the lips of Jesus with a strongly negative connotation (cf. 4:48). In all the other cases, the thrust of a σημεῖον reference appears to be prophetic-symbolic: the sign's

---

12. It is indeed possible, and even likely, that John had a view that Jesus was the new Moses especially in light of John's repetition of the motif of "the Prophet" referring back to Deut. 18:15-18 (cf. John 1:21, 25; 6:14; 7:40). Yet, it must be kept in mind that although Ezekiel was not "the Prophet," he was in the long line of "prophets" leading up to the revelation of Jesus. This is why several of the Old Testament prophets performed Moses-like signs (e.g., Elijah, Elisha, Isaiah). See T. F. Glasson, *Moses in the Fourth Gospel*, SBT 40 (London: SCM, 1963), 20–32.
13. So too Fortna, *Gospel of Signs*, 101. Smith, "Exodus Typology," 335, recognizes this problem but sidesteps it by suggesting that some of the plagues/signs were "expendable." He does this in order to align the plagues with the seven signs of Jesus. Some of Smith's connections (336–37) are extremely tenuous (e.g., the plague of darkness = Jesus healing the blind man in John 9:1-41).
14. The closest John gets to this is perhaps the proposed parallels to the Decalogue in John 7–10. On this see George J. Brooke, "Christ and the Law in John 7–10," in *Law and Religion: Essays on the Place of the Law in Israel and Early Christianity*, ed. Barnabas Lindars (Cambridge: James Clarke & Co., 1988), 102–12.

symbolism is developed and the prophetic component is emphasized, in the case of John's Gospel the authentication of Jesus' Messianic claims.[15]

Köstenberger is indeed correct to connect the Johannine σημεῖα to "prophet-symbolic" actions. It goes without saying that the signs performed by the Old Testament prophets were to legitimate the message and the work of God through the prophet. Sometimes these were miraculous such as raising the dead (cf. 1 Kgs. 17:22; 2 Kgs. 4:35) or healing of diseases (2 Kgs. 5); at other times they were merely symbolic acts that when performed were *expected* to bring forth legitimacy and praise directed to God (Isa. 20:1-6; Ezek. 4–5; 12; 24).[16] However, can we move beyond the broad nomenclature of "prophetic-symbolic" to identify a specific prophet?

Sign Acts in the Prophets

Some may suggest that other prophets' sign acts were the influence behind John's use of the motif rather than Ezekiel. Indeed, Isaiah's sign act of walking barefoot and naked for three years (Isa. 20:3) immediately comes to mind as a memorable action. However, frequency and specific identification of the sign acts as "signs" is important to our discussion. Few would disagree that Jesus performed *signs* in the Synoptic Gospels; however, they are not identified as such, nor do they garner special rhetorical attention as they do in John.[17] Similarly, while it is true that both Jeremiah and Ezekiel

---

15. Andreas J. Köstenberger, *Studies on John and Gender: A Decade of Scholarship*, SBLit 38 (New York: Peter Lang, 2001), 103–104. So too Rengstorf, "σημεῖον," 244–45.
16. Contra Rengstorf, "σημεῖον," 250, who tries to sever the connection between Johannine signs and the Old Testament symbolic actions based upon the failure of the Old Testament acts to generate faith in the onlooker. However, it is possible to conclude that Ezekiel's sign acts must have enlightened at least some people in the knowledge of who Yahweh was and the nature of Yahweh's power. In turn this would have generated a level of faith.
17. Riga, "Signs of Glory," 402–10, suggests that the signs of John are parallel to the parables of the Synoptics. This may be true but one still has to answer the question of why John made the switch.

have an almost equal number of sign acts (cf. Jer. 13:1-11; 18:1-12; 19:1-15; 27:1-22; 32:6-15; 35:1-19; 43:8-13; 51:59-64), it is only in Ezekiel where we actually see them identified by the terms אות (*'ôṯ*) and מופת (*môp̄ēṯ*).[18]

Furthermore, Ezekiel is the only prophet that is told by God that he and his sign acts are a "sign for the house of Israel" (cf. Ezek. 4:3; 12:6, 11; 24:24, 27). In light of our ongoing thesis there can be no doubt that one prophet—Ezekiel—stands out as performing the most specifically identified sign acts of any of the prophets, many of which find parallels with Johannine usage.[19]

Ezekiel's Sign Acts and the Fourth Gospel

Apart from the general connections to the Exodus and prophetic traditions noted above, it seems a bit too coincidental that John's six to eight signs match closely in number to the six to eight sign acts performed by Ezekiel.[20] Second, and more importantly, it is perhaps telling that both Jesus and Ezekiel used signs as a means of authenticating their message and themselves as spokesmen for God.[21] Third, the numerous other connections between John and Ezekiel prove that John was very familiar with Ezekiel's message (e.g., Ezek. 1–3//John 1; Ezekiel 34//John 10; Ezek. 15//John 15; Ezek. 37:1-14//John 20).[22] Finally, all of the undisputed signs and sign

---

18. There are of course "signs" directly related to a given oracle (e.g., Isa. 8:18; 19:20; 37:30; 38:7; 55:13; 66:19; Jer. 10:2; 32:20; 44:29) but nothing compares with the way Ezekiel uses sign acts as a means of vindicating his ministry and calling.
19. As we will see below, Jeremiah has just as many sign acts as Ezekiel, but his are not labeled as such.
20. I realize there is a major debate concerning the exact identification of the number of signs and sign acts in each book. But the general consensus is that there are approximately six to eight for each book. See more on this in the discussion below.
21. In Ezek. 33:33 Yahweh tells Ezekiel that when all of the things he has shown the people come to pass, then they will know a prophet has been in their midst.
22. Many of these will be developed below. The general scholarly consensus is that the Good Shepherd motif is drawn from Ezek. 34 and the vine imagery of Ezek. 15 influenced John 15.

acts of Jesus and Ezekiel fall within the first half of their respective books when Ezekiel and Jesus are involved in their public ministries (Ezek. 4–24 and John 2–12, respectively).[23] Ezekiel's public ministry included his direct words to the exiles (Ezek. 3:11, 15; 11:25), his sign acts, and his meetings with the elders of Israel (cf. Ezek. 8:1; 14:1; 20:1). After chapter 24, Ezekiel's book shifts from a focus on Israel to oracles of judgment against the nations.

In light of these observations and connections it does not seem farfetched to draw the conclusion that John had Ezekiel's sign acts in mind when he opted rhetorically to fashion Jesus' ministry around a series of signs to legitimate his claims of divinity. However, one also needs to discuss how to determine what a legitimate sign/sign act is in the Fourth Gospel and Ezekiel.

What Constitutes a Sign or a Sign Act?

At least seven clearly identified sign acts appear in Ezekiel, the first four of which occur in Ezek. 4–5. In the very first instance, Ezek. 4:1-3, the prophet is told by Yahweh that his divinely dictated actions are to be a "sign" (אות /*ʾôt*) for the house of Israel (Ezek. 4:3). After the appearance of the term אות in 4:3, the word that is used to identify the sign act is מופת (*môpēt*; cf. Ezek. 12:6, 11; 24:24, 27), which is a synonym for אות.[24] This explains why the LXX translates both אות and מופת with the term σημεῖον (*sēmeion*).[25] At the same time, in some cases such as Ezek. 5:1-4, neither of these two terms appear even though a sign act is clearly in view. In this case, the use

---

23. On this concept in John, see Köstenberger, *Studies on John and Gender*, 109; or Riga, "Signs of Glory," 417–18, 423.
24. So too Daniel Block, *The Book of Ezekiel: Chapters 1–24*, NICOT (Grand Rapids: Eerdmans, 1998), 164–65.
25. E.g., Exod. 7:3 and 11:9. In Ezekiel, the LXX also uses the term τέρας (*teras*) when translating מופת (*môpēt*; cf. Ezek. 12:6; 24:24, 27), but, based upon the Exodus examples, this seems more arbitrary than nuanced.

of אות in Ezek. 4:3 appears to govern the four signs appearing in close canonical proximity (i.e., 4:1-3, 4-6, 9-17; 5:1-4). As for the remaining three sign acts, the use of מופת identifies them as such (Ezek. 12:6, 11; 24:24, 27). The double appearance of the term מופת in Ezek. 12:6 and 12:11 is clearly dealing with the same sign act and thus we can group the entire section under one event (Ezek. 12:1-20). There is one other debated sign act in Ezekiel: the unification of the two sticks in Ezek. 37:15-28. In this case, the account does not have a specific designation as a sign act, but it could be argued that it is utilized as one.[26]

In the case of the Fourth Gospel, Köstenberger avers that "In John's Gospel . . . a sign is a symbol-laden, but not necessarily 'miraculous' public work of Jesus selected and explicitly identified as such by John for the reason that it displays God's glory in Jesus who is thus shown to be God's true representative (cf. 20:30-31)."[27] Köstenberger's definition of Johannine signs and their use summarizes well the heart of how and why John used signs.[28] There can be little doubt that John used signs (σημεῖα *sēmeia*) as a key structural and rhetorical device.[29] Köstenberger also correctly notes that Jesus' signs in the Fourth Gospel were: 1) publicly performed to appeal particularly to the visual sensory mode and thus to go beyond mere words and utterances; 2) they were "explicitly identified" as signs in John; and 3) they served to prove that Jesus was "God's authentic representative."[30] These criteria could easily be applied to

---

26. For a discussion on the parameters of behaviors considered sign acts, see Kelvin Friebel, *Jeremiah's and Ezekiel's Sign Acts*, JSOTSup 283 (Sheffield: Sheffield Academic, 1999), 13–19. However, Friebel's criteria (14) seems to be too broad.
27. Köstenberger, *Studies on John and Gender*, 107. See also Thompson, "Signs and Faith in the Fourth Gospel," 93–95.
28. These include: 2:11, 18, 23; 3:2; 4:48, 54; 6:2, 14, 26, 30; 7:31; 9:16; 10:41; 11:48; 12:18, 37; and 20:30; these as noted by Köstenberger, *Studies on John and Gender*, 100.
29. Ibid., 100.
30. Ibid., 104–107.

Ezekiel's use of sign acts, although the second criterion can be a bit unclear at times. Nonetheless, in every case within each book, the signs were used to convince people of some facet of who Yahweh/Jesus was and what God was capable of doing.

When Jesus performed his signs before an unbelieving crowd, many hardened their hearts and refused to believe (John 12:37), a similar outcome experienced by Ezekiel. As early as the call of the prophet, Yahweh warned him that the people he was ministering to were a "rebellious house"[31] (בית־המרי; cf. Ezek. 2:3, 5-8; 3:9, 26, 27; also Ezek. 12:2, 3, 9, 25; 24:3) and hard-headed (Ezek. 3:8). Even when Ezekiel performed these vivid signs, the people refused to listen (cf. John 1:11).

Finally, just as sign acts were a common prophetic device during the sixth century, in John's era, the people had actually been expecting their Messiah to perform such acts (John 6:14; 7:31; cf. b. Sanh. 98a).[32] Yet, according to John, the people still failed to accept Jesus when he performed the miraculous before their very eyes. In this vein Guthrie notes, "In further support of the special emphasis given to Messianic claims is the fact that only in this gospel is the Hebrew form of the word 'Messiah' found, once on the lips of Andrew (i. 41) and once on the lips of the Samaritan woman (iv. 25)."[33] Jesus as Messiah in the Fourth Gospel had used signs as evidence of who he was. Yet, like Ezekiel's "hard-headed" audience, the hard-hearted people Jesus ministered to, as depicted in the Fourth Gospel, rejected his message.[34]

---

31. In Ezekiel, the phrase "rebellious house" forms an inclusio to the oracles against Israel (i.e., Ezek. 2–24). Because the people rejected the prophet's words, destruction and exile were assured (Ezek. 24:3-24), a reality that finds fulfillment in Ezek. 33:21.
32. See Alfred Edersheim, *The Life and Times of Jesus the Messiah* (McLean: VA, MacDonald Publishing Co., 1988), 2:68; and Riga, "Signs of Glory," 411.
33. Guthrie, "Importance of Signs in the Fourth Gospel," 72.
34. Riga, "Signs of Glory," 403.

With this brief overview of the macro similarities between John's signs and Ezekiel's sign acts in hand, we are now ready to focus on the micro-level correspondences. The important thing to remember when looking at John's signs is answering the question: why did he choose specific signs out of the numerous possibilities available to him (John 20:30-31)? A comparative analysis of John's signs vis-à-vis Ezekiel's sign acts will help answer this question.

Signs and Sign Acts in the Fourth Gospel and Ezekiel Identified

As noted in our introduction to this chapter, there is no shortage of studies on John's signs.[35] The major problem in this regard has been the identification of the number of signs that John actually used.[36] Köstenberger has pointed up this problem and has highlighted the most frequently noted six signs while moving on to suggest the possibility of a seventh.[37] At the same time, he rightly cautions that if a thorough study were done in this regard, perhaps others could be identified.[38] Thus, Köstenberger is correct to caution when trying to narrow the number to seven, namely, as a parallel to John's seven "I Am" Sayings, or, in my case, even to find a perfect parallel with Ezekiel's seven or eight sign acts, a caution I take to heart.[39] What is more, John 1:19—12:50 is often assigned the ascription "The Book of the Signs," although this is perhaps not the best designation in light of the assertion by the author himself in 20:30-31 that the entire book serves just such a function.[40] Not surprisingly, when trying to

---

35. For an example of these studies as of 2001, see Köstenberger, *Studies on John and Gender*, 99–100n1.
36. For solid criteria for what constitutes a sign in John's Gospel, see ibid., 107.
37. Ibid., 100–102.
38. Ibid., 100. Köstenberger (114–16) concludes that the temple cleansing may be the seventh sign.
39. Ibid., 100–102.
40. Francis J. Moloney, *Love in the Gospel of John: An Exegetical, Theological, and Literary Study* (Grand Rapids: Baker, 2013), 99; and D. A. Carson, *The Gospel according to John*, PNTC (Grand Rapids: Eerdmans, 1991), 103.

identify the sign acts of Ezekiel, there is just as much controversy.[41] Nevertheless, I will follow the general consensus that there are at least eight possible signs in John. Similarly I will adopt the eight most identified signs acts from Ezekiel. They may be listed as follows:

John's Signs

1. Turning water into wine (2:1-11)
2. The cleansing of the temple (2:14-17, 21)[42]
3. The healing of the official's son (4:46-54)
4. The healing of the man by the pool (5:1-9)
5. The feeding of the five thousand (6:1-15)[43]
6. The healing of the blind man (9:1-7)
7. The raising of Lazarus (11:1-44)
8. The miraculous catch of fish (John 21:1-11 cf. Luke 5:1-11)[44]

---

41. Block, *The Book of Ezekiel: Chapters 1–24*, 166n15, points out the issues with determining how many sign acts there are in Ezekiel. See also Friebel, *Jeremiah's and Ezekiel's Sign Acts*, 14–15.
42. So George Beasley-Murray, *John*, WBC 36 (Nashville: Thomas Nelson, 1999), 42; Carson, *Gospel according to John*, 181; and Dodd, *Interpretation of the Fourth Gospel*, 300–303, 370.
43. Fortna, *The Gospel of Signs*, 70, 101, combines the feeding of the 5000 and Jesus' walking on the water.
44. Paul N. Anderson, *The Riddles of the Fourth Gospel: An Introduction to John* (Minneapolis: Fortress Press, 2011), 13; and Stephen S. Smalley, *John: Evangelist & Interpreter* (Downers Grove, IL: InterVarsity, 1998), 130. It is possible that if chapter 21 was part of the original Gospel that this may be included. Gary T. Manning, *Echoes of a Prophet: The Use of Ezekiel in the Gospel of John and in Literature of the Second Temple Period* (London: T & T Clark, 2004), 189–94, draws a connection to Ezek. 47:9-10 and the abundance of the messianic age. Here in Ezekiel, an abundance of fish will be caught in the river flowing from the temple to the Dead Sea. This connection is at best tangential. Other signs have been posited: Jesus' comments about the serpent in the wilderness being lifted up (3:14-15; cf. Brown, *Gospel according to John I–XII*, 528); Jesus' anointing (12:1-8; cf. Dodd, *Interpretation of the Fourth Gospel*, 438); the triumphal entry (12:12-16; cf. ibid., 371, 438); the crucifixion and resurrection (John 18–19; cf. Carson, *Gospel according to John*, 661); and the resurrection appearances (John 20–21; cf. Beasley-Murray, *John*, 387). These additional signs as cited by Köstenberger, *Studies on John*, 108–109. For a refutation of these possibilities with the exception of the cleansing of the temple, see ibid, 109–14. Fortna, *Gospel of Signs*, 102–109 (108), suggests that John's "source" originally had the signs in the following order: 1) Cana (John 2); 2) official's son (John 4); 3) draught of fish (John 21); 4) feeding of the people and walking on the water (John 6); 5) Lazarus (John 11); 6) blind man healed (John 9); and 7) lame man healed (John 5).

Ezekiel's Sign Acts

1. Ezekiel drawing Jerusalem on a brick and mimicking laying siege to the city (4:1-3)
2. Ezekiel lying on his side (4:4-6)
3. Ezekiel eating rationed food over dung (4:9-17)
4. Ezekiel cutting his hair (5:1-4)
5. Ezekiel mimicking going into exile (12:1-20)[45]
6. Ezekiel not mourning his wife's death (24:15-18, 24)
7. The opening of Ezekiel's mouth (24:27)
8. The unifying of the two sticks (37:15-28)[46]

Regardless of the exact number, although the eight-to-eight ratio is appealing for my argument, the important thing for our discussion is how these signs/sign acts were rhetorically and structurally utilized. Why did John follow up his introduction of Jesus by the first sign at Cana? The answer to this question may again rest upon John's parroting of Ezekiel's structural presentation of Yahweh and the prophet Ezekiel.

Before moving on with our comparisons I need to make it clear that I am not asserting that there is a verse-to-verse parallel or a chapter-to-chapter connection when it comes to the length of a given literary link. The forty-eight chapters of Ezekiel serve more as a structural pattern for the much shorter twenty-one chapters of John. My discussion in chapter 2 above is a good example of this whereby John 1 has a number of motifs connected to the first three chapters of Ezekiel.[47] John appears to be borrowing from Ezekiel's structure and narrative flow in an effort to equate Jesus to both the

---

45. While it is possible that Ezek. 12:18-20 may constitute a separate sign, the entire context of Ezek. 12:1-20 seems to be in keeping with the theme of exile.
46. This is rarely noted as a sign per se but is listed as a possibility.
47. However, as I noted at the beginning of chapter 2 there is a closer one-to-one parallel in the length of the material being compared in John 1 and Ezek. 1–3 than elsewhere.

prophet Ezekiel and his presentation of the exalted Yahweh. In this regard, I am not suggesting that every sign act of Ezekiel has a direct parallel with Jesus' signs. Rather, select sign acts find structural and rhetorical connections with John's presentation of Jesus, particularly, the thematic connections throughout. It is to an assessment of these connections that we now turn.

Turning Water into Wine in Cana

It is in no way novel to draw connections between the first sign of Jesus and the work of Ezekiel. For example, Hugh Montefiore asserts that the water motif of Ezek. 47:1-12 lays behind Jesus' act of turning the water into wine.[48] However, Montefiore's connections are tangential at best. The living water imagery of Ezek. 47 finds better thematic ties to John 4 or 7:38-39.[49] Moreover, there appears to be more purposeful parallels in light of geographical, structural, and rhetorical concerns.

To begin, Jesus' first sign act falls within the narrative sequence of John 2–4, material unique to the Fourth Gospel. There is no reason to question the historicity of this material based upon this fact alone any more than one would question whether Jesus actually delivered the parables of the Good Samaritan, the Rich Man and Lazarus, the Prodigal Son, or spoke to the leaders in the temple when he was a child—events all recorded in Luke's Gospel. The first sign covers the first eleven verses of chapter 2 and takes place when Jesus and his

---

48. Hugh Montefiore, "Position of the Cana Miracle and the Cleansing of the Temple in St. John's Gospel," *JTS* 50, no. 2 (1949): 183–86, esp. 184–85. Keener, *The Gospel of John*, 1:278, notes a possible connection to Moses' turning the Nile into blood (Exod. 7:20). However, I doubt that John would want to draw this connection especially due to the fact that the Exodus passage is in a context of judgment on another nation.
49. See the discussion by Anthony T. Hanson, *The Prophetic Gospel: A Study in John and the Old Testament*, second ed. (Edinburgh: T & T Clark, 2006), 104–12; Thomas R. Hatina, "John 20:22 in Its Eschatological Context: Promise or Fulfillment?," *Bib* 74, no. 2 (1993): 196–219 (209); and Manning, *Echoes of a Prophet*, 179–86.

family attend a wedding at Cana of Galilee. John recounts that after the crowd had consumed all the celebratory wine, Jesus is approached by his mother, who intimates that he should perform a miracle by providing more wine. Now, while the specific details of the miracle are not important to my thesis, the location/setting of Cana is, both geographically and structurally.

Geographically, John situates the reader in Jesus' "home" region (about ten miles northeast from Nazareth) to perform the first sign before going to Jerusalem to cleanse the temple.[50] As we will see in a moment, the importance of the movement between Jesus' "home" region of Galilee and Jerusalem is a clue to John's reliance on Ezekiel's structure. It does not appear to be a coincidence that Ezekiel performs his first sign acts at his "home" in Babylon by the River Chebar. Ezekiel's first sign acts are followed up by his movement, in a vision, back to Jerusalem to witness the corruption of the Jerusalem temple; a similar picture is evinced in the Fourth Gospel when Jesus travels from Cana/Galilee to Jerusalem to cleanse the temple (cf. John 2:13-22). We will handle the temple cleansing in more detail in the next chapter.

Structurally, in the first two chapters of the Fourth Gospel we have the revelation of Jesus' glory as God (John 1:1-14), the introduction and/or calling of a prophet and disciples (John 1:6-51), Jesus' first sign at home in Galilee (John 2:1-11), followed by the cleansing of the temple in Jerusalem (John 2:13-22). Comparatively, in Ezekiel chapters 1–8 we find the revelation of Yahweh's glory as divine Suzerain (Ezek. 1), the introduction/calling of the prophet (Ezek. 1:1-3; 2–3), Ezekiel's first sign acts at home at Chebar (Ezek. 4–5), followed by his visionary movement to Jerusalem to witness the

---

50. I note Nazareth as Jesus' "home" because his home was really heavenly, just as Ezekiel's "home" was not by Chebar at Tel-Aviv but rather in Judah. On the former point, see comments by R. H. Lightfoot, *St. John's Gospel* (repr., Oxford: Oxford University Press, 1966), 34–36.

needed cleansing of the temple (Ezek. 8).[51] Now to be sure some may protest that this is mere coincidence; however, when viewed in the light of the amassing of these parallels and similar motifs, the weight of the argument begins to gain momentum.

Finally, as just noted, the obvious rhetorical purpose of the first sign was to reveal Jesus' "glory" (δόξα/*doxa*), a similar image that we noted in chapter 2 above (cf. John 1:14; Ezek. 1:28; 3:12, 23; 8:4; 9:3; 10:4, 18, 19; 11:22-23). However, some also assert that Jesus' turning water into wine "suggests creation's renewal"[52] as reflected in the eschatological hope of plentitude as promised in Amos 9:11-13. In this vein, Irenaeus recorded (*Adv. haer.* 5.33.3f; c. 180) that by the period of Papias, Bishop of Hierapolis, some believed that the millennial reign of Jesus would be one of astronomical bounty.[53] Now, while Amos 9:11-13 does present this hope in a succinct fashion, the picture of eschatological blessing in the form of plentitude is actually handled in much more detail in the revivification of the land of Israel in Ezek. 44–48. Nowhere in all of the Old Testament is a clearer picture of eschatological fecundity presented.[54]

---

51. Chapters 6–7 of Ezekiel serve as a basic introduction/overview to the judgment oracles of chapters 13–24 and thus do not have the same structural importance as do the visions. See more on this in Brian Neil Peterson, *Ezekiel in Context: Ezekiel's Message Understood in Its Historical Setting of Covenant Curses and Ancient Near Eastern Mythological Motifs*, PTMS 182 (Eugene, OR: Pickwick Publications, 2012), 140–42.
52. Jeannine K. Brown, "Creation's Renewal in the Gospel of John," *CBQ* 72, no. 2 (2010): 276–90 (288); and Brown, *Gospel according to John I–XII*, 121. Riga, "Signs of Glory," 421–22, suggests that the abundance of wine has Eucharistic overtones.
53. Papias said that the sayings came directly from the Apostle John. Cf. Ernst Haenchen, *John*, Hermeneia (Philadelphia: Fortress Press, 1984), 1:10–11. Haenchen (11) rightly notes that this is a legend based upon 2 Bar. 29:5. For the text of Irenaeus, see Alexander Roberts and James Donaldson eds., *The Ante-Nicene Fathers: The Writings of the Fathers Down to A.D. 325*, 10 vols (Buffalo: Christian Literature Publishing Co., 1885–97 repr., Grand Rapids: Eerdmans, 1951–56), 1:562–63.
54. See Peterson, *Ezekiel in Context*, 322–25.

The Temple Cleansing

Even though this event will be handled in greater detail in the next chapter, a few points seem to be in order, especially in light of the fact that scholars have also included the temple cleansing as Jesus' second sign.[55] Jesus' movement to Jerusalem to confront those defiling the temple with their acts of commerce has an interesting metaphorical parallel with Ezekiel. At the heart of the opening sign acts of Ezekiel, the prophet is portrayed as laying siege, metaphorically, against Jerusalem (Ezek. 4:1-3, 7). In Jesus' actions in the temple, one can easily see that he laid spiritual siege to the city and in essence also prophesied the city's destruction by his use of the metaphor of his destroyed body (John 2:19). The fact that Jesus actually likens himself to the temple by saying, "Destroy this temple and in three days I will rebuild it" (John 2:19), finds affinity to what Ezekiel does in his first series of sign acts. According to Donna Petter, Ezek. 4:8 places "Ezekiel in the role of the city." She continues, "in the dramatic performances of Ezek. 4:1—5:4, Ezekiel identifies with the siege, famine and destruction by becoming the city."[56] Both Ezekiel and Jesus identified with the city, or an aspect of it, in a metaphorical manner. Scholars have noted that Jesus' reference to the destruction of the temple of his body has prophetic overtones of impending disaster

---

55. So too Köstenberger, *Studies on John and Gender*, 114–16; Dodd, *Interpretation of the Fourth Gospel*, 303; and Edwyn Hoskyns, *The Fourth Gospel Vol. 1* (London: Faber and Faber Limited, 1940), 205. Closely connected to this is the implication of Jesus' body being the temple that will be raised in three days (e.g., Brown, "Creation's Renewal," 287). Brown also lists Jesus resurrection as a possible eighth sign.

56. Donna Lee Petter, *The Book of Ezekiel and Mesopotamian City Laments*, OBO 246 (Göttingen: Vandenhoeck & Ruprecht, 2011), 74. Petter aptly notes the use of the possessive "your siege" (מצורך) in Ezek. 4:8, thus equating Ezekiel with the city.

of the actual city and temple (see my discussion in the next chapter).[57] Thus, as goes the temple so goes the city and vice versa.

Closely associated with the metaphor of becoming the temple is the role of bearing the sins of the nation (cf. John 1:29). As noted above, the sign acts that appear in Ezek. 4:1-17 deal with the sin of the people and the punishment/destruction of the city and temple. In the midst of the cluster of sign acts, Ezekiel is told to lie on his left side for 390 days and then afterward on his right side for another forty days to "bear the iniquity" (נשאת עון) of Israel and Judah respectively (Ezek. 4:5-6). The priestly language abounds in these passages. According to God's instructions to the priests and Levites, they were to "bear the iniquity" (נשאת עון) of the nation as the spiritual representatives of Israel (cf. Lev. 10:17; Num. 18:1, 23; see also Exod. 28:43; Lev. 16:22; in Num. 14:18 Yahweh bears the guilt). Here Yahweh is calling on Ezekiel to perform a priestly duty in a foreign land far from the temple and the sacrificial system. Not only does Ezekiel metaphorically become the city (Ezek. 4:8), here the prophet becomes a *savior figure* that the author of the Fourth Gospel may have seen as prefiguring Jesus and his work on the cross![58] In this regard, Walther Zimmerli has suggested that Ezekiel was the inspiration behind the Suffering Servant figure in Isaiah who bore the sins of the people as noted in Isaiah 53.[59] However, as Hassell Bullock rightly notes, if one does not follow the post-exilic dating for the Isaiah passage, then "Ezekiel takes his place as an intermediate link between the portrait of the Suffering Servant and the Servant himself as we see him in Christ."[60] Of course Ezekiel could not take away the

---

57. So too the conclusion of Mark Matson, "The Animal Sellers/The Money Changers in the Temple: Driven Out—But Why?," in *Character Studies in the Fourth Gospel: Narrative Approaches to Seventy Figures in John*, ed. Steven A. Hunt, D. Francois Tolmie, and Ruben Zimmermann, WUNT 314 (Tübingen: Mohr Siebeck, 2013), 245–48 (248).
58. So too Bullock, "Ezekiel," 28.
59. Walther Zimmerli, *Ezekiel 1*, Hermeneia (Philadelphia: Fortress Press, 1979), 165. So too Bruce Vawter, "Ezekiel and John," *CBQ* 26, no. 4 (1964): 458.

sins of Israel and Judah in a literal sense, but Yahweh does expect him to play out the sign act before the people so that they might know the gravity of their sin.[61] For John, Ezekiel's priestly act is a ready-made motif pregnant with meaning needing only to be applied to Jesus' life (John 1:29, 36; 3:16; cf. Isa. 53:6). That John used these themes in light of the numerous other parallels is very likely (cf. Heb. 4:14; 9:26; 10:12).

The Healing and Feeding Signs

Signs 3–6 all have a similar theme of providing either healing or food for the individual: the healing of the official's son (4:46-54); the healing of the man by the pool (5:1-9); the feeding of the five thousand (6:1-15); and the healing of the blind man (9:1-7). Because many of these signs are associated with the "I Am" Sayings and will be handled in more detail in chapter 5, I will only highlight a few of the Ezekielian and Johannine connections here.

Jesus' work/signs in these specific areas were meant to show that as God/Messiah he could provide for his people all that was needed both physically and spiritually (cf. Ezek. 43–48; Isa. 61), an essential aspect of his salvific work.[62] In this vein, Karl Heinrich Rengstorf comments, "The feeding of the multitude and the miracle at Cana fit into this pattern [of the Messianic age] inasmuch as they correspond to the expectation that the Messianic age will put an end to hunger and thirst."[63] Of course to this I would add healing as well (Ezek. 47:12; cf. Isa. 53). The immediate Old Testament connection that comes to mind is the provision of Yahweh for his people in the wilderness (Exod. 16). Although this is a solid point of reference it

---

60. Bullock, "Ezekiel," 28.
61. So too ibid., 31.
62. Claus Westermann, *The Gospel of John in the Light of the Old Testament*, trans. Siegfried S. Schatzmann (Peabody, MA: Hendrickson, 1998), 13.
63. Rengstorf, "σημεῖον," 246.

fails to take into account the numerous prophetic passages, Ezekielian in particular, associated with Yahweh's provision for Yahweh's people in the last days/eschaton (cf. Ezek. 34:14, 18; 36:8-12; 37:26; 39:26-29; 47:1-12).

For the early church, the coming of Jesus initiated this eschatological hope. Therefore, John opts to use these "provision" signs to prove that Jesus was the promised hope for all Israel. As of the time of John's writing, the sting of the present political situation in light of the 70 C.E. disaster (and the exile of 586 B.C.E.) must have caused a level of psychological anxiety about God's ability to sustain Israel.[64] Recollections of the privation associated with the First Jewish War and the siege of Jerusalem must have been foremost in John's mind as he incorporated these signs to prove who Jesus was. Not surprisingly, the common theme in the majority of Ezekiel's sign acts actually revolves around privation associated with siege warfare (see sign acts 1–5 above). Jesus' provision of food, wine, and healing is a reversal of the curses once placed upon the nation and at the same time, are a direct fulfillment of the prophecies of Yahweh's provision and sustaining power in Ezekiel (e.g., Ezek. 34:29; 36:29-30; 47:8-12).

The Raising of Lazarus

It is impossible to determine why the account of the raising of Lazarus is never mentioned by the authors of the Synoptic Gospels. While some have posited theories for the lacuna[65] others have denied

---

64. Some note that the absence of any notation on the destruction of the temple may betray an early date for the writing of the Gospel, that is, pre-70 C.E. Cf. Saeed Hamid-Khani, *Revelation and Concealment of Christ: A Theological Inquiry into the Elusive Language of the Fourth Gospel*, WUNT 120 (Tübingen: Mohr Siebeck, 2000), 284. Hamid-Khani goes on to note, however, that "it is possible that the prominence given to this story [the temple cleansing], and to the festivals, may be John's way of addressing the trauma" (284).
65. E.g., Kenneth K. Maahs, *The John You Never Knew: Decoding the Fourth Gospel* (New York: Peter Lang, 2006), 151–56. Maahs suggests that the earlier Synoptic writers may have been

its historicity altogether.⁶⁶ Nevertheless, one cannot deny the Ezekielian connections.⁶⁷ Indeed, perhaps the best answer to why John chose to include this sign, the last of Jesus' public ministry, lies in the fact that it finds a parallel with one of the last of Ezekiel's public-ministry sign acts: the death of Ezekiel's *beloved* wife.⁶⁸ Thus, the ordering of John's signs vis-à-vis Ezekiel's sign acts may be telling of John's rhetorical intent.

In John 11 we see that Jesus' last sign of his public ministry (John 2–12) prior to the rhetorical shift in the Fourth Gospel to the Passion narrative (John 13–21) finds parallels with Ezekiel's last sign act prior to the major shift in his prophetic content (i.e., the oracles against the nations in Ezek. 25–32).⁶⁹ In each case, the sign or sign act is directly connected to the death of someone. But it was not just anyone who died. In each case, it was someone who was special/beloved by Jesus and Ezekiel: Lazarus and Ezekiel's wife. John records that Jesus "loved" (ἀγαπάω/*agapaō*) Lazarus, and Yahweh tells Ezekiel that Yahweh will take away the "desire of your eyes" (מחמד עיניך), that is, the person he loves (Ezek. 24:16).

Also similar to both accounts is the fact that the impending death of the person in question is known by the main character before it happens. Ezekiel knows a few hours before his wife dies and

---

protecting the younger Lazarus by not drawing attention to him in their gospels. See a similar conclusion by David Wenham, "The Enigma of the Fourth Gospel: Another Look," in *Understanding, Studying and Reading: New Testament Essays in Honour of John Ashton*, ed. Christopher Rowland and Crispin H. T. Fletcher-Louis, JSNTSup 153 (Sheffield: Sheffield Academic, 1998), 128n51.

66. Rudolf Bultmann, *The Gospel of John: A Commentary*, trans. G. R. Beasley-Murray (Philadelphia: Westminster John Knox, 1971), 396n3. The fact that the raising of Lazarus only appears in John does not make the account any less historical than those events unique to each of the other Gospels.
67. See for example the comments by Frederic Manns, *L'Evangile de Jean à la Lumière du Judaïsme*, SBFA 33 (Jerusalem: Franciscan Printing Press, 1991), 242–49.
68. See more on this in chapter 5 below. For a detailed discussion of this sign act in the context of Ezekiel, see Friebel, *Jeremiah's and Ezekiel's Sign Acts*, 337–51.
69. While the promise to Ezekiel that he would regain his speech falls in close proximity to the loss of his wife (Ezek. 24:27), the sign does not actually happen until Ezek. 33:22.

Jesus knows the exact day Lazarus actually died.[70] In each account, these deaths serve as a sign for something greater. The death of Ezekiel's wife served as the precursor to the destruction of the temple in Jerusalem, the "desire" of the nation's eyes (עיניכם).[71] Similarly, John's use of the sign of Lazarus' death served as a sign and symbol of the death and resurrection of Jesus, the "temple" spoken of in John 2:19. As Jeannine Brown rightly notes, the sign of Lazarus's resurrection is a foreshadowing of the coming resurrection of Jesus himself in a "re-creation" of sorts.[72]

What is more, several of the Ezekielian motifs in the above-noted sign act are important to our thesis of motif borrowing in an antithetical way. For example, Ezekiel's wife is not raised from the dead whereas both Lazarus, and eventually Jesus, are. Yet, in the midst of Ezekiel's loss and despair displayed in this sign act, he goes on to promise a brighter day by describing a rebuilt temple and city (Ezek. 40–43). Here John's use of the Ezekielian motif in a nuanced fashion fits well in the setting of Jesus' promised death, burial, *and* his resurrection as the new "temple."

Another one of the motifs that serves antithetically is the fact that Ezekiel was not allowed to mourn his wife, which in turn showed that Yahweh would not mourn the loss of Yahweh's temple at the hands of the Babylonians (Ezek. 24:16). In the raising of Lazarus pericope, one of the things that is stressed is the mourning of the people and how it moved Jesus to act (John 11:33). Furthermore, where Ezekiel is forbidden to show remorse, Jesus wept at the

---

70. The messenger would have taken a day to get to the Transjordan but Jesus knew even at that time that Lazarus had died. He remained another two days and then took another day to travel to the graveside in Bethany for a total of four days (John 11:17). Cf. Carson, *Gospel according to John*, 407.
71. Note the use of the second masculine plural suffix.
72. Brown, "Creation's Renewal," 288.

graveside of Lazarus. His weeping served as a means of showing his humanity in the midst of the mourners' despair.[73]

In the LXX version of Ezekiel's sign act, the relevant phrase in Ezek. 24:16 is οὐ μὴ κοπῇς οὐδὲ μὴ κλαυσθῇς ("you may neither mourn nor shall you weep"). Notice that the Greek words κόπτω and κλαίω are used to speak of the restriction placed upon the prophet: he was neither to mourn/κόπτω nor to weep/κλαίω (cf. also Ezek. 24:23).[74] It is κλαίω which is used in John 11:31 and twice in verse 33. Conversely, Jesus' weeping in John 11:35 is designated by the word δακρύω (cf. Ezek. 27:35), perhaps an indication of John's desire to show a distinction between the crowd's mourning and Jesus' weeping.[75] Thus, one of the last clearly indicated sign acts in each book rests in the context of death and mourning; however, for John, Jesus reverses the people's weeping as a sign of who Jesus truly is: Messiah and God incarnate.

The Catch of Fish

The eighth sign that I have chosen to include falls within the second section of the Fourth Gospel (John 13–21). Scholars have long noted that the great catch of fish serves as a metaphor for the ingathering and unity of the Church (John 21:1-11).[76] Peter and the disciples were to become "fishers" of people (John 21:15-17; Mark 1:17). Also, unlike the other signs, this sign is not performed in the midst of a crowd but rather is given to the disciples privately, and is only

---

73. There are many theories as to why John records the weeping of Jesus especially since Jesus knew that he would soon turn the people's weeping into joy. It may have been because of the people's unbelief or it may have been done as a means of showing his empathy for their sorrow.
74. κλαίω is used only twice in Ezekiel, both in the context of this sign act!
75. This verb is used only here in the New Testament and appears only in the LXX in Ezek. 27:35. See also *BDAG*, "δακρύω," 211.
76. F. F. Bruce, *The Gospel of John: Introduction, Exposition and Notes* (Basingstoke: Pickering and Inglis, 1983), 401–402; and Barnabas Lindars, *The Gospel of John*, NCBC (repr., Grand Rapids: Eerdmans, 1982), 629. See also Carson, *Gospel according to John*, 673.

later played out in public when the Church is birthed (Acts 2). Similarly, Ezekiel's last sign act of the two sticks in Ezek. 37:15-28 falls within the second section of his book (viz., the oracles of hope; see esp. Ezek. 34–48). We also see that the prophet performs the sign in private (37:15-17), and then explains it publicly (37:18-28). In both the Fourth Gospel and Ezekiel, the sign/sign act represents the unification of God's people with eschatological importance (see more in chapter 7 below).

The Muteness of Ezekiel

As I noted in my introduction to this chapter, it is my belief that not every Johannine sign and Ezekielian sign act are expected to be exact parallels. Nevertheless, as we have seen in several instances thus far, the signs of John do in fact bear thematic, rhetorical, and structural resemblances to Ezekiel's sign acts. One instance where Johannine correspondences seem to be lacking is with the unique Yahweh-enacted sign act of Ezekiel's muteness (Ezek. 3:26-27; 24:27; 33:22), even though Ezekiel did pronounce oracles when Yahweh would open his mouth to do so (Ezek. 3:27).[77] The fall of Jerusalem and the destruction of the temple not only signaled the completion of his public ministry, which was marked by oracles of doom (Ezek. 4–24), but also marked the moment when Ezekiel regained the ability to speak and issue final warnings and oracles of hope (cf. Ezek. 33:22; chs. 34–48). Interestingly, and I offer this only as something to ponder, many unique aspects of the Fourth Gospel *may* possibly be explained by this Ezekielian sign act/motif.

---

77. On the muteness of Ezekiel, see Peterson, *Ezekiel in Context*, 80–83; Robert R. Wilson, "An Interpretation of Ezekiel's Dumbness," *VT* 22, no. 1 (1972): 91–104; and Ellen S. Davis, "Swallowing Hard: Reflections on Ezekiel's Dumbness," in *Signs and Wonders: Biblical Texts in Literary Focus*, ed. J. C. Exum, SBLSS (Atlanta: Scholars, 1989), 217–37.

There are several places in the Fourth Gospel where one may postulate that John had Ezekiel's muteness motif in mind, especially before the marked shift in Jesus' public ministry to his final days, death, burial, and resurrection. For example, many times Jesus' ministry focused on individuals (e.g., John 2–4; 11; 13–17), a similar reality to that found in Ezekiel (Ezek. 8:1; 14:1; 20:1). John also does not include Jesus' parables to crowds perhaps for the very purpose of focusing more on the "muted" ministry of Jesus, focused instead on signs.[78] Moreover, only in the Fourth Gospel do we see Jesus repeatedly withdrawing from crowds, hiding himself (John 5:13; 6:15; 7:1; 8:59; 11:54; 12:36 cf. also 2:4), or refusing to reveal himself to them (John 7:4, 6, 10). However, just like the transition in Ezekiel's ministry, when Jesus' public ministry comes to a close and he commits himself to go to the cross for the destruction of the "temple" of his body, John, more than any of the Synoptic writers, presents Jesus as "talkative."

During Jesus' trial the Synoptic writers note Jesus' silence before his accusers (Matt. 26:63; 27:12, 14; Mark 14:60-61; 15:4-5; Luke 23:9), especially Jesus' minimal interaction with Pilate (Matt. 27:11; Mark 15:2; Luke 23:3). In the Fourth Gospel, while John does note Jesus' silence once (John 19:9), Jesus also is presented as having extended dialogue with his accusers (John 18:20-21, 23; cf. Matt. 26:64; Mark 14:63; Luke 22:67-70), especially Pilate (John 18:34, 36, 37; 19:11).[79] Similarly, John records more of Jesus' speeches on the cross than any of the other writers (John 19:26-28, 30; cf. Matt. 27:46, 50; Mark 15:34, 37; Luke 23:43, 46). Finally, in the post-cross sections of the Gospels, it is once again John who records Jesus' extended dialogues with his followers offering them words of encouragement

---

78. John does note Jesus' interaction with crowds, but more so in a general sense (John 18:20).
79. Craig L. Blomberg, *The Historical Reliability of John's Gospel: Issues and Commentary* (Downers Grove, IL: InterVarsity, 2001), 242, also notes the distinct Johannine "talkativeness" of Jesus during his trial.

and hope (John 20–21; cf. Matt. 28:9-10, 17-20; Mark 16:12-20;[80] Luke 24:13-53).

Even though both Ezekiel and Jesus used words to accompany their actions, their sign acts and signs tend naturally towards non-verbal communication. Ezekiel moved away from the sign acts to more oracular communication after the reversal of his muteness in Ezek. 33:22. It is indeed possible that John's presentation of a more vocal Jesus in the closing chapters of the Fourth Gospel has its roots in the similar transition Ezekiel had from muteness to being able to speak.

The Absences of Exorcisms

Before leaving the topic of signs, which vindicate the divinity of Jesus, one must at least consider why, unlike the Synoptic Gospels, John fails to include among his signs the temptation of Jesus and any miracles involving the casting out of demons. After all, what better way to show the power of Jesus than to record the casting out of a legion of demons (Mark 5:2-20; Luke 8:29-37)![81] Is this omission due to the fact that the author of John was a Sadducee?[82] Or did John not know that Jesus was an exorcist?[83] Perhaps John's source material did not contain any exorcisms, that is, the author of the source did not know Jesus was an exorcist.[84] Was it due to the fact that there was

---

80. This section of Mark does not even appear in the earliest manuscripts.
81. So too Eric Plumer, "The Absence of Exorcisms in the Fourth Gospel," *Bib* 78, no. 3 (1997): 350–68 (350).
82. E.g., R. H. Strachan, *The Fourth Evangelist: Dramatist or Historian?* (London: Hodder and Stoughton, 1925), 157–60, esp. 158; and D. E. H. Whitely, "Was John Written by a Sadducee?," *ANRW* II.25.3 Berlin/New York: de Gruyter, 1985), 2481–2505, esp. 2494–2502. With the exception of a brief notation on page 2486, Whitely does not go into any discussion about the absence of exorcisms, only that the author was a Sadducee.
83. See the refutation of this and similar proposals by Graham H. Twelftree, "Exorcisms in the Fourth Gospel and the Synoptics," in *Jesus in Johannine Tradition*, ed. Robert T. Fortna and Tom Thatcher (Louisville: Westminster John Knox, 2001), 135–43 (135–36).
84. For a refutation of this position, see Plumer, "Absence of Exorcisms in the Fourth Gospel," 352.

nothing exceptional about exorcists at this time?[85] Several important studies have been conducted in an attempt to answer these questions and to account for this lacuna. Ronald Piper's solution is one of the more persuasive.[86] Piper suggests that the absence of exorcisms is perhaps due to John's focus on the *accusations* of demonic activity throughout the Gospel (e.g., John 7:20; 8:44, 48-52). He suggests that these accusations are reflected in three narrative facets: 1) "group identity conflict," the "us versus them" mentality (i.e., the followers of God/Jesus on one side and those associated with the Evil One on the other); 2) the Johannine worldview of Jesus' victory over the "ruler of this world" (John 12:31); and 3) the "opposition within" the ranks of the believers where certain members of Jesus' band leave and join the Evil One (e.g., Judas; John 17:12).[87] Therefore, as noted in these three situations, the accusations of being a demon or being possessed are reserved as a label for those outside of the given group. For the Jewish elite, it is Jesus and his followers (John 7:20; 8:48-52); for Jesus, conversely, it is those who reject his divinity and authority (John 8:44; 17:12). The rhetorical needs of the author, therefore, supersede any positive role exorcisms would have played in the gospel as a sign demonstrating Jesus' power.

Now while this proposal is noteworthy, perhaps a simpler conclusion can be drawn based upon Piper's second point (i.e., John's

---

85. Cf. Josephus, *Antiquities*, 8:46–49 (8.2.5 § 46 alternate ordering).
86. Ronald A. Piper, "Satan, Demons and the Absence of Exorcisms in the Fourth Gospel," in *Christology, Controversy, and Community: New Testament Essays in Honour of David R. Catchpole*, ed. David Horrell and Christopher M. Tuckett, NovTSup 99 (Leiden: Brill, 2000), 253–78. Note also the work of Graham H. Twelftree, *Jesus the Exorcist: A Contribution to the Study of the Historical Jesus* (repr., Peabody, MA: Hendrickson, 1993); and Plumer, "Absence of Exorcisms in the Fourth Gospel," 350–68. Plumer (361–62) suggests that the Jewish allegations against Christians that Jesus was a pawn of Satan may have caused John to avoid the entire topic. This may be the case, but the same concern would be applicable to the other Gospel writers as well, yet they chose to include the exorcism accounts. Further, like Mark, John could have simply included the rebuke of Jesus to this allegation (Mark 3:22–30).
87. Piper, "Satan, Demons," 268–78. Piper (277) also notes a similar "us vs. them" perspective in the Qumran literature, namely, the *Manual of Discipline* and the *Damascus Rule*.

worldview), and my proposed Ezekielian parallels. John's worldview is indeed one in which Jesus is equal with God and is in fact to be seen as God (John 10:30; 17:11, 21). As such, Satan and his cohorts are already a defeated foe and need not be given a place of recognition in the narratives (John 16:11).[88] This would also account for the glaring absence of the temptation of Jesus (cf. Matt. 4:1-11; Mark 1:12-13; Luke 4:1-13). As already covered in our discussion of John 1 in chapter 2 above, John's Jesus is God and does not need to prove himself vis-à-vis Satan and his cohorts.

Secondly, neither demons nor Satan appear in Ezekiel.[89] Now, while some may respond that this has a lot to do with a sixth-century understanding and development of demonology and the like, the fact still remains that Ezekiel does not address these issues in relation to Yahweh's demonstrated power and glory even though the concept of demons was prevalent in ancient Babylon.[90] Because Ezekiel does not address this issue, John may have followed this pattern.

---

88. Contra Twelftree, "Exorcisms in the Fourth Gospel," 141, who suggests Jesus' whole ministry in John is pervaded by "a battle with Satan." The series of verses Twelftree cites from John are hardly what one could call "promoting" a pervasive atmosphere. With the exception of two of his noted references in John 12:31 and 14:30, the use of the citations where demons and Satan are mentioned fall more in the realm of what we could call "school-ground name calling."
89. This concept is in no way novel. Fortna, *Gospel of Signs*, 230–31, says as much concerning John's use of the lives of Moses, Elijah, Elisha (and perhaps Joseph)—who did not perform exorcisms—as his exemplars.
90. For example, the Poem of Erra relates the work of the Sebetti (the seven demon gods). Cf. Daniel Bodi, *The Book of Ezekiel and the Poem of Erra*, OBO 104 (Freiburg: Universitätsverlag/Göttingen: Vandenhoeck & Ruprecht, 1991). For a full translation of the *Poem of Erra*, see Benjamin R. Foster, *Before the Muses: An Anthology of Akkadian Literature* (Bethesda, MD: CDL, 2005), 880–911. See also the work of Rintje Frankena, *Kanttekeningen van een Assyrioloog bij Ezechiël* (Leiden: Brill, 1965), and his comparison of Ezekiel with the *Poem of Erra*; and Peterson, *Ezekiel in Context*, 145–53. JoAnn Scurlock, *Magico-Medical Means of Treating Ghost-Induced Illnesses in Ancient Mesopotamia*, AMD III (Leiden: Brill, 2006), 178–677, lists 352 full or partial texts (with transliterations and translations) dealing with the vast array of incantations and prayers to ward off ghosts and to heal ghost-induced illnesses. For further reading, see Jerrold S. Cooper, "The Fate of Mankind: Death and Afterlife in Ancient Mesopotamia," in *Death and Afterlife, Perspectives of World Religions*, ed. Hiroshi Obayashi (New York: Greenwood, 1992), 19–33, esp. 27–30; JoAnn Scurlock, "Ghosts in the Ancient Near East: Weak or Powerful?," *HUCA* 68 (1997): 77–96; and Peterson, *Ezekiel in Context*, 232–35. The use of curses and divination to ward off evil spirits that cause sickness also appears in Egyptian

Furthermore, Victor Hamilton rightly points up the fact that the worldview of the Old Testament authors "is not one in which Yahweh shares power or competes for power with other supernatural forces" rather Yahweh "alone is the power."[91] In this vein, not surprisingly Yahweh is pictured as the sovereign God throughout the book of Ezekiel, with Yahweh performing wonders and judgments in their midst in order that they might know that Yahweh is God. Nothing, not even an archenemy (Ezek. 38–39), can stand in Yahweh's way to complete what Yahweh has set out to do.[92] Similarly, Jesus, from the outset of the Fourth Gospel is sovereign and God over all.[93] Indeed, one of the key purposes of Jesus' signs is to serve as a witness and evidence that he was God.[94] That is, Jesus did the very things that a human being was not supposed to be able to do. He turned water into wine, healed the sick, fed 5000 (and walked on water), and raised the dead. Jesus was God, and did not need to prove it to the spirit world. Furthermore, the cross was the "legal defeat" of Satan, who is cast out of heaven.[95] Therefore, the absence of Satan's temptation of Jesus and the acts of exorcism in the Fourth Gospel may have more to do with John's rhetorical intents rooted in Ezekielian precedent.

---

curse literature. Cf. Katarina Nordh, *Aspects of Ancient Egyptian Curses and Blessings: Conceptual Background and Transmission* (Stockholm: Gotab, 1996), 103.

91. Victor P. Hamilton, *Handbook on the Historical Books* (Grand Rapids: Baker, 2001), 256.

92. It is perhaps telling of authorship concerns or rhetorical intents that the author of Revelation uses Gog and Magog as the prototypical archenemy in Revelation 20.

93. One might also add to this list of omissions John's failure to mention the baptism of Jesus by John. David Wenham, "The Enigma of the Fourth Gospel: Another Look," in *Understanding, Studying and Reading: New Testament Essays in Honour of John Ashton*, ed. Christopher Rowland and Crispin H. T. Fletcher-Louis, JSNTSup 153 (Sheffield: Sheffield Academic, 1998), 123, has rightly noted that "the strong emphasis on the supreme, heavenly status of Jesus in the fourth Gospel" is no doubt the reason for this lacuna. He points this out in the context of a possible rivalry between Jesus and John's followers as to who was the greatest. Therefore, John is not depicted as baptising the Son of God.

94. Allison A. Trites, *The New Testament Concept of Witness*, SNTSMS 31 (Cambridge: Cambridge University Press, 1977), 78–127, esp. 93–110.

95. Ibid., 113.

Is John Anti-Jewish?

While this topic is not necessarily a part of the sign acts per se, it does fit with our discussion on John's use of prophetic method.[96] John has been labeled as presenting a message that is at best anti-Jewish and at the worst, straight up "anti-Semitic."[97] However, one must keep in mind that to be against a group of people (i.e., the religious elite), *within* a larger ethnic group (no doubt the same as the author), does not necessarily merit a label of disdain for the entire group.[98] What John is decrying is how the religious elite had understood what it meant to follow God, that is, their perspective of religious "Judaism" that in turn was affecting the perspective of the people vis-à-vis Jesus. In this vein, John is functioning in the realm of Old Testament types, figures, and motifs and needs to be interpreted in this light. Under the criteria adduced by most in determining what makes someone anti-Jewish, most, if not all of the Old Testament prophets would be candidates! But again it must be stressed that the Old Testament prophets, like John, were addressing a misperception, within his own community, of what it meant to follow God.

---

96. For detailed studies of this topic in John, see Reimund Bieringer, D. Pollefeyt, and F. Vandecasteele-Vanneuville eds., *Anti-Judaism and the Fourth Gospel: Papers of the Leuven Colloquium 2000*, JCHS 1 (Assen: van Gorcum, 2001); Ruben Zimmermann, "'The Jews': Unreliable Figures or Unreliable Narration," in *Character Studies in the Fourth Gospel: Narrative Approaches to Seventy Figures in John*, ed. Steven A. Hunt, D. Francois Tolmie, and Ruben Zimmermann, WUNT 314 (Tübingen: Mohr Siebeck, 2013), 71–109; and Urban C. von Wahlde, "The Johannine 'Jews': A Critical Survey," *NTS* 28, no. 1 (1982): 33–60. Note also the concise, but astute, discussion in John W. Pryor, *John: Evangelist of the Covenant People: The Narrative and Themes of the Fourth Gospel* (London: Darton, Longman, and Todd, 1992), 181–84.
97. Wahlde, "Johannine 'Jews,'" 54, rightly notes that scholars who suggest that John is anti-Semitic tend to "assert their positions rather than present evidence for them." Wahlde (33–54) has also presented conclusive evidence that John's references to the "Jews" were directed at the authorities not the Jewish people themselves. See also Whitely, "Was John Written by a Sadducee?," 2488–92.
98. I chose the religious elite in light of the apparent ongoing struggle between this group and Jesus. So too the conclusion of Wahlde, "Johannine 'Jews,'" 45–46. For a full listing of the proposed groups of Jews in view, see ibid., 35; and Zimmermann, "The Jews," 73.

On this topic a few further points need to be made. First, John is addressing the issues of his day, through which he had lived. The reality was that John may very well have seen the destruction of the city and temple, and in turn interpreted the Jewish authorities' rejection of Jesus as the Messiah as the cause that precipitated this devastating event. Indeed, based upon the dating of the book (see chapter 1 above), the author appears to have lived post-70 C.E. and was evaluating the losses of city, temple, and, no doubt friends and family, in light the Roman destruction of Jerusalem. Second, John Pryor is correct when he notes that John's message no doubt was heard in a predominant Jewish setting. Only later when the Church became dominated by Gentiles would the language of John sound anti-Jewish even though that was not his intent.[99] Third, as we have shown throughout, John's use of Ezekiel may in fact explain the harsh tone John uses against the Jewish religious elite of his day. One need only read Ezek. 16 and 23 to find some of the most graphic allegations leveled against the Jewish nation of Ezekiel's day. A quick reading of Ezek. 20 reveals that, according to Ezekiel, at no point in Israel's history had the nation reflected the actions of a truly covenanted people.[100] From Ezek. 4–24 the prophet goes on an almost unbroken diatribe revealing through sign acts, visions, and metaphors, the waywardness of his nation. Yet, in the midst of this prophetic tirade, Yahweh offered hope for those who would listen and yield; for Yahweh certainly did not take pleasure in the death of any person (Ezek. 18:32; 33:11). It is this background that informed the New Testament authors, especially John.

Finally, as will be further developed in chapter 5 below, John seeks to present Jesus as God (see also chapter 2 above). For the author

---

99. Pryor, *John*, 184.
100. See Brian Neil Peterson, "Ezekiel's Perspective of Israel's History: Selective Revisionism?," in *Prophets and Prophecy and Ancient Israelite Historiography*, ed. Mark J. Boda and Lyssa Wray Beal (Winona Lake, IN: Eisenbrauns, 2013), 295–313.

of the Fourth Gospel, no people, not even the elite of the "chosen people," have the right to thwart God's plan.[101] They may have had their own concept of what theocracy looks like, but Yahweh would have the last say. And even though the words "We have no king but Caesar" (John 19:15)[102] spoken by the elite may pulsate in the reader's ears, when understood in the light of Ezekiel Yahweh's words prevail: "As I live declares the Lord Yahweh, surely with a strong hand and with an outstretched arm and with outpoured rage, I will be king over you!" (Ezek. 20:33). For John, those who oppose Jesus/God, a God of judgment awaits (John 3:18; 5:24-30; 12:48); to those who believe that Jesus is the I Am, the same God reaches for a towel and washes his people's feet (John 13:4-16)—the choice is for the people to make. John's presentation of Jesus in this milieu makes sense. Ezekielian motifs and tone informed the author in such a way that Jesus is seen as God (John 1) with the full privilege that entails. He can speak and act for his Father.

Conclusion

As we have demonstrated above, the signs of John find a number of parallels with Ezekiel's sign acts, especially the first and seventh of these signs: the miracle at Cana and the raising of Lazarus. Building upon our conclusions of chapter 2, John appears to be following the structural and rhetorical pattern of Ezekiel. This rhetorical strategy helps to explain John's choice of particular signs and their strategic

---

101. Pryor, *John*, 183, comments, "Every religion is entitled to claim for itself absoluteness, and John does this most forcefully for Jesus. 'Before Abraham was, I am' is a mighty claim to absoluteness and finality. This is not anti-Semitic, but it certainly is anti-Judaism, if by Judaism one means a religion which sees itself as self-contained apart from finding its meaning in Jesus Christ. But one must add that it is no more anti-Judaism than anti-Islam or anti-Hinduism (or even anti-Anglicanism or anti-Catholicism when they stand apart from the Lord they presume to worship)."
102. Of the four Gospels, only John mentions this statement. This again points to a particular intent of the author to juxtapose Jesus' right to be King as opposed to Caesar's claim.

placement in the Fourth Gospel. Our brief analysis of the eighth sign and sign act helped to bolster this conclusion. At the same time, scattered throughout the "Book of the Signs" are accounts where individuals either misunderstood or completely missed the purpose and message behind Jesus' actions. For example, the religious elite at the temple cleansing event misunderstood Jesus' sign and sought further explanation, although Jesus refused the request (John 2:18-20; see also Jesus' interaction with Nicodemus and the woman at the well; John 3:3-4; 4:9-12). Not surprisingly, the motif of the misunderstood saying also finds parallels with at least two sign acts of Ezekiel (cf. Ezek. 12:3-11 and 24:19). Of course, nothing was misunderstood more than Jesus' exploits in the temple, the first defining action against the religious status quo in the Fourth Gospel. Here Jesus exerts his authority over that which is supposed to be his abode: his Father's house, the temple. We therefore see a movement from Cana to Jerusalem where Jesus, following the lead of Yahweh almost six centuries early, enacts the cleansing of the temple. It is to this we now turn.

4

John's Placement of the Cleansing of the Temple in Light of Ezekiel 8–11

Given this central historical significance of Jesus' action in the temple in the Synoptic tradition, it would seem to me that the strange positioning of the temple episode in John's Gospel could provide the interpretive key for the understanding of the whole.[1]

In the Fourth Gospel, in contrast to the Synoptics, the scene in which Jesus "cleanses" the temple is located near the outset of his public ministry (John 2:13-22). This is perhaps the most evident and problematic difference between the Johannine and Synoptic accounts. . . .[2]

J. A. Draper's astute analysis of the importance of the temple-cleansing pericope cannot be overstated. The temple-cleansing

---

1. J. A. Draper, "Temple, Tabernacle and Mystical Experience in John," *Neot* 31, no. 2 (1997): 263–88 (265).
2. N. Clayton Croy, "The Messianic Whippersnapper: Did Jesus Use a Whip on People in the Temple (John 2:15)?," *JBL* 128, no. 3 (2009): 555–68 (555).

pericope as the "interpretive key" is not only important for the overall rhetorical thrust of the Fourth Gospel, but is also vital in understanding and appreciating the author's purposes vis-à-vis Ezekielian motifs. Furthermore, N. Clayton Croy's assessment of the temple-cleansing pericope vis-à-vis the Synoptics highlights well the problematic nature of this pericope. Indeed, the temple-cleansing pericope in the Synoptics and John differ both in location *and* length.[3] On the one hand, John places his *extended* rendition of the event at the beginning of the Fourth Gospel as the watershed moment when Jesus' ministry goes "public" in Jerusalem. Here, the reader is given a preview of the outcome of Jesus' earthly ministry: opposition from the "Jews" and Jesus' eventual death.[4] On the other hand, the Synoptic writers place the cleansing at the end of their gospels to serve as the spark that would lead to Jesus' arrest during the final days of his ministry. Which location—early or late—is historically correct? And, if in fact his location is historically inaccurate, why does John make the switch? While the former question is virtually impossible to answer with certainty, the answer to the latter may be more attainable in light of our ongoing discussion.

In this chapter I will argue that the placement of the temple-cleansing pericope is an integral part of the Fourth Gospel's structure.[5] In what follows, we will examine the scholarly theories for John's placement of the temple-cleansing pericope and offer an alternate solution based upon Ezekielian rhetorical and structural considerations. In this vein, the second key event in Ezekiel's prophetic work is highlighted by what I have classified in the chart

---

3. For a discussion on this issue, see Ernst Haenchen, *John 1*, Hermeneia (Philadelphia: Fortress Press, 1984), 1:186–90.
4. Again, my use of "Jews" here is focused on the religious elite who opposed the message of Jesus.
5. So too the conclusion of Mark Matson, "The Temple Incident: An Integral Element in the Fourth Gospel's Narrative," in *Jesus in Johannine Tradition*, ed. Robert T. Fortna and Tom Thatcher (Louisville: Westminster John Knox, 2001), 145–53 (145, 148).

in chapter 1 above as the second "peak" to his overall structure. The first two peaks are basically the same: two visions of the glory (*kābôd*) of Yahweh, one taking place in Babylon to serve as the hallmark of the prophet's call, and the second set within Jerusalem to serve as the proverbial moment of truth when the glory of Yahweh departs the temple due to the defiling practices of the people. Having covered the first peak in chapter 2, in this chapter I will show how Ezekiel's second vision/peak, in the midst of the sign acts, parallels the cleansing of the temple, one of the key structural differences between the Fourth Gospel and the Synoptics.

The Location of the Temple-Cleansing Pericope

A number of monographs and articles have been written about the temple-cleansing pericope in John 2:13-22.[6] The biggest issue surrounding this event is scholars' attempts to answer two basic questions: 1) which Gospel placement is correct: John or the Synoptics?; and 2) if the Synoptics are correct, why did John alter its placement? Several solutions to the first dilemma have been proffered. Some posit that there were two cleansings of the temple—one at the beginning and one at the end of Jesus' ministry.[7] Others insist that

---

6. E.g., Ernest F. Scott, *The Crisis in the Life of Jesus: The Cleansing of the Temple and Its Significance* (New York: Scribner, 1952). See more in the footnotes below and Steven M. Bryan, "Consumed by Zeal: John's Use of Psalm 69:9 and the Action in the Temple," *BBR* 21, no. 4 (2011): 479–94 (479n1).

7. E. Randolph Richards, "An Honor/Shame Argument for Two Temple Clearings," *TJ* 29 NS, no. 1 (2008): 19–43; R. V. G. Tasker, *The Gospel according to St. John* (repr., Grand Rapids: Eerdmans, 2002), 61; William Hendriksen, *Exposition of the Gospel according to John*, NTC, seventh ed. (Grand Rapids: Baker, 1976), 120; Leon Morris, *The Gospel according to John*, NICNT (Grand Rapids: Eerdmans 1971), 196 (intimated); and D. A. Carson, *The Gospel according to John*, PNTC (Leicester: IVP, 1991), 177–78. Cecil Roth, "The Cleansing of the Temple and Zechariah xiv. 21," *NovT* 4, no. 3 (1960): 174–81 (176), argues against the possibility of there being two temple cleansings due to the supposed redundancy of the action. See also the rejection of two accounts by Scott, *Crisis in the Life of Jesus*, 18. However, Francis J. Moloney, *The Gospel of John: Text and Context*, BIS 72 (Leiden: Brill, 2005), 62n68, 64, arguing for two cleansings/temple incidents perhaps conflated, suggests that, according to the Fourth Gospel, Jesus was a regular "nuisance" in the temple based upon his numerous appearances in

there could only be one—the Synoptic tradition being the correct one.[8] Some settle the issue by suggesting that John's placement is most accurate.[9] On the other hand, Ivor Buse suggests that neither is correct but, rather, "that the happening had no fixed chronological place in the tradition and that it might have occurred at a time different from that indicated by either of the Gospels," perhaps due to competing sources.[10] Some sidestep the entire issue by negating the importance of the chronological setting and noting that the theological focus is the most important, namely, the event was a precursor to the cross.[11] Finally, and I could go on, others see this as just another example of the untrustworthy nature of the gospel record/history.[12]

---

the temple. See a similar intimation by Judith M. Lieu, "How John Writes," in *The Written Gospel*, ed. Markus Bockmuehl and Donald A. Hagner (Cambridge: Cambridge University Press, 2005), 172.

8. E.g., Rudolf Schnackenburg, *The Gospel according to St. John Vol. I: Introduction and Commentary on Chapters 1–4*, HTCNT, trans. Kevin Smyth (New York: Herder and Herder, 1968), 344, 354.

9. James F. McGrath, "'Destroy this Temple': Issues of History in John 2:13-22," in *John, Jesus, and History, Vol. 2: Aspects of Historicity in the Fourth Gospel*, ed. Paul N. Anderson, Felix Just, S. J., and Tom Thatcher (Atlanta: SBL, 2009), 35–43 (42–43); Victor Taylor, *The Gospel according to St. Mark* (London: Macmillan, 1952), 462; and Richard Bauckham, "John for Readers of Mark," in *The Gospels for All Christians: Rethinking the Gospel Audiences*, ed. R. Bauckham (Grand Rapids: Eerdmans, 1998), 147–72 (159–60). For a further list of scholars holding this position, see Raymond E. Brown, *The Gospel according to John I–XII*, AB 29 (New York: Doubleday, 1966), 117.

10. Ivor Buse, "The Cleansing of the Temple in the Synoptics and John," *ExpTim* 70, no. 1 (1958): 22–24 (22).

11. Paul Trudinger, "The Cleansing of the Temple: St. John's Independent, Subtle, Reflections," *ExpTim* 108, no. 11 (1997): 329–330. Trudinger notes that, like the Synoptics, John's presentation is still a precursor/sign pointing to the cross.

12. E.g., David Seeley, "Jesus' Temple Act," *CBQ* 55, no. 2 (1993): 263–83, esp. 273–76; idem, "Jesus' Temple Act Revisited: A Response to P. M. Casey," *CBQ* 62, no. 1 (2000): 55–63; and Jürgen Becker, *Jesus of Nazareth* (New York: de Gruyter, 1998), 332–33. Seeley ("Jesus' Temple Act," 276–82) focuses on Mark's version of the event and propounds that Mark made the entire account up. This of course is not that appealing in light of the fact that every Gospel writer records the falsified (?) account. See further refutation by Nicholas Perrin, *Jesus the Temple* (Grand Rapids: Baker, 2010), 82–83; P. M. Casey, "Culture and Historicity: The Cleansing of the Temple," *CBQ* 59, no. 2 (1997): 306–32; and Mark A. Matson, "The Contribution of the Temple Cleansing by the Fourth Gospel," SBLSP 31 (Atlanta: Scholars, 1992): 499. See also the

The second question dealing with John's reason for moving the account has garnered numerous responses as well.[13] F. A. Cooke suggests that it had to do with the author's desire not to detract from the last sign of Jesus, the raising of Lazarus (John 11).[14] Therefore the author moved the temple-cleansing pericope to the beginning of the book just after the first sign. Larry J. Kreitzer suggests that that the quotation of Ps. 69:9 is a clue to the author's rhetorical purposes for its placement. He posits that the use of the phrase, "zeal for the temple will consume me" in 69:9 is forward-looking in that it is not the temple that is consumed but rather Jesus' body.[15] Therefore, John placed the temple-cleansing pericope in its present location in order to set the tone and agenda for the rest of the book, namely, the coming crucifixion. This position has its merits to be sure even though Kreitzer's linguistic argument regarding being "consumed" is not as convincing.[16]

In a similar vein, R. H. Lightfoot's theory also follows an Old Testament connection. He suggests that the prophecy of Mal. 3:1-3 (cf. also Hos. 9:15 or Zech. 14:21) is the prophetic impetus that lies behind John's odd ordering of the event. He posits that this is due to both Malachi's and John's mentioning of the coming of the

evaluation by R. J. Miller, "The (A)historicity of Jesus' Temple Demonstration: A Test Case in Methodology," SBLSP 30 (Atlanta: Scholars, 1991): 235–52.

13. Hugh Montefiore, Position of the Cana Miracle and the Cleansing of the Temple in St. John's Gospel," *JTS* 50, no. 2 (1949): 183–86, posits that Ezekiel 47 may be the structural guiding principle behind John's choice to place the temple cleansing early. Because the LXX tradition at 47:8 places the water as beginning from Galilee, Montefiore suggests that the Johannine structure of Jesus' ministry starting in the Galilee has in view Ezekiel 47. This seems too far of a stretch to be plausible.

14. F. A. Cooke, "The Cleansing of the Temple," *ExpTim* 63, no. 10 (1952): 321–322 (322). So too the conclusion of Brown, *The Gospel according to John I–XII*, 118.

15. Larry J. Kreitzer, "The Temple Incident of John 2:13-25: A Preview of What is to Come," in *Understanding, Studying and Reading: New Testament Essays in Honour of John Ashton*, ed. Christopher Rowland and Crispin H. T. Fletcher-Louis, JSNTSup 153 (Sheffield: Sheffield Academic, 1998), 93–101 (97).

16. For example, Kreitzer (ibid., 97) looks at the Hebrew verb for consume אכל ('ākal) and suggests it can mean "to cause to be put to death." While this is possible, he offers no examples where this translation is used as such.

forerunner in close proximity to the Lord's coming to his temple to purify the sons of Levi (cf. John 1–2).[17] In light of my overall presentation, I feel Lightfoot's connection to the Old Testament prophets moves the discussion in the right direction. However, in Malachi it is the Levites who are purged and not the temple per se.[18]

Similar to Lightfoot's perspective is that of Paul Trudinger who suggests that Hezekiah's cleansing of the temple at the period of the Passover is what John had in mind (cf. 2 Chr. 29:2-8, 14-19; 30:1).[19] Trudinger's perspective is insightful by virtue of considering the messianic parallels. However, to what degree Hezekiah is an ideal messianic parallel for Jesus is questionable. Hezekiah was far from the ideal king, especially in his abject failure with the Babylonian envoys (2 Kgs. 20:12-18; Isa. 39) and the stripping of the temple to pay the Assyrians (2 Kgs. 18:16). We may rightly wonder then whether Hezekiah would have been an attractive model for John's portrayal of Jesus.

Finally, I believe that Edwyn Hoskyns is on the right track when he notes that, "The fourth Evangelist is concerned more with the meaning of the words and actions of Jesus than with their original setting or relative order."[20] In this vein, Rudolf Schnackenburg's astute comments summarizes the basic rhetorical intent of John when he notes, "The Johannine narrative does not become worthless if one does not follow it for the dating of the cleansing of the temple. The profound insights which it communicates allow us to recognize the

---

17. R. H. Lightfoot, "Unsolved New Testament Problems: The Cleansing of the Temple in St. John's Gospel," *ExpTim* 60, no. 3 (1948): 64–68, esp. 66–67.
18. So too the critique of William W. Watty, "Jesus and the Temple Cleansing: Blessing or Cursing," *ExpTim* 93, no. 8 (1982): 235–39 (236). Nevertheless, Lightfoot's perspective is definitely an important advancement in why John is doing what he is doing with the temple-cleansing pericope.
19. Trudinger, "The Cleansing of the Temple," 329. Trudinger suggests that, according to the work of David Daube, *He that Cometh* (London: Tooley, 1966), 1–6, in the New Testament era Hezekiah was seen as a messianic figure.
20. Edwyn Hoskyns, *The Fourth Gospel Vol. 1* (London: Faber and Faber, 1940), 209–10.

secret forces at work in unbelief, to see the gulf between Jesus and official Judaism and to sense the coming catastrophe from the start."[21] Indeed, John's purpose was, from the start, to set in plain view for the reader the "coming catastrophe."

As we have seen, no one theory that we have examined satisfactorily answers the structural dilemma. However, before I offer my own solution to the enigma, we need to examine *why* Jesus actually cleansed the temple. Did he have Old Testament exemplars in mind? Was he truly outraged at something that may have been going on for some time, or was this just a good piece of street theatre to introduce his public ministry? Answers to these questions are certainly germane to the discussion.

Why Did Jesus Cleanse the Temple?

When trying to answer this "why" question, scholars generally fall into one of the following three positions: 1) the act was non-eschatological and merely reflects actions germane to the immediate circumstances in the temple, namely, corruption of the sacred space and temple-sanctioned "banditry"; 2) the act had eschatological import for the coming destruction of the temple and its replacement with Jesus the "Temple"; or 3) it is some combination of both 1 and 2.[22] In the discussion that follows I will give a sampling of different scholars and their positions in light of these three categories. Due to the hybrid nature of some of these scholarly positions, I will only loosely follow the above categories.

To begin, John Ferguson suggests that Jesus cleansed the temple as a statement against the defilement of the non-Jewish section of

---

21. Schnackenburg, *Gospel according to St. John*, 1:355.
22. For a brief discussion on these perspectives along with a list of scholars holding each position, see Perrin, *Jesus the Temple*, 88–92. See also Craig S. Keener, *The Gospel of John: A Commentary*, 2 vols. (Peabody, MA: Hendrickson, 2003; repr., Grand Rapids: Baker, 2012), 1:522–27.

105

the temple, the court of the Gentiles.[23] Therefore, Jesus was being "international" in his actions in an effort to show his desire for the inclusiveness of the Gentiles in the plan of God. To a degree, Ferguson is no doubt correct, but, as will be developed below, there is much more going on especially in light of John's use and structural placement of the event. Victor Eppstein proposes that the cleansing may have been the direct result of a new fiscal policy put in place by Caiaphas after the expulsion of the Sanhedrin.[24] This new policy allowed for the selling of sacrificial animals in the temple precincts, from which the high priest profited.[25] Eppstein's theory merits serious consideration due to the thorough historical context from which he argues. Yet, this still leaves one wondering if Jesus' actions have more purpose behind them than merely protesting against a new business venture.[26] The Old Testament links must be considered when evaluating Jesus' actions.

In this regard, Andrew Lincoln suggests that John was creating a dichotomy between the old order and the new order in an effort to set up a lawsuit format.[27] Lincoln's position is valid and does strengthen the Old Testament connections; yet once again the commercial circumstances in the temple also seem to be a part of

---

23. John Ferguson, "The Cleansing of the Temple," *Modern Churchman* 24, no. 1 (1981): 27–30, esp. 30.
24. Matson, "Temple Incident," 145–53 (147), objects to this conclusion. Richard Bauckham, "Jesus' Demonstration in the Temple," in *Law and Religion: Essays on the Place of the Law in Israel and Early Christianity*, ed. Barnabas Lindars (Cambridge: James Clarke & Co., 1988), 72–89, suggests that Jesus was opposing the commercialism of the temple. However, contra Bauckham (74), it is hardly likely that Jesus was opposed to "theocratic taxation" seeing how the Old Testament laws legislated "theocratic taxation" in the form of required offerings and tithes (Exod. 13:15; 22:29; 34:20; Lev. 27:26; Num. 3:13; 18:15-18, 28; Deut. 12:6-17).
25. Victor Eppstein, "The Historicity of the Cleansing of the Temple," *ZNW* 55, no. 1 (1964): 42–58. Alfred Edersheim, *The Life and Times of Jesus the Messiah* (McLean, VA: MacDonald, 1988), 1:370, notes that the salesmen were gouging the poor people by charging as much as four dollars for a pair of doves worth a nickel.
26. So too the conclusion of Evans, "Jesus' Action in the Temple," 269.
27. Andrew T. Lincoln, *Truth on Trial: The Lawsuit Motif in the Fourth Gospel* (Peabody, MA: Hendrickson, 2000), 233.

the picture. Next, Hartmut Stegemann posits that Jesus may have been influenced by the Essenes at Qumran who believed that the messianic era had dawned.[28] As such the need for sacrifices had ended. However, this is a very tenuous thesis that relies heavily on a direct link between Jesus and the Qumran community of which there is no supporting textual evidence.[29] Finally, E. P. Sanders averred that the actions of Jesus in the temple cleansing may be linked to the Old Testament prophetic warnings of coming judgment. Thus Jesus' actions are not to be connected with a priestly act of cleansing/purifying the temple, but rather serve as a prophetic harbinger of the coming destruction of the temple in 70 C.E.[30]

Focusing more on the hybrid nature of Jesus' actions, Craig Evans rightly takes exception with Sanders's view by arguing that the purification of the temple was in fact the intent of Jesus with the eschatological/prophetic nuance also as a possible motive.[31] This is especially true in light of the numerous Old Testament references to corruption at the priestly level, a similar reality in the days of Jesus.[32] It is therefore more likely that both of these motifs were in view as Jesus cleansed the temple.[33]

Also important to this discussion are the conclusions of William Watty. In studying the Markan version of this event, Watty correctly

---

28. Hartmut Stegemann, "Some Aspects of Eschatology in Texts from the Qumran Community and in the Teachings of Jesus," in *Biblical Archaeology Today*, ed. Janet Amitai (Jerusalem: Israel Exploration Society, 1985), 408–26, esp. 412–13.
29. Ibid., 408–26, esp. 412–16. I must concur with Craig Evans's ("Jesus' Action in the Temple: Cleansing or Portent of Destruction?," *CBQ* 15, no. 2 [1989]: 237–70 [264–65]) critique of Stegemann's thesis. Passages such as Matt. 5:23-24 push against Stegemann's thesis.
30. E. P. Sanders, *Jesus and Judaism* (Philadelphia: Fortress Press, 1985), 61–76. So too the conclusion of Watty, "Jesus and the Temple Cleansing," 237; and Willard M. Swartley, *John*, BCBC (Waterloo, Ontario: Herald Press, 2013), 99.
31. Evans, "Jesus' Action in the Temple," 237–70. For a similar view, see Andreas J. Köstenberger, *John*, BECNT (Grand Rapids: Baker, 2004), 102.
32. Evans, "Jesus' Action in the Temple," 248–64.
33. So too the conclusion of Stephen Motyer, *Your Father the Devil?: A New Approach to John and 'the Jews'* (Milton Keynes, England: Paternoster, 1997), 39.

notes the possible prophetic symbolism in Jesus' "walking around" and "surveying" the defilement of the temple precincts (Mark 11:11). Much like Joshua encircled the city of Jericho and "surveyed" the city under the "ban"/*ḥerem* (Joshua 6), and similar to the surveying of the temple in Rev. 11:1-2 prior to its destruction/defilement by the Gentiles, Jesus performs a prophetic-inspired symbolic action against the temple and its leaders.[34] Watty goes on to conclude that, "It therefore seems that in looking around and walking around Jesus was performing symbolic actions which might be interpreted as a survey and an encirclement preliminary to the desecration and destruction of the temple now placed under a ban."[35] Even though John does not mention "walking around" the temple, the prophetic overtones cannot be dismissed. Nicholas Perrin's conclusion highlights this well: "In entering the temple that day, Jesus was primarily interested in, first, issuing a *prophetic indictment* against the regnant temple administration on the grounds of fiscal abuse and, second, indicating his own role of (re)builder of the eschatological temple" (italics mine).[36] Even though I am more in line with Evans's perspective, Perrin's *prophetic indictment* perspective meshes well with that of the sixth-century prophet Ezekiel.

In light of the possible intermingling of motives attributed to Jesus' actions in the temple, many scholars are now coming to realize that limiting Jesus' actions to one purpose alone may be too restrictive. A growing number of scholars are now suggesting that Jesus' actions in the temple reflect both his actions against the temple's defilement by the priests of his day and an eschatological outlook of the temple's destruction by the Romans. Furthermore, for John, Jesus' actions

---

34. Watty, "Jesus and the Temple Cleansing," 239. See a similar conclusion by R. H. Lightfoot, *The Gospel Message of St. Mark* (Oxford: Clarendon, 1950), 74–79.
35. Watty, "Jesus and the Temple Cleansing," 239.
36. Perrin, *Jesus the Temple*, 92.

foreshadowed Jesus' death burial, and resurrection as the new Temple (John 2:21; see also Perrin's position above).[37] Again Watty's position reflects shades of this conclusion. He suggests that the cleansing was symbolic of the replacement of the earthly temple with a spiritual one, that is, the believer's body (1 Cor. 6:19), a position not readily accepted by some.[38] Also, Rev. 21:22 makes it clear that Jesus will be the new temple in the eschaton.[39] This latter interpretation takes seriously the statement in John 2:19: "Destroy this temple and in three days I will build it again." John seems to intimate what the author of Revelation comes out and says clearly.[40]

As will be discussed below, in light of our thesis John no doubt had both nuances in view: cleansing and symbolic action reflecting the replacement of the temple with Jesus' body. As John fashioned his temple-cleansing pericope he seems to have had the Ezekielian exemplar in mind.[41] For Ezekiel, the priesthood and elders had defiled the temple precincts (Ezek. 8). This desecration had forced the departure of Yahweh's glory/*kābôd* from the first temple.[42] In John's presentation, even though Jesus symbolically cleanses the temple of its impurities—allowed by not only the temple clergy but the high priest himself[43]—the fate of the second temple is sealed. The people's

---

37. See comments by D. A. Carson, "Adumbrations of Atonement Theology in the Fourth Gospel," *JETS* 57, no. 3 (2014): 513–22 (515); and Bryan, "Consumed by Zeal," 480.
38. Watty, "Jesus and the Temple Cleansing," 235–39. On the other hand, Francis J. Moloney, *Belief in the Word: Reading the Fourth Gospel: John 1–4* (Minneapolis: Fortress Press, 1993), 102n35; and Schnackenburg, *Gospel according to St. John*, 1:357, object to the connection with the believer.
39. Carson, "Adumbrations," 519, notes the possibility of the continuity between the authorship of the Fourth Gospel and Revelation.
40. It seems quite clear that for John his "portrayal" of Jesus is to be equated with the "historical" Jesus.
41. So too Perrin, *Jesus the Temple*, 88–89. Evans, "Jesus' Action in the Temple," 257, does suggest that "Jesus' actions in the temple may very well have been inspired by the oracles of the classical prophets."
42. See Perrin, *Jesus the Temple*, 112n86, where he lists Ezek. 8–10 as an example in concert with John's temple cleansing.
43. See Evans, "Jesus' Action in the Temple," 264. By listing and interacting with a number of first-century texts, Evans (256–64) presents a cogent argument discussing the likelihood of the

failure to worship God with a pure heart, and the rejection of Jesus' message as God's spokesperson, had assured their downfall (cf. John 12:37; Luke 19:44). In essence, John is showing that Jesus had authority over the earthly temple to cleanse it at will and to symbolically predict its demise. Nothing could be closer to the reality of Yahweh's interaction with Ezekiel in Ezek. 8–11.

That such a message resembled, to a degree, the Qumranic and other sectarian hopes and expectations for a messiah in a first-century context may be more coincidental than purposeful, at least in the case of the Fourth Gospel. Nevertheless, this does not negate the possibility that Jesus chose to adopt, in a way, the role of fulfilling the people's messianic expectations, an idealized role that he would break with as the cross loomed large (John 12:12-36; 13:26-29; 14:1-4; 16:16-19; 18:10-11; cf. Matt 16:21-28; Mark 8:31-33; Acts 1:6).[44] At the same time, one also must bear in mind that for the Johannine readers, post-70 C.E., Jesus did indeed become their new "temple" in place of the earthly one.[45] Similarly, Ezekiel's second vision sets before his readers the reality that the defiled temple needed to be cleansed (Ezek. 8–10). This would happen during the catastrophic event of 586 B.C.E. (Ezek. 12:1-28; 17:12-24; 21:19-26; 24:1-14; 33:21-22).[46]

To summarize what we have covered thus far, scholars have failed to reach a consensus on why John placed the temple-cleansing pericope early in the Fourth Gospel. Even though I am cautious to offer yet another theory, the number of other parallels with Ezekiel

---

corruption of the priesthood during the time of Jesus. By extension this would include the corruption of the second temple.

44. According to Acts 1:6, the disciples expected an earthly kingdom to be established immediately. However, once again Jesus' plan was not in line with the messianic thinking of the day.

45. Moloney, *Belief in the Word*, 102. See also Swartley, *John*, 97.

46. For a discussion of the looming Babylonian destruction of the temple in 586 B.C.E. as evidenced in the rhetorical intent in Ezekiel's second vision, see Brian Neil Peterson, *Ezekiel in Context: Ezekiel's Message Understood in Its Historical Setting of Covenant Curses and Ancient Near Eastern Mythological Motifs*, PTMS 182 (Eugene, OR: Pickwick Publications, 2012), 142–56.

pushes me to do so.[47] Second, most recognize that the cleansing of the temple had symbolic as well as practical connotations, a conclusion that best fits the data. Third, Jesus may have been playing upon his generation's hopes for the messianic figure. However, John puts a twist on their expectations by presenting Jesus as a spiritual temple (John 2:19). Finally, in Jesus' act of temple cleansing, he was showing the religious elite, and his generation, that he had authority over God's/his house to demand those who used it to follow a strict holiness code. Through this symbolic act, Jesus prophesied the destruction of the old order and the inbreaking of the new. In many ways this resonates with the events leading up to the fall of the city more than six centuries earlier. It was Ezekiel who prophesied the destruction of the first temple and the city. And it was Ezekiel who foretold it through visions and sign acts. Yahweh had every right to cleanse Yahweh's house because the nation was not following a strict holiness code.

It is my contention that John looked to this moment in Israel's past and saw in that tragic snapshot of time ready-made parallels and symbols ripe for the picking in a first-century context, especially writing *ex post facto* of the temple destruction. It was the literary and historical context of Ezekiel's prophecy and the temple's destruction that shaped John's rhetorical purposes. More specifically, it was the second vision of Ezekiel that served as the impetus behind his literary uprooting of the temple cleansing from the final days of Jesus' life—if it indeed is historically in the correct place in the Synoptics—in order to place it at the opening stages of Jesus' public ministry. It was both ingenious and in concert with the events of Ezekiel's era. It is to this analysis that we now turn.

---

47. Draper, "Temple, Tabernacle and Mystical Experience," 264, suggests Isaiah and Ezekiel as the backdrop for the temple cleansing.

The Location of the Temple-Cleansing Pericope Vis-à-vis Ezekiel's Second Vision[48]

In what follows I will organize my discussion into three categories: 1) general parallels of the motifs between the Johannine temple-cleansing pericope and Ezekiel's second vision of the departure of Yahweh's glory/*kābôd*; 2) the general structural similarities between the two; and 3) the more specific connections linking the two. In the latter case I will first show the unique features of John's presentation of the temple-cleansing pericope vis-à-vis the Synoptics in order to demonstrate that John includes features unique to his account in order to draw motif and thematic connections with Ezekiel's vision.

General Parallels of Motifs

As noted in the previous chapter, both Ezekiel and Jesus arrive in Jerusalem to witness the desecration of the temple, one in a visionary mode and the other physically.[49] Both the prophet and Jesus are spiritually sickened by what they see. On the surface, the things that defiled the temple of Jesus' day seem to pale in comparison to that of Ezekiel's era. However, the similar spiritual condition of the leaders in both periods is a unifying factor. Unbelief in God in the book of Ezekiel and unbelief in God/Jesus in the Fourth Gospel is the central reason for the departure/need for cleansing in both accounts (cf. Ezek. 2; 3:1-11; 8; John 1:11; 2:18).[50] The defiling of Yahweh's

---

48. Bruce G. Schuchard, *Scripture within Scripture: The Interrelationship of Form and Function in the Explicit Old Testament Citations in the Gospel of John*, SBLDS 133 (Atlanta: Scholars, 1992), 25–26, also connects the early cleansing of the temple with Ezekiel's second vision. Hassell Bullock, "Ezekiel: Bridge between the Testaments," *JETS* 25, no. 1 (1982): 29, intimates this connection as well.
49. J. Ramsey Michaels, *The Gospel of John*, NICNT (Grand Rapids: Eerdmans, 2010), 158, notes that Jesus goes to Jerusalem specifically to visit the temple.
50. John's notation in 1:11 concerning the rejection of Jesus by his own people sets the tone for the rest of the book. This is clearly meant to serve as an introduction with the end already in view. Jesus' signs used to bring about belief in Jesus thus become a rhetorical device for John. Indeed,

presence with idols in Ezekiel's vision, and commercial ventures in Jesus' day, are merely symptoms of the religious elites' greater heart problem: unbelief in the message of God through his P/prophet.

The temple-cleansing pericope also appears after Jesus' sign at Cana in John 2:1-11. And, according to some scholars, Jesus' cleansing of the temple should itself be labeled a sign, a position I adopt (see chapter 3 above). As we have pointed out already, Jesus' cleansing of the temple also serves as an overview for the rest of the book, namely, as a symbolic precursor to the crucifixion and the rejection of Jesus, and as evidence of the open hostilities between Jesus and the religious elite.[51] The act of the temple cleansing was performed as a sign before the religious elite with the purpose of proving that Jesus had the authority of God. Also, the phrase "destroy this temple and in three days I will raise it up" sets a somber tone for Jesus' earthly ministry: he was on a collision course with the cross (John 2:19). Even the disciples did not realize what this meant until after the fact (John 2:22). But for the first readers of the Fourth Gospel it was clear that the tone was one of foreboding: the Jewish elite were waiting for their opportunity to kill Jesus (John 5:18; 7:1, 19, 25, 8:37, 40; 11:53). From chapters 3–12 Jesus battles the unbelief of the people as he performs his signs. According to John, it will be their unbelief that will bring about their judgment (John 3:18; 12:37).[52] John clearly must have had the events of 70 C.E. in mind when he chose to include these warnings.[53]

---

the request for a sign from Jesus when he cleansed the temple betrays the unbelief of the temple leaders. By the end of Jesus' life few would actually accept the signs as evidence that he was in fact God incarnate.

51. Francis J. Moloney, "Reading John 2:13-22: The Purification of the Temple," *RB* 97, no. 3 (1990): 432–52 (439).

52. Ernst Käsemann, *The Testament of Jesus: A Study of the Gospel of John in Light of Chapter 17*, trans. Gerhard Krodel (London: SCM, 1968), says, "The glory of the earthly Jesus manifests itself in time and space and in a world of rebellion against God (20)"

Nevertheless, Jesus' words also sound a note of hope. Inherent in the phrase "in three days I will raise it [his body] up" is the message of hope that looks forward to Jesus' return from the grave to dwell among his followers (John 14:2-3, 18, 28; 20:19-31; the eternal abiding presence of the Paraclete is also in view here; cf. John 14:16-17, 26).[54] Finally, due to the clear connections between the temple cleansing and the Passion Week, one must handle these topics together. Not surprisingly, in the book of Ezekiel one cannot address the departure of Yahweh's glory/*kābôd* without considering Yahweh's return in Ezek. 43:1-5 (see chapter 7 below).

The parallels become clear when these general motifs are juxtaposed with Ezekiel's second vision. The vision falls in the midst of the sign acts of the prophet (Ezek. 4-5 and chapters 12 and 24), and serves a similar function in relation to its importance for the entire book of Ezekiel as does the temple-cleansing pericope for the Fourth Gospel. That is, the departure of Yahweh's glory/*kābôd* in chapter 11 serves as a central theme for most of the book (viz., the loss of Yahweh's presence), beginning with the sign act of the exile in Ezek. 12, a foreshadowing of the city and temple's destruction. Throughout chapters 13-24 the oracles take on an ominous tone as the prophet outlines the many sins of the people, with a special focus on the religious and political elite (cf. Ezek. 13, 14, 17, 19), who have caused the nation to be judged. Even though Ezekiel performs sign acts and delivers oracles, the people still will not believe (Ezek. 33:32). Thus, from the second temple vision onward the rest of the first half of Ezekiel depicts the rapid slide into exile. Yet, a glimmer

---

53. See also comments by Andreas J. Köstenberger, "The Destruction of the Second Temple and the Composition of the Fourth Gospel," in *Challenging Perspectives on the Gospel of John*, ed. John Lierman, WUNT 2.219 (Tübingen: Mohr Siebeck, 2006), 69–108 (80).
54. For a discussion on the distinctness of the Paraclete in the Fourth Gospel, see J. T. Forestell, "Jesus and the Paraclete in the Gospel of John," in *Word and Spirit: Essays in Honor of David Michael Stanley, S. J. on His 60th Birthday*, ed. Joseph Plevnik (Toronto: Regis College Press, 1975), 151–97.

of hope is still present within the sullen presentation of the second vision. Ezek. 11:16-20 offers this hope while promising the coming of the new covenant (Ezek. 11:19)! In this regard, after the departure of Yahweh's glory/*kābôd*, the remainder of the book looks forward to the return of the same as depicted in Ezek. 43:1-5, which is marked by Yahweh's blessing and peace.[55] This latter facet also resonates with the picture found in the Fourth Gospel whereby Jesus' return as the rebuilt and resurrected "temple" brings about everlasting "peace" (John 20:19, 21, 26; see chapter 6 below). While these broad strokes of the narrative content show similarities in motifs between the two books, a closer analysis, which we will undertake in a moment, will reveal even more thematic parallels.

Finally, the defiling aspects in the temple caused Yahweh to depart his abode and move to the foreign land of Babylon where Yahweh had driven the exiles. Yahweh chose to be among the outcasts, whom most in Jerusalem felt had been judged by God already. There Yahweh promised to be a "sanctuary" for the outcasts (Ezek. 11:16).[56] Yahweh's pledge to dwell among the exiles is in the immediate context of the promise of the messianic age when a new spirit would be given to the people (Ezek. 11:19, 20). Interestingly, in John 1:14 Jesus is depicted as leaving his abode in heaven and tabernacling among humankind for the purpose of ministering to them in this inaugurated messianic age.

Much like the depiction in Ezekiel, John not only shows that Jesus, as God, is not restricted to an earthly building, but also that the messianic age had arrived. That is why these unique chapters in the Fourth Gospel (i.e., John 2–4) must be read together. After Jesus cleansed the temple, John records a series of encounters with people

---

55. See Peterson, *Ezekiel in Context*, 297–302. It is fitting that in the eschaton Jerusalem will be named "Yahweh is there" (יהוה שמה cf. Ezek. 48:35).
56. See also Köstenberger, "Destruction of the Second Temple," 82.

as Jesus goes out from the temple/Jerusalem to minister to the least likely of people, namely, Nicodemus, the Samaritan woman, and the royal official (John 3–4). By these acts Jesus was showing that the new messianic age had dawned, the time when a new spirit would be given to his "people" (John 3:5-8; 4:23-26). Jesus not only emphasizes the role of the Spirit in the lives of Nicodemus and the Samaritan woman, but he stresses that the messianic age had arrived and that he was the Messiah (John 4:23, 26)! Indeed, Jesus says as much during his discussion with the woman at the well just a chapter and a half later: neither Jerusalem nor Mt. Gerizim will be the place of worship but rather those who worship God must do it in spirit and in truth (John 4:21, 23)! Thus, John shows that Jesus can minister in the most unlikely of places (e.g., Samaria, a region of "outcasts"!) without a temple. This of course mirrors Yahweh's/Ezekiel's ministry in the unlikely setting of the Babylonian exile without a temple (cf. Psalm 137).

Similar Structural Patterns

In light of our discussion about the thematic similarities, it is now possible to formulate a structural picture. The basic structural pattern of Ezekiel's vision in chapters 8–11 is as follows: 1) Ezekiel comes to the temple and sees/hears the abominations in the temple (Ezek. 8); 2) the enactment of judgment takes place (Ezek. 9); 3) Yahweh's glory/*kābôd* departs from the temple (Ezek. 10); and 4) the visionary/symbolic destruction of the city ensues in Ezek. 11 after the departure of Yahweh's glory from the city (Ezek. 11:23).

A number of noticeable parallels emerge when this structure is superimposed on the Johannine temple-cleansing pericope. First, much like Ezekiel's visionary arrival at the first temple, Jesus comes to the second temple and sees the defiling actions of the money changers (John 2:13-14a).[57] Immediately a possible answer to the dilemma of why John has Jesus appearing in Jerusalem early in his Gospel (contra the Synoptic writers) finds a solution in the structural parallels with Ezekiel (cf. Matt. 20:18; Mark 10:32; Luke 17:11). Next, whereas in Ezekiel's day the people thought that Yahweh did not see them because he had abandoned them (Ezek. 8:12), in John's case God, in the person of Jesus, is indeed present and sees what they are doing in the courts of the temple (see also Mark 11:11). In Ezekiel, the prophet prefaces the departure of Yahweh's glory/*kābôd* by enumerating the abominations in the temple. In Ezek. 8 these defiling things include: the idol of jealousy (vv. 3-5); the elders practicing idolatry with carved images of every creeping thing, in secrecy (vv. 7-12); the worship of Tammuz (v. 14); and the worship of the sun (v. 16). Whereas in Ezekiel's day the blatant idolatry included animal images, Tammuz, and the sun, in the Fourth Gospel Jesus sees the idolatry not in the images per se, but rather in the priests' quest for wealth and money at the expense of the Gentiles' ability to worship.[58] The nation may have learned their lesson not to practice blatant idolatry after 586 B.C.E., but, just like in Ezekiel's era for many (the religious elite in particular) in Jesus' day, their hearts were still far from God.

Second, the judgment that is enacted upon the temple/Jerusalem comes at the hands of Yahweh's servants (cf. Ezek. 9:1-2; John 2:15-16). In Ezekiel's case, seven selected "men"/divine beings (Ezek. 9:2; 10:2) carry out the judgment in a visionary/symbolic act, an act brought to fruition by the Babylonians in 586 B.C.E. For John, it is Jesus, the Man/Divine Being, who carries out the symbolic judgment, a judgment brought to fruition by the Romans in 70 C.E.

---

57. Note also 2 Macc. 10:5-9 and the cleansing of the temple by Judas Maccabeus.
58. Cf. Eppstein, "Cleansing of the Temple," 42–58. Eppstein suggests that the issue was more related to a dispute between the new high priest, Caiaphas, and the exiled Sanhedrin. Caiaphas was thus trying to muscle his way into a lucrative enterprise that was once monopolized by the Sanhedrin on the Mount of Olives.

Moreover, both destructions come at the will/permission of God (cf. Ezek. 9:5-6; 10:2; 11:7-13; Luke 23:28-29).[59]

The third structural parallel is the departure of Yahweh's glory/*kābôd* from the temple. In Ezekiel this happens in two phases.[60] First the *kābôd* of Yahweh moves from the Holy of Holies to the threshold of the temple (Ezek. 9:3; 10:4, 18). Then it moves out of the temple and rests on the Mount of Olives to the east of the city (Ezek. 11:23). It is this last position that serves as a picture of Yahweh's presiding presence as a judge as Yahweh oversees the total destruction of the city and temple. In the Fourth Gospel, Jesus too has a phased departure from his ministry/presence in the temple. In John 2:22, the temple-cleansing pericope ends with the intimated departure of Jesus from the temple. Craig Keener rightly notes that for Jesus the temple is a place of conflict with people wanting to kill him (John 8:59).[61] From the point of Jesus' cleansing of the temple until chapter 10, Jesus makes only sporadic appearances in the temple (John 5:14; 7:14, 28; 8:2, 20, 59). The final appearance of Jesus in the temple comes in John 10, but here it ends with Jesus being driven out of the temple by the unbelief of the people and their attempts to stone him (John 10:31-39 cf. also 8:59). The people's rejection of Jesus/Yahweh in both accounts effects the departure of God from the temple (see more on temple abandonment below). What is more, Yahweh moves to a hill outside of the city to effect judgment on Jerusalem, whereas Jesus is crucified outside of the city (John 19:17-20), an act that will have "judgment" repercussions both literally and spiritually.[62] Thus, the temple cleansing scene begins the

---

59. Cf. William A. Tooman, "Ezekiel's Radical Challenge to Inviolability," *ZAW* 121, no. 4 (2009): 498–514 (508, 511).
60. Ibid., 498. Here Tooman notes that midrash Pesiqta de-Rab Kahana breaks Yahweh's departure into ten steps.
61. Keener, *Gospel of John*, 1:519.
62. It is only in the Fourth Gospel that the crucifixion site is explicitly noted as being "near the city."

phased departure of Jesus from the temple, the final aspect of which comes just prior to Jesus' crucifixion, that is, the destruction of the temple of his body (cf. John 2:19).

The final structural parallel between Ezekiel and John is the destruction of the city and temple. Ezekiel's vision of the temple's destruction occurs approximately six years before the city and the temple's destruction takes place. This can be determined from the dated prophecy in Ezek. 8:1: "In the sixth year, in the sixth month, on the fifth day" (i.e., September 18, 592 B.C.E.).[63] Similarly, in the Johannine account the fulfillment of Jesus' symbolic actions takes place at a later period, approximately forty years later for the destruction of the city and temple and approximately three years for the destruction of the temple of Jesus' body. Thus, the real-time events in both books have a future-looking fulfillment.

Finally, it is important to note that the temple-cleansing pericope literarily falls within the midst of the signs that John uses to prove Jesus' divinity (e.g., turning the water into wine [2:1-11]; the healing of the official's son [4:46-54]; the healing of the man by pool [5:1-9]). Not surprisingly, the departure of Yahweh's glory/*kābôd* in Ezek. 8–11 also falls within the sign acts of Ezekiel (the brick [4:1-3]; laying on his side [4:4-6]; baring his arm [4:7-8]; eating rationed food over dung [4:9-17]; cutting his hair [5:1-17]; and mimicking going into exile [12:1-16]). In both cases the signs served to prove the trustworthiness of the person and their connection to God; in Jesus' case, his very divinity.

A Note on Temple Abandonment

Before finishing this topic it seems appropriate to briefly discuss the importance of temple abandonment for an ancient audience. Temple

---

63. For a full listing of the dates in Ezekiel, see Daniel Block, *Ezekiel 1–24*, NICOT (Grand Rapids: Eerdmans, 1997), 28–29.

abandonment was the worse curse imaginable for the ancients, Israel included.[64] In a New Testament context, temple abandonment may not have had the exact same stigma, but John's presentation of Jesus' departure from the temple (i.e., temple abandonment; cf. John 8:59[65]), served a symbolic function paralleling that of Ezekiel: the fate of Jerusalem and the temple was sealed. In Ezekiel's presentation, the defilement of the temple had forced Yahweh to leave, a precursor to the invasion of the Babylonians and the destruction of the city and temple. This is eerily similar to the events leading up to the final destruction of the second temple in 70 C.E. by the Romans. For John, the religious elite, through their defilement and rejection of Jesus, had in essence forced Jesus to abandon his house (John 2:13-22; 8:59). The end result in both John and Ezekiel was the certain destruction of the temple and the city.[66]

Closely associated with this idea is the concept of mourning the loss of the temple after the departure of the Divine. Matthew and Luke record Jesus mourning over the loss of the city, and, by extension, the temple, once Jesus knew his work on earth was over (Matt. 23:37; Luke 13:34; 23:28-31). However, in light of John's reliance on Ezekiel, this picture did not fit the parallel in Ezekiel. Because Ezekiel was told not to mourn the death of his wife—a sign act depicting the loss of the city and temple (Ezek. 24:16)—John may have purposely avoided this Synoptic motif.

---

64. See more in Peterson, *Ezekiel in Context*, 153–72; and Daniel Block, "Divine Abandonment: Ezekiel's Adaptation of an Ancient Near Eastern Motif," in *The Book of Ezekiel: Theological and Anthropological Perspectives*, ed. Margaret S. Odell and John T. Strong, SBLSymS 9 (Atlanta: SBL, 2000), 15–42.
65. See also comments by Köstenberger, "Destruction of the Second Temple," 103–104.
66. See also ibid., 80.

Specific Parallels vis-à-vis the Synoptics

Our preliminary assessment showed that there are a number of general thematic and structural parallels between Ezek. 8–11 and John 2:13-22. More of the rhetorical intent becomes apparent in the details John includes/excludes when one considers the differences between the Synoptic traditions and John vis-à-vis Ezekiel. The following section highlights the differences in how the Synoptic writers present Jesus' cleansing of the temple compared to John's usage.[67]

Placement of Pericope

The Synoptic writers present Jesus' cleansing of the temple during the last week of his life whereas John presents it in the first year of Jesus' ministry (see above discussion). Having covered this point in some detail in the above discussion, I will only make a few passing comments here. To begin with, if there was only one account of the temple cleansing, John bypasses or alters many of the Synoptic parallels of the event for a greater purpose.[68] Further, John clearly wanted the reader to grasp the righteous anger and judgmental tone of the event as opposed to the kingly aura that is a key part of the Synoptic writers' placement of the temple cleansing during the triumphal entry (cf. Zech. 9:9; Matt. 21:1-14; Mark 11:1-17; Luke 19:29-46).[69] Now, to be sure, while Jesus' kingly nature is evident in the Fourth Gospel, John may have removed the triumphal entry

---

67. For a discussion on the differences between John's and Mark's presentation of the temple-cleansing pericope, see Matson, "Contribution of the Temple Cleansing," 495–99. Matson contends that John was relying on an "independent version of the same episode (499)." See also idem, "Temple Incident," 145–53 (152–53). Schnackenburg, *Gospel according to St. John*, 1:353, suggests that the accounts in all the Gospels are the same event. The differences can be explained due to the fact that John is only relating his details from memory.

68. The complete dismissal of many of the differences between John and the Synoptics as later additions or falsehoods by Scott (*Crisis in the Life of Jesus*, 17–21) is not at all satisfactory or convincing.

into Jerusalem with Jesus sitting on a colt for the very purpose of highlighting the theme of judgment in the temple-cleansing pericope. In this regard, this tone of judgment fits well with the content of Ezek. 8–11 (see above).

Length of the Account

The Synoptic writers spend two to three verses on this event (cf. Matt. 21:12-14; Mark 11:15-17; Luke 19:45-46) whereas John devotes ten verses to the account, thus showing John's desire to draw attention to this event (John 2:13-22). As noted in the first observation, the desire of John to connect Jesus' actions to Ezekiel's vision may help explain why John gives a protracted temple-cleansing pericope. John's extended, yet select, rendition of the account may point to the heightened rhetorical importance that he placed upon the event. Further, the extended focus in John is on the actual act of the temple cleansing, not on the teaching about the actions (as noted in Mark 11:17).[70] This makes sense in light of the focused vision in Ezekiel where the prophet sees the abominations and desecrations in the temple and then the departure of Yahweh.

The Inclusion of Specific Animals

Only John mentions the oxen, sheep, and doves (John 2:14-15). John's inclusion of the sacrificial animals, which are mentioned here as opposed to the Synoptics, may have been triggered by the drawings/carvings of "every creeping thing, beasts, and detestable things" (כל־תבנית רמש ובהמה שקץ) that defiled the temple as

---

69. William Loader, "Jesus and the Law in John," in *Theology and Christology in the Fourth Gospel: Essays by the Members of the SNTS Johannine Writing Seminar*, ed. Gilbert van Belle, Jan G. Van Der Watt, and Petrus J. Maritz, BETL 184 (Leuven: Leuven University Press, 2005), 135–54 (140–41), also draws a connection between the temple-cleansing pericope and Ezek. 8 and 9.
70. Cf. Matson, "Contribution of the Temple Cleansing," 499.

depicted in Ezek. 8:10. The LXX misses the three designations and conflates them under the heading "vain abominations" (μάταια βδελύγματα). In Ezek. 8:10 the key word is בהמה (*bĕhēmâ*), which accounts for sacrificial animals (perhaps with the exception of doves; cf. Gen. 1:25; Lev. 1:2; 7:25; 27:11; Num. 31:30; Deut. 14:4).[71] In Ezekiel's day, the priests and elders had made idols and carvings of all these sacrificial animals (along with other creeping things and idols) and had placed them in the temple as part of their worship practices. Here John lists the sacrificial animals, which are fine in their rightful place but are now defiling the temple. In both texts, it was not the animals themselves that were unclean, but how they were used by the people in worship and where the animals and/or their images were placed in the temple. Further, in both texts, this is the very first thing that Ezekiel and Jesus mention and see (Ezek. 8:10; John 2:14).

Missing Quotations from the Prophets

In the Synoptics, Jesus quotes Isa. 56:7, "My house shall be called a house of prayer,"[72] and alludes to Jer. 7:11 with the phrase "den of robbers" (cf. Matt. 21:13; Mark 11:17; Luke 19:46). The omission of these Old Testament quotations by John may be rooted in John's desire not to detract from the motif of "zeal" as found in Ps. 69:9 (on this, see more below).

Temple Metaphor

None of the Synoptic writers note Jesus' metaphor of destroying the temple and rebuilding it in three days (John 2:19). The reason for the inclusion of this aspect in the Fourth Gospel finds a suitable answer

---

71. Swartley, *John*, 100, rightly points out that Jesus does not drive out the doves (John 2:15) because they were the sacrifice most often used by the poor.
72. For a discussion on the use of the Old Testament allusions in this passage, especially as they relate to the inclusion of the Gentiles, see Roth, "Cleansing of the Temple," 174–81.

in John's rhetorical needs to connect the temple cleansing with the crucifixion as well as the temple destruction and abandonment motifs in Ezek. 8–11 (see above discussion).

Jesus' Whip

Only John notes that Jesus used/made a "scourge from cords" (φραγέλλιον ἐκ σχοινίων) (John 2:15).[73] John's inclusion of this fact appears to be a minor detail on the surface.[74] While most attempt to determine *how* or *if* Jesus used the whip (i.e., on the animals *and* the people)—a valid question to ask for sure—few ask the glaring question of *why* John even included this fact in the first place.[75] However, in light of Ezek. 9:1-2, this notation takes on rhetorical significance.[76] In the Ezekiel account, the destroyers come to destroy the city (and temple) "each with his destroying weapon in his hand" (ואיש כלי משחתו בידו; Ezek. 9:1).[77] John specifically notes that Jesus made this scourge for the purpose of judging/driving out the moneychangers

---

73. B. F. Westcott, *The Gospel according to St. John* (London: John Murray, 1892), 41, notes that the whip was made of rushes twisted together and that it was a "symbol of authority." However, see the critique of Westcott's position by Hoskyns, *Fourth Gospel*, 1:203.
74. Of course it is possible that there were two cleansings of the temple and John only utilizes the first one. However, I am moving forward under the general consensus that there was only one and that the Gospel writers chose to include select aspects of that one event for rhetorical reasons. Scott, *Crisis in the Life of Jesus*, 19, 25, suggests that Jesus did not touch anyone, but rather that an eager crowd of sympathetic onlookers did the actual casting out of the moneychangers and animal traders. However, there is no textual evidence for this position.
75. Andy Alexis-Baker, "Violence, Nonviolence and the Temple Incident in John 2:13-15," *BibInt* 20, no. 1-2 (2012): 73–96, goes to great lengths in his attempt to downplay the aggressive/"violent" nature of Jesus in this pericope. He postulates that Jesus did not beat any person but merely herded the animals out of the temple with his makeshift "whip" (94). Now, while it is no doubt true that Jesus probably did not beat the moneychangers senseless, it is also true that the context and tenor of the pericope seems to imply more than a mere herding of the animals. I am sure that not too many of the moneychangers would have sat idly by and allowed Jesus to overturn their tables. Some "gentle persuasion" must have taken place. See also a similar conclusion by Croy, "Messianic Whippersnapper," 555–68.
76. Contra McGrath, "'Destroy this Temple,'" 35–43 (36), who avers that John's notation about the whip "serves no Johannine purpose."
77. Bullock, "Ezekiel," 29, also draws a connection to the six destroyers but not to the specific weapons.

and animals. It is very likely that he included this detail of the story to draw a closer parallel to Ezekiel's account.

John's Use of Psalm 69

The only clear Old Testament reference in the Johannine version of the temple cleansing is Ps. 69:9 [68:10 LXX], an imprecatory psalm; the Synoptic writers do not mention this.[78] John stresses that Jesus' actions are rooted in his "zeal" (ζῆλος; *zēlos*),[79] whereas the Synoptic writers focus on the "house of prayer" angle (John 2:17; cf. Matt. 21:13; Mark 11:17; Luke 19:46).[80] Jesus' righteous indignation accompanied the act of his forced removal of the moneychangers.[81] While modern sensibilities try to downplay this aspect of Jesus' actions,[82] it is clear by the use of the imprecatory psalm terminology (see more on this below) that Jesus was upset.[83] In Ezekiel, Yahweh's anger also is emphasized as Yahweh determines that the temple is to be cleansed/destroyed (Ezek. 8:4-18, esp. v.18).[84] Yahweh's passion for a pure Israel and a clean cultic setting are apparent throughout the book of Ezekiel. Claus Westermann concludes, "Jesus is gripped with anger over the profaning of the temple. His action is akin to the work

---

78. On the change in verb tenses from the past perfect to the future, namely, "Zeal for your house has/will consume(d) me," see Rudolf Schnackenburg, *Gospel according to St. John*, 1:347. See also Bryan, "Consumed by Zeal," 479–94.
79. So too Jo-Ann A. Bryant, *John* (Grand Rapids: Baker, 2011), 70.
80. There are those who interpret the text as referring to the zeal of the religious elite, not Jesus'. See for example Bryan, "Consumed by Zeal," 481–82. Now, to be sure, this is indeed possible; however, one should not miss the double entendre intended by John. One group is zealous for their temple cult, the other is zealous for temple purity, a temple understood to be symbolic of the greater temple of Jesus' body. Further, the very fact that Jesus took matters into his own hands shows a level of zeal for the purity of the temple. Why else did he perform such an act?
81. On this use of rage, see T. Torrance, "The Cleansing of the Temple: John ii.13-25," *EvQ* 9, no. 2 (April 1937): 180–91 (184–85).
82. E.g., Alexis-Baker, "Violence, Nonviolence," 73–96; Swartley, *John*, 100.
83. Frederick Dale Bruner, *The Gospel of John: A Commentary* (Grand Rapids: Eerdmans, 2012), 144, has "The Very Angry Jesus" as the heading for this portion of the Fourth Gospel.
84. So too Donna Lee Petter, *The Book of Ezekiel and Mesopotamian City Laments*, OBO 246 (Göttingen: Vandenhoeck & Ruprecht, 2011), 96. Schuchard, *Scripture within Scripture*, 25, also connects Ezekiel's zeal in Ezek. 8–11 with Jesus' in John 2:13-22.

of the prophets of judgment."[85] Of course, one should not exclude the priestly prophet Ezekiel as a man who was zealous for the purity of the temple and worship.[86]

Not surprisingly, only two texts in the LXX use the same Greek term to describe Yahweh's zeal (ζῆλος; *zēlos*) for purity, both in Ezekiel (Ezek. 5:13 and 38:19). The first text is of the most importance because it is situated in the midst of the sign acts. More specifically, it comes as an oracle of doom after the four-part sign act of Ezek. 5:1-4. Here the prophet is told to cut his hair and then divide it into three lots; spreading a third into the wind, burning a third in the center of the city, binding a few pieces onto his belt, and then burning the rest. Yahweh then goes on to declare that Yahweh will pour out his rage on the city of Jerusalem because of their corruption of the law (Ezek. 5:6-7), their abominations (Ezek. 5:9, 11), and their desecration of the temple (Ezek. 5:11). The key verse in the oracle falls in verse 13, which states: "And my anger will be fulfilled and I will satisfy my fury on them and I will be consoled, then they will know that I Yahweh have spoken in my *zeal* (ζῆλος) when I have fulfilled my wrath on them." Ezek. 5 is a prophetic sign act serving as a precursor to the temple destruction! Therefore, in many ways, Jesus' zeal for the temple matches Yahweh's zeal for the temple. Even though the quoting of the imprecatory psalm (Ps. 69:9) is fitting within the context, the prophetic connections are present as well.

Apart from these comparative issues there are also a couple of linguistic points that need to be made before leaving this topic. First, John, like the Synoptic writers, uses the term ἱερός (*hieros*/temple) to describe the temple precincts. However, in John when Jesus speaks of his body being the temple he uses ναός (*naos*/temple or sanctuary)

---

85. Claus Westermann, *The Gospel of John in the Light of the Old Testament*, trans. Siegfried S. Schatzmann (Peabody, MA: Hendrickson, 1998), 13.
86. Bullock, "Ezekiel," 29.

three times (John 2:19-21). Now, while ναός is used for the temple proper, not the outer courts, both in John and the Synoptics (cf. Matt. 23:16, 17, 21, 35; 26:61; 27:5, 40, 51; Mark 14:58; 15:29, 38; Luke 1:9, 21, 22; 23:45), in the LXX it is the book of Ezekiel where ναός appears more than any of the prophets to describe the temple proper, not the outer courts (Ezek. 8:16 [2x]; 41:1, 4, 15, 21, 23, 25; Jer. 7:4; 24:1; 37:18).[87] In fact, the LXX translators used ναός as the term to introduce the reader to the inner court of the temple in Ezek. 8:16. Therefore, although John could have used ἱερός or ναός to speak of the temple, when Jesus identifies himself as the temple in the Fourth Gospel, John appears to be purposely using the dominant term used for the temple proper (i.e., ναός) in the LXX text of Ezek. 8:16.

Second, John also uses the term οἶκος (*oikos*/house) for the temple, which is the dominant term used in the LXX of Ezekiel for identifying the temple as a whole (cf. John 2:16-17; Ezek. 8:12, 14, 16, 17 etc.).[88] And only in John do we have the designation "house of my Father" (τὸν οἶκον τοῦ πατρός μου; cf. John 2:16). In the Synoptics, the authors only note Jesus identifying the temple as "my house" (μου οἶκος; cf. Matt. 21:13; Mark 11:17; Luke 19:46). However, in John this is not merely an indication of a place of worship, this is the dwelling place of Jesus' Father.[89] While the connections are not conclusive, they do add to our theory regarding John's use of Ezekiel.

Conclusion

In this chapter we have looked at a range of scholarly theories dealing with the placement of John's temple-cleansing pericope along with

---

87. The LXX translators also used οἶκος (house) as a designation for the temple because of the use of בית (*bayit*/house) in the Hebrew (cf. Ezek. 9:3, 6, 7; 10:3, 4, 18; 40:5).
88. Cf. Matt. 21:13; Mark 11:17; Luke 19:46.
89. Moloney, "Reading John 2:13-22," 441–42.

the possible reasons *why* Jesus cleansed the temple. While some of the theories were innovative, none offered a satisfying solution to the dilemma. In light of my ongoing theory, I posited a possible parallel between John 2:13-22 and Ezek. 8–11. I then examined a number of structural, thematic, and motif parallels between these two accounts and found that there is good reason to conclude that John placed the temple-cleansing pericope early in his Gospel in order to match Ezekiel's rhetorical agenda, structure, and motifs. This conclusion was bolstered by the features unique to John's rendition of the temple-cleansing pericope vis-à-vis the Synoptics. Many of the peculiarities that John includes in his telling of this transitional event find connections with Ezekiel's visionary account of the departure of Yahweh's glory/*kābôd* and the ensuing destruction of the city. As the tone of foreboding overtakes each book within their early chapters, the reader is alerted to the conclusions of each. For John, it is Jesus being driven from his Father's house, going to the cross, and being resurrected to initiate the new covenant; for Ezekiel, it is Yahweh departing the temple, going into exile, and returning to initiate the new era/covenant (Ezek. 34:25; 37:26). While this chapter continued to build upon the parallels between John and Ezekiel highlighted in our previous two chapters, the prototypical Johannine "I Am" Sayings offer even more support for our thesis. It is to this evaluation that we now turn our attention.

5

John's "I Am" Sayings in Light of Ezekiel

Almost half of the occurrences of the word [εἰμί] in the New Testament (141 times) appear in the Johannine literature, and 54 of these occurrences are in the Fourth Gospel. Forty-five times the word is uttered from the lips of Jesus, 38 of which include the emphatic use of the personal pronoun ἐγώ.[1]

As these findings of William Fowler make clear, of all the Gospel writers, John stands out for his utilization of the term εἰμί (*eimi* "I am"). As a matter of fact, only John uses the unique terminology known as the "'I Am' Sayings." Due to its uniqueness to the Fourth Gospel, one inevitably raises the question regarding the writer's intent. In light of these types of questions, in this chapter I will demonstrate how many of these "I Am" Sayings are meant to connect Jesus to a number of Ezekielian attributes assigned to Yahweh as well as to the coming messianic figure. Moreover, I will juxtapose the general, yet frequent, use of the phrase "I am" (ἐγώ εἰμί/*egō*

---

1. William Glenn Fowler, "The Influence of Ezekiel in the Fourth Gospel: Intertextuality and Interpretation" (PhD diss., Golden Gate Baptist Theological Seminary, 1995), 67–68.

eimi) throughout the Fourth Gospel, especially the reference in John 8:28 ("then they will know I am he"), with the more than sixty occurrences of the similar phrase in Ezekiel: "then they/you will know I am Yahweh." In light of our ongoing thesis, I will conclude that John intends to draw further direct links to Ezekiel in an effort to show that the people needed to know/believe that God had sent Jesus as the Messiah. I also will argue that John used the concept in the same way Ezekiel used the phrase, namely, for the purpose of re-educating his generation. Whereas six hundred years earlier Ezekiel's audience needed to be re-educated concerning who Yahweh was as their covenant God, John sought to educate his audience concerning misconceptions about Jesus as Messiah. The re-education of Ezekiel's day was to be realized only after the destruction of the city and temple, an eerily similar picture in John's day as he wrote after the events of 70 c.e. Even though Jesus' ministry lasted for roughly three years, the numbers of those who actually believed and followed him were few. It would be the work of the apostles to expand this nascent community into the thriving church. It is in this context that John, writing well after Jesus' earthly ministry, writes with the intent of convincing his audience that true belief and knowledge of God through Jesus would bring new life (John 20:22).

Old Testament Linguistic Roots of John's "I Am" Sayings

John's utilization of the "I am" (ἐγω εἰμι/*egō eimi*) sayings along with Jesus' self-identification as "*I am* he"/"It is I" (John 6:20; 8:18, 24, 28, 58; 13:19; 18:5, 6, 18) is derived from the Greek verb εἰμι meaning "to be." This usage cannot be divorced from the similar Hebrew terminology used for Yahweh in the Hebrew Bible (cf. Exod. 3:15 cf. Exod. 6:3).[2] The appellative Yahweh derives from the Hebrew verb היה (*hāyāh*) meaning "to be." It is self-evident that John desired to draw direct connections between Jesus and Yahweh.³ In this regard, Dorothy Lee comments, "In fact, to see Jesus in this Gospel is to see God, since sight of the Johannine Father is through, and only through, the palpable presence of the Son (12:45; 14:7-9; 17:24). The invisible God is thus made visible in the Johannine Jesus (1:18; 5:37; 6:46), making possible the *visio Dei*."⁴ Now, that is not to say that John was suggesting that Jesus was in fact Yahweh, for John constantly shows the subordination of Jesus to the Father and to his will,⁵ but rather that John wanted to present Jesus as equal to God in his divinity (John 5:18; 10:30; 17:21).⁶ Indeed, a number of these concepts have been handled in chapter 2, where I showed the parallels between John 1 and Ezek. 1–3.

Linguistically, the Greek phrase ἐγώ εἰμι is used in the LXX in direct connection with Yahweh 107 times.⁷ Not surprisingly,

---

2. For a detailed listing of many of the Old Testament allusions to the "I Am" Sayings in John, see Paul N. Anderson, *The Riddles of the Fourth Gospel: An Introduction to John* (Minneapolis: Fortress Press, 2011), 191. When dealing with the background influences on John's use of the phrase, Raymond E. Brown, "The Egō Eimi ("I am") Passages in the Fourth Gospel," in *A Companion to John: Readings in Johannine Theology (John's Gospel and Epistles)*, ed. Michael J. Taylor (New York: Alba, 1977), 117–26, esp. 120–24, fails even to mention Ezekiel! J.-A. Bühner, "The Exegesis of the Johannine 'I Am' Sayings," in *The Interpretation of John*, ed. John Ashton, second ed. SNTI (Edinburgh: T & T Clark, 1997), 207–18, posits that the "I Am" Sayings are not self-revealing in an epiphany-type way, but rather link the "I Am" Sayings to the messenger motif whereby Jesus becomes the mediator for God. While I like the connections to the Old Testament, to argue that Jesus is not primarily revealing his divinity through the sayings, seems to push against a straightforward reading of the texts.
3. The Synoptic writers make reference to Jesus using the term but rarely with what appears to be a direct inference to Yahweh (cf. Matt. 14:27; 22:32; Mark 6:50; 14:62; Luke 22:70; 24:39). On the latter concept, see Mark 14:62; Luke 22:70; 24:39.
4. Dorothy Lee, "The Gospel of John and the Five Senses," *JBL* 129, no. 1 (2010): 115–27 (117). See also Marianne Meye Thompson, "'Every Picture Tells a Story': Imagery for God in the Gospel of John," in *Imagery in the Gospel of John: Terms, Forms, Themes, and Theology of Johannine Figurative Language*, ed. Jörg Frey, Jan G. van der Watt, and Ruben Zimmermann, WUNT 200 (Tübingen: Mohr Siebeck, 2006), 259–77.
5. Cf. John 3:35; 5:19-20; 6:37, 44, 57; 8:28, 38, 49, 54; 10:18, 29; 12:49, 50; 13:3; 14:28, 31; 20:17, 21.
6. So too the conclusion of Peter Riga, "Signs of Glory: The Use of Semeion in John's Gospel," *Int* 17, no. 4 (1963): 421.
7. Gen. 17:1; 26:24; 31:13; 46:3; Exod. 3:6, 14; 7:5; 8:18; 14:4, 18; 20:2; 29:46; Lev. 11:44, 45; 19:10, 12, 14, 16, 18, 25, 28, 30-32, 34, 36, 37; 21:23; 22:30; 24:22; 25:17; 26:1, 13, 44, 45; Deut.

it is Ezekiel that has the most appearances with thirty-two while Leviticus, a priestly text, is second with twenty-three. Isaiah and Jeremiah are third and fourth with thirteen and nine occurrences respectively. When the phrase is extended to "I am the Lord" (ἐγώ εἰμι κύριος/*egō eimi kurios*) the numbers tilt even more dramatically in favor of Ezekiel with thirty occurrences, with Exodus and Leviticus both having just five appearances, Jeremiah with two, and Deuteronomy with one. Finally, when the phrase is extended further to include "*then* they will know that I am the Lord" (γνώσονται ὅτι ἐγώ εἰμι κύριος/*gnōsontai hoti egō eimi kurios*) it is only Ezekiel that remains in play with seventeen occurrences.[8] Once again, while it is possible that John had Exodus, Leviticus, or even one of the other prophets in mind when adopting this language, the weight of the linguistic evidence pushes in favor of Ezekiel as a source of the borrowing. Moreover, in both John and Ezekiel it is Yahweh and Jesus who use the phrase to self-identify and to highlight the purpose of their work! In light of these conclusions, we will now examine how John's "I Am" Sayings find thematic, and at times, structural connections to Ezekiel.

An Analysis of John's "I Am" Sayings Vis-à-vis Ezekiel

In the Fourth Gospel, John uses seven distinct "I Am" Sayings. These include:

- I am the Bread of Life (John 6:35, 41, 48, 50, 51 [3x], 58 [2x])
- I am the Light of the world (John 8:12; 9:5)

5:9; 32:39; Judg. 6:8; Ps. 45:11; Hos. 5:14; 11:9; Joel 2:27; Hag. 1:13; 2:4; Mal. 1:14; Isa. 41:4; 43:10, 25; 45:8, 18, 19, 22; 46:4, 9; 48:12, 17; 51:12; 52:6; Jer. 1:8, 17, 19; 3:12; 9:23; 23:23; 24:7; 26:28; 49:11; Ezek. 7:6; 28:22-24, 26; 29:6, 9, 16, 21; 30:8, 19, 25, 26; 32:15; 33:29; 34:15, 27, 30; 35:4, 9, 12, 15; 36:11, 23; 37:6, 13, 28; 38:23; 39:6, 7, 22, 28.

8. When the second person plural form of the verb is added into the mix, the number goes back up to over sixty for Ezekiel.

- I am the Door (John 10:9)
- I am the Good Shepherd (John 10:11)
- I am the Resurrection and the Life (John 11:25)
- I am the Way the Truth and the Life (John 14:6)
- I am the True Vine (John 15:1)

As with my earlier disclaimer concerning the signs of Jesus in chapter 3 above, I am not proposing that every "I Am" Saying has a perfect one-to-one fit with Ezekiel. Yet, as I have noted throughout, there are clear hints within the Fourth Gospel that point to John's dependence on Ezekielian motifs. None are as clear as the charred vine in Ezek. 15 (cf. John 15) and the evil shepherds of Ezek. 34 (cf. John 10)—both connected to Jesus' "I Am" Sayings. While I will examine these more overt connections in detail below, I will also demonstrate that there are a number of the other "I Am" Sayings that find affinity with Ezekiel's message. Now to be sure, some may contend that the Ezekielian motifs with which I will make connections to the Fourth Gospel could just as easily be found in Isaiah, Jeremiah, or elsewhere. While on the surface this may be true, one is forced to narrow the focus to Ezekiel when one considers the numerous motif and thematic parallels with Ezekiel that have been addressed above and below. One such area that we have been examining is the structural overlap.

The structural connections between John and the book of Ezekiel continue to resonate with John's presentation of Jesus' earthly life and ministry through the "I Am" Sayings. As we have noted in chapter 3, the sign acts served as a possible backdrop to John's use of signs to frame Jesus' public ministry. After the temple-cleansing sign (see chapter 4 above), which paralleled the second peak of my proposed structure of Ezekiel (see chart in chapter 1 above), John goes on to present Jesus through a number of other signs and "I Am" Sayings. When these sayings are juxtaposed to Ezekiel's structure an interesting parallel begins to emerge. In Ezek. 13–24, 33, and 34, Ezekiel describes the many sins of the people that brought about, deprivation, death, destruction, and separation from Yahweh.[9]

In what follows, I will show that through the use of the "I Am" Sayings John demonstrates how Jesus reverses these former curses on Israel while fulfilling the many prophetic pronouncements from Ezekiel. Indeed, John 3–11 presents "I Am" Sayings (and signs) whereby Jesus is pictured as the answer to the sins that plagued Israel.[10] Further, even in the midst of the foreboding of the cross, there is a theme of hope if the people will believe in Jesus' message and signs (John 1:7; 11:42[11]). This is accomplished by Jesus' becoming the metaphorical temple and bringing spiritual life, bread, water, leadership, and sustenance to Israel, and, by extension, to the world. During this process, Jesus reveals aspects about his character that teach the nation about God.[12] In the discussion that follows I will demonstrate how the "I Am" Sayings reveal these character traits of Jesus while sharing a number of thematic and structural affinities with Ezekiel.

---

9. The oracles against Israel/Judah are predominantly handled in chapters 13–24. Chapters 25–32 cover the oracles against the nations, which would not have suited John's rhetorical intent. However, chapter 33 serves as a transition to the final judgment oracle against Israel's shepherds in chapter 34. From chapter 34 onward, a message of hope predominates in the book of Ezekiel. Indeed, it is in Ezek. 34:25 that the first appearance of the covenant of peace appears. On the use of chapter 33 as a transitional chapter, see Brian Neil Peterson, *Ezekiel in Context: Ezekiel's Message Understood in Its Historical Setting of Covenant Curses and Ancient Near Eastern Mythological Motifs*, PTMS 182 (Eugene, OR: Pickwick Publications, 2012), 263–64.

10. Note also the parable of the mustard seed as it relates to the coming of Jesus' Kingdom (Mark 4:30-32; cf. Matt. 13:32; Luke 13:19). Some have seen connections to Ezek. 17:22-24 in this parable. Cf. R. W. Funk, "The Looking-Glass Tree Is for the Birds," *Int* 27, no. 1 (1973): 3–9, esp. 5, 7.

11. Note that in these verses the third person plural aorist subjunctive form of the verb πιστεύω (*pisteuō*) "they might believe" forms an inclusio to the public ministry of Jesus.

12. Mark Matson, "The Temple Incident: An Integral Element in the Fourth Gospel's Narrative," in *Jesus in Johannine Tradition*, ed. Robert T. Fortna and Tom Thatcher (Louisville: Westminster John Knox Press, 2001), 145–53 (151).

I Am the Bread of Life

Six times in chapter 6 John notes spiritual bread coming out of heaven (John 6:32, 33, 41, 50, 51, 58). Jesus' declaration that he is this spiritual bread immediately brings Exod. 16 to mind and God's gift of manna to Israel, especially considering the explicit comments of John connecting his act to the wilderness miracle (John 6:31-32, 49, 58).[13] Nevertheless, Jesus' words take on importance beyond this immediate context when one looks at possible connections to Ezekiel. For Israel during Ezekiel's day, privation of the necessities of life, that is, bread and water, was the norm especially during the long periods of siege (Ezek. 4:16, 17; 5:16, 17; 6:11, 12; 7:15; 12:16, 18, 19; 14:13, 21). At these moments, Israel no doubt longed for the new age. In this vein, in two of the three places where Ezekiel prophesies the coming new age (Ezek. 34:25; 36:26-27), Ezekiel also prophesies that the hallmark of the new covenant era, and by default the messianic age (cf. Ezek. 34:23-24; 37:24-25), would be an end of famine and privations (Ezek. 34:29; 36:29-30) especially grain/bread (Ezek. 36:29)—the feeding of the five thousand in John does just that. Therefore, while Jesus' actions do recall the wilderness period, John also draws a direct connection between Ezekiel's prophesied new age and the miraculous signs that will accompany this era.[14] In this context, this "I Am" Saying is a fitting parallel to Ezekiel.

Next, one also must bear in mind the structural connections between the two books. John places the miracle of the feeding of the five thousand and the first of the "I Am" Sayings in the midst of the signs and after the cleansing of the temple (John 2:13-22).

---

13. See discussion in Edwin D. Freed, *Old Testament Quotations in the Gospel of John*, NovTSup 11 (Leiden: Brill, 1965), 11–16; and Bruce G. Schuchard, *Scripture within Scripture: The Interrelationship of Form and Function in the Explicit Old Testament Citations in the Gospel of John*, SBLDS 133 (Atlanta: Scholars, 1992), 33–46.
14. Messianic expectation of this period involved the miraculous feeding of the people with manna from heaven on Passover; cf. Fowler, "The Influence of Ezekiel," 69.

Immediately before chapter 6, chapter 5 deals with the authority, which Jesus has on earth to supersede even the established law (i.e., healing on the Sabbath cf. John 5:9, 10, 16, 18; cf. 5:30) and Israel's interpretation of it.[15] Some interesting parallels emerge when these events are juxtaposed with Ezek. 8–11 and 12. First, as we saw in our last chapter, the cleansing of the temple in many ways parallels Ezek. 8–11. Second, just as Yahweh chooses to minister to the exiles (Ezek. 11:16), after the cleansing of the temple Jesus ministers to "outcasts" (e.g., the Samaritan woman). Third, during Ezekiel's vision the reader is made aware that Yahweh has the authority to supersede the "sacred" temple by departing from it and destroying it as Yahweh sees fit (Ezek. 9–11; cf. Jer. 7:4). Thus Yahweh showed Yahweh's authority to override earthly institutions. Similar to Yahweh's actions, in John 5 Jesus showed that he had authority even over the Sabbath by healing the lame man (cf. John 2:18).[16] Finally, Ezek. 12, the next of Ezekiel's sign acts, depicts the nation going into exile and being deprived of food; bread in particular (cf. Ezek. 12:18, 19). In John 6, Jesus feeds the multitude with bread thus showing them that the new age had arrived and the former curses could be done away with, that is, if they believed in him.[17] We can summarize the above structural parallels as they relate to the first "I Am" Saying as follows:

John 2:13-22 = Ezek. 8–10: cleansing of the temple.

John 3–4 = Ezek. 11:16: Jesus/Yahweh ministers to the outcasts (see ch. 4 above).

---

15. See also comments by Marianne Meye Thompson, *The Humanity of Jesus in the Fourth Gospel* (Philadelphia: Fortress Press, 1988), 58.
16. Gary T. Manning, *Echoes of a Prophet: The Use of Ezekiel in the Gospel of John and in Literature of the Second Temple Period* (London: T & T Clark, 2004), 160–62, draws a loose connection between John 5:25-28 and Ezek. 37:4, 9, and 12. I feel these are not as strong as those I will propose in chapter 6 below.
17. One must remember that in the midst of Ezek. 8–12 the prophet prophesies the coming messianic age in Ezek. 11:19 (see chapter 4 above for the discussion there).

John 5 = Ezek. 11 (esp. vv. 22-23): Yahweh/Jesus have authority to overrule sacred laws/institutions.

John 6 = Ezek. 12 (cf. 11:17-21): privation of food is reversed as the sign of the messianic age.

I Am the Light of the World

Next to Jesus' discussion on the bread of life in John 6, the "light" motif occurs by far the most frequently in the Fourth Gospel. The second "I Am" Saying, "I am the light of the world" (ἐγώ εἰμι τὸ φῶς τοῦ κόσμου) is found in John 8:12 and 9:5 (cf. John 12:46). In chapter 2, we already have seen the connections between Jesus as the light of the world (John 1:4, 5, 7, 8 [2x], 9 cf. also 3:19-21 [5x]; 5:35; 11:10; 12:35 [2x], 36 [3x], 46) and Ezekiel's vision of the radiance of Yahweh in Babylon (Ezek. 1:4, 27-28). However, there are other important thematic and structural connections in light of our discussion immediate above. For instance, where the last "I Am" Saying ended its primary parallels with Ezek. 12, the light metaphor picks up only with much more detail. Even though the two "I am the light of the world" sayings appear in separate contexts in John, they both find parallels with Ezek. 12 only with different foci. John appears fixated on the sign act of Ezek. 12 as the prophet enacts the fall of the city, the attempted escape of the king, the promised scattering and exile of the people, and the spiritual blindness of all involved.

The first appearance of the "light" "I Am" Saying is in John 8:12. Here Jesus presents himself as the light to follow in a leadership role (spiritual and messianic/kingly). Ezekiel's sign act in chapter 12 was to be partially performed in the dark (Ezek. 12:6, 7, 12) to show that the prince (i.e., Zedekiah) would slink out of the city shirking his leadership responsibilities (Jer. 52:6-9; Ezek. 12:12-13) by leaving the people to fend for themselves (Ezek. 12:14). The use of the word "prince" (נשיא/*nāśî*) in the singular within the context (Ezek. 12:10, 12; cf. 7:27; 21:25) must be understood in light of the messianic parallels in Ezek. 34:24 and 37:26 (cf. 44:3; 45:7, 16, 22; 46; 48:21-22).[18] The king was to be a leader: the one at the front of the people serving as their "light." However, Judah's kings had failed at this and had brought death to their people. Into this context, Jesus, the messianic Prince, affirms that he is the Light of the world and will bring life (John 8:12).

In the second appearance of the phrase in John 9:5, the context deals with both spiritual and literal blindness, the former of which brings judgment. The chapter begins with Jesus seeing a blind man (9:1), and being asked by his disciples about the sin of the man and his parents (9:2-3). The narrative then moves to the concept of working in the day for the night is coming (9:4). It is at this juncture that Jesus declares himself to be the light of the world. This is immediately followed up by his healing of a blind man, which he uses as a metaphor for Israel's leaders' spiritual blindness (John 9:6-41).[19] Jesus finishes this by noting his role in bringing judgment because of the spiritual blindness of those who should be attuned to the spiritual realities of which he speaks (John 9:39-41).[20]

In Ezek. 12 we also see a double entendre with the concept of blindness, both spiritual and literal. Ezek. 12:2 sets the tone with an allusion to Isa. 6:10: "they have eyes to see but do not see and ears to hear but do not hear" (cf. John 12:40).[21] The spiritual blindness motif is also carried forward in 12:9, 22, 27 (cf. John 9:39-41) as are

---

18. The use of נשיא (*nāśî*) in the singular is predominantly in an eschatological context. Whenever נשיא does appear in the singular without an eschatological bent, it is in the context of judgment on Zedekiah (Ezek. 7:27; 12:10, 12; 21:30). Apart from the oracles against the nations, the remaining references to נשיא are in the plural (Ezek. 19:1; 21:17; 22:6).
19. John also records that the man who is healed calls Jesus a "prophet" (John 9:17); perhaps in an effort to connect the event back to the prophet Ezekiel. This is the only time the term is used where it does not have messianic overtones (cf. John 4:19; 6:14; 7:40).
20. George Beasley-Murray, *John*, WBC 36 (Nashville: Thomas Nelson, 1999), 149, correctly entitles this section "Jesus the Light of the World that Brings Judgment to the World (9:1-41)."

the motifs of darkness (Ezek. 12:6, 7, 12; cf. John 9:4), the covering of the eyes (Ezek. 12:6, 12; cf. John 9:6), and literal blindness (Ezek. 12:13; cf. John 9:1-7). The covering of the eyes in Ezek. 12:12 serves as a metaphor for the literal blinding of Zedekiah for his treachery against Nebuchadnezzar (Ezek. 12:13; cf. Jer. 52:11). Ezekiel ends his discourse by predicting judgment on the people for their spiritual blindness (Ezek. 12:28; cf. John 9:39-41). These parallel motifs may be listed as follows:

1. Jesus performs a sign (John 9:1-7, esp. vv. 3-4) = Ezekiel performs a sign act (Ezek. 12:6).
2. Spiritual blindness predominates and forms an inclusio for both accounts (John 9:2, 40, 41) = Ezek. 12:2, 9, 22, 27.
3. Day/night motif appears in both (John 9:4//Ezek. 12:3-7).

Interjection of "I Am" Saying: Jesus identifies himself as the light of the world, that is, the One to follow (John 9:5).

4. Covering eyes with clay (John 9:6) = Covering eyes with cloth (Ezek. 12:6, 12).
5. Blind man gains his sight (John 9:6-7) = Zedekiah loses his sight (Ezek. 12:13).
6. People don't believe (John 9:8-34) = People ask Ezekiel, what are you doing? (Ezek. 12:9).
7. John 9 ends with an allusion to Isa. 6:10[22] (John 9:39) = Ezek. 12 begins with a reference to Isa. 6:10 (Ezek. 12:2).

---

21. See also comments by Marianne Meye Thompson, "Signs and Faith in the Fourth Gospel," *BBR* 1 (1991): 106–7. For a discussion on John's use of Isa. 6:10 at John 12:40, see Schuchard, *Scripture within Scripture*, 91–106, or Craig A. Evans, "The Function of Isaiah 6:9-10 in Mark and John," *NovT* 24, no. 2 (1982): 133–37.
22. So too Andreas Köstenberger, "John," in *Commentary on the New Testament Use of the Old Testament*, ed. G. K. Beale and D. A. Carson (Grand Rapids: Baker, 2007), 461.

8. Judgment for spiritual blindness is the outcome in both accounts (John 9:39-41//Ezek. 12:28).

With so many connections, it is clear that John continues to draw upon the material of Ezekiel, especially these early chapters. Although John presents Jesus in the prophetic office like Ezekiel, Jesus is greater because, as God, he can perform the works of God. In light of John 8:12 and John 9, Jesus becomes the princely leader who serves as the spiritual light and healer.

Before leaving this second "I Am" Saying, one further point needs to be made in light of Jesus' words in John 9:4. Until the dawn of modern electricity and the light bulb, sunlight was the only means by which one could work and travel. Lamp light played an integral part of the ancient world and was highly valued within the home.[23] Lamps were used to study and read the Torah, an important way to learn about who God was. Thus, the ancients realized the value of lamps and the light that they afforded every person. It was in this setting that Jesus used the metaphor of being the light of the world. Jesus' metaphor showed that he was the one who shines spiritual light into the darkness of unbelief and ignorance. As M. de Jonge states, "Light means Life, but at the same time it discloses darkness as darkness. . . ."[24] Bringing this type of spiritual light to the world brings understanding of who God is[25]—a close connection to the revelatory formula of Ezekiel (see below).

---

23. The Mishnah (e.g., Bava Metzia 7:1; Kelim 3:2; Shabbat 2:4), Jerusalem Talmud (e.g., Shabbat 2:1), Babylonian Talmud (e.g., Berakhot 60b; Shabbat 23b, 29b, 30a), and Tosefta (Ketubot 5:8; Shabbat 1:13) are replete with sayings focused on the importance of the oil lamp in daily life and Torah study. See more in Joan Goodnick Westenholz, ed., *Let There be Light: Oil Lamps from the Holy Land* (Israel: Bible Lands Museum, 2004), 8; and Brian Neil Peterson, "The Lamps of Khirbet el-Maqatir," *Bible and Spade* 26, no. 4 (Fall 2013): 98–102.
24. Marinus de Jonge, "Signs and Works in the Fourth Gospel," in *Miscellanca Neotestamentica* 2, ed. T. Baarda, A. F. J. Klijn and W. C. van Unnik, NovTSup 48 (Leiden: Brill, 1978), 107–25 (118).
25. Craig R. Koester, *The Word of Life: A Theology of John's Gospel* (Grand Rapids: Eerdmans, 2008), 189.

I Am the Door

While this "I Am" Saying is often addressed within the context of the Good Shepherd account, which will be handled in our next section, a few comments still can be made in relation to Ezekiel. John 10:1-10 sets up the metaphor of Jesus fulfilling the messianic shepherd promises of Ezek. 34 (cf. also Ps. 118:20). As the "door," Jesus is the only way of entering the new covenant (John 10:9), with Jesus also serving as the Good Shepherd of his flock. Jesus makes it clear that those who came before him were thieves and robbers; his true sheep did not listen to their voice (John 10:8).

From an Old Testament perspective, the negative impact that the profane priests and false prophets had on the pre-exilic and exilic generations cannot be overstated. Both Ezekiel and Jeremiah battled this problem (cf. Jer. 2:8, 26; 5:13, 31; 14:13-15; 23:14-32; 27:9-18; 29; 32:32; 37:19; Ezek. 13; 22:25, 28). These evil leaders had tried to get Israel to follow another way and enter into worship of Yahweh through a "door" of their own making. Prophet, priests, and rulers were all alike (Ezek. 22:25-31). Priests had instituted idolatry and the worship of Tammuz as a means of approaching Yahweh (Ezek. 8:1-18, esp. v. 14; cf. Jer. 7:18; 44:17-25). Prophets had directed the people falsely (Ezek. 13:1-16), and prophetesses had used talismans and divination to circumvent the protective hand of Yahweh (Ezek. 13:17-23). Ezekiel also declared that the prophets, priests, and leaders did not stand in the breaches/openings (פרצות/*perāṣôṭ*) in the walls to protect Israel (Ezek. 13:5; 22:30), clear shepherding imagery related to the "door" metaphor of John 10:1-10.[26] This shepherding imagery is extended to the leaders who behave like "wolves" (λύκοι/*lukoi*;

---

26. The connections here must be understood in light of the watchman motif (Ezek. 3:17; 33:6-7). While the context may connote military action, as the leaders of the people they were to guard and serve as watchmen over the "sheep" in the "sheepfold" of the city/walls.

Ezek. 22:27). Interestingly, this is the same term used by Jesus to speak of those who misuse his sheep (John 10:12).

Moreover, as James Martin points out, Jesus becomes the "door" to life for those cast out of the synagogue because of their faith in him.[27] Of course, the account of the blind man in John 9 immediately comes to mind (John 9:34-38). In this vein, in the Fourth Gospel Jesus opens the "door" to life on the Sabbath (cf. John 5:9-18; 9:14-16). This Sabbath/door motif finds further connections to the messianic era described in Ezek. 43–48. On this William Fowler posits that

> There is a gate (the east gate that God Himself entered by according to 44:2) that is to remain open on the Sabbath to provide the people access to the Temple (46:1). According to Ezek. 46:1-12, the gate remains shut except on the days when the prince enters through it (and exits, 46:8) for worship. On those days the people can "go in and out" (46:10) with the prince. Once he leaves the gate is shut (46:12). This connection seems a bit strained until one remembers that the prince in Ezekiel is also the Good Shepherd (34:23, 24).[28]

Finally, it is also important to point out the structural similarities thus far. Structurally there is movement from Ezek. 12, paralleled to John 9 (as noted in our previous "I Am" Saying), to Ezek. 13 and 22, which now have potential connections to John 10. This sequence is in keeping with the next "I Am" Saying, which focuses on chapter 34 of Ezekiel. While every "I Am" Saying is not necessarily canonically sequential such as here, it is telling of the way John uses Ezekielian motifs.

The Good Shepherd

Johannine scholars have long noted the clear connections between John 10 and Ezek. 34 (cf. Ezek. 37:24).[29] Despite other possible

---

27. James P. Martin, "John 10:1-10," *Int* 32, no. 2 (1978): 171–75 (173).
28. Fowler, "Influence of Ezekiel," 74.

literary links (e.g., Ps. 23; Jer. 10:21; 12:10; 23:1-4; Zech. 11:1-17), Gary Manning correctly points out that

> The two passages [John 10 and Ezek. 34] share three phrases, eleven key words, five close synonyms, and four weaker synonyms. The amount of verbal parallelism makes it clear that John is not merely drawing on everyday shepherd life, as a few scholars have claimed. Furthermore, no other shepherd metaphor in the OT comes close to having this many verbal parallels to John 10. For example, John has in common with Zech. 11:1-17 only 5 shepherding terms. John and Jer. 23:1-4 share only four shepherding terms. The rest of the occurrences of the shepherd metaphor in the OT (LXX or MT) show even fewer parallels with John 10. There are about 60 passages in the OT that use shepherding terminology metaphorically; the rest of these have only one, two, or three significant words in common with John 10. These other passages become even less likely as background passages when it is realized that at least one of the terms they usually share with John is "sheep" or "shepherd."[30]

In light of the general consensus and the detailed comparative work done by others such as Manning, I will move the discussion forward with a broader thematic and motif analysis. Interestingly, it is common motifs such as those found in John 10 and Ezek. 34 that

---

29. E.g., R. V. G. Tasker, *The Gospel according to St. John* (repr., Grand Rapids: Eerdmans, 2002), 129; Craig S. Keener, *The Gospel of John: A Commentary*, 2 vols (Peabody, MA: Hendrickson, 2003; repr., Grand Rapids: Baker, 2012), 1:802; C. H. Dodd, *The Interpretation of the Fourth Gospel* (Cambridge: Cambridge University Press, 1953), 358–62; Rudolf Schnackenburg, *The Gospel according to St. John Vol. III: Commentary on Chapters 13–21*, HTCNT, trans. David Smith and G. A. Kon (London: Burns & Oates, 1982), 210; Karoline M. Lewis, *Rereading the "Shepherd Discourse": Restoring the Integrity of John 9:39—10:21*, SBLit 113 (New York: Peter Lang, 2008), 8; Andreas J. Köstenberger, *John*, BECNT (Grand Rapids: Baker, 2004), 303–307; Gail R. O'Day, "The Gospel of John: Introduction, Commentary and Reflections," in *New Interpreter's Bible: A Commentary in Twelve Volumes*, ed. Neil Alexander (Nashville: Abingdon, 1995), 9:669; Saeed Hamid-Khani, *Revelation and Concealment of Christ: A Theological Inquiry into the Elusive Language of the Fourth Gospel*, WUNT 120 (Tübingen: Mohr Siebeck, 2000), 115; Donald L. Fowler, "The Background to the Good Shepherd Discourse in John 10," in *New Testament Essays in Honor of Homer A. Kent, Jr.*, ed. Gary T. Meadors (Winona Lake, IN: BMH Books, 1991), 153; and Manning, *Echoes of a Prophet*, 100–35. Manning (100–11) also connects John 10 to Numbers 27 and the institution of Joshua as leader after Moses.

30. Manning, *Echoes of a Prophet*, 113.

bring poignancy to my ongoing thesis.[31] Because of the numerous connections to this portion of Ezekiel, I will develop this section at length.

While it is true that John quotes other Old Testament prophets and texts (e.g., Isa. 6//John 1 and 12; Ps. 69//John 2 and 12; Gen. 2//John 20), never do we see comparisons on the macro level such as seen here.[32] Now, while passages like Ps. 23 (Ps. 22 in the LXX) have shepherd motifs, it is only in John 10 and Ezek. 34 that the positive and negative attributes of shepherds are juxtaposed—in both cases, earthly versus heavenly shepherds.[33] At the same time, Karoline Lewis asserts that "the Evangelist . . . seems to be suggesting that one does not have to have read Ezekiel to understand the meaning of this imagery."[34] While this *may* be correct, if John's audience were in fact Jewish, they would have known the Ezekielian text and as such would have gained the fullest understanding of the rhetorical nuances.[35] Only when one undertakes a close analysis of John 10 and Ezek. 34 is it the case that the assertions of Lewis and others are minimized.[36] In this regard, Mary Katharine Deeley correctly comments: "That Ezekiel's text speaks of faithless shepherds as well as the One who is faithful, points to John's purposeful selection of

---

31. For a detailed chart discussing the verbal parallels between John 10 and 11 and Ezek. 34 and 37, see ibid., 112–13.
32. Cf. Johannes Beutler, S. J., "The Use of 'Scripture' in the Gospel of John," in *Exploring the Gospel of John: In Honor of D. Moody Smith*, ed. R. Alan Culpepper and C. Clifton Black (Louisville: Westminster John Knox, 1996), 147–62, esp. 148–53.
33. See also, Charles K. Barrett, The Old Testament in the Fourth Gospel," *JTS* 48, no. 2 (1947): 163.
34. Lewis, *Rereading the "Shepherd Discourse,"* 157.
35. Ibid. Lewis posits that "the Gospel itself becomes the referent for the imagery found in John 9:39—10:21." It is true that immediate context must govern one's interpretive methodology; however, failure to grasp the larger literary/tradition context can handicap the reader when it comes to rhetorical purpose and intent of the author.
36. Barrett, The Old Testament in the Fourth Gospel," 164, avers that John's use of the shepherd motif "is not based on any single O.T. text or passage." On the other hand, Herman Ridderbos, *The Gospel of John*, trans. John Vriend (Grand Rapids: Eerdmans, 1997), 358, 361, correctly makes the connections between the two texts.

this text [i.e., Ezek. 34] as one which helped to articulate his own understanding of the significance of Jesus in the world."[37] It is to this analysis that we now turn our attention.

A number of shepherding motifs appear in Ezek. 34, which we will in turn parallel with those of John 10 below. To begin, Yahweh's flock has been misused by evil shepherd (i.e., those who have stolen, and mistreated the flock), thus meriting Yahweh's judgment (34:1-8). Because of this mistreatment, Yahweh will deliver the flock and take over the role of Shepherd (34:9-12), care for them, and bring back those that were scattered (34:12-13 cf. Ezek. 36:37-38; John 11:52). Yahweh, the responsible Shepherd, will in turn lead them to good grazing grounds (in Israel 34:14), give them rest (34:15), bind their wounds, and strengthen the sick (34:16a).[38] As part of the judgment on the evil shepherds, Ezekiel identifies them as "fat sheep" fit for judgment. Indeed, Yahweh will judge between the "rams" and the "goats" (34:16b-22). At this juncture, Ezekiel invokes messianic language/expectation when he notes that Yahweh will place his "servant David" over the flock (34:23 cf. Ezek. 37:24, 25), and in turn, establish a covenant of peace with them (34:25 cf. Ezek. 37:26). With Yahweh's servant "David" in charge blessings will abound.[39]

Not surprisingly, John's account in 10:1-18 has many similar motifs. From the very beginning we see false shepherds and thieves entering the fold by a means other than the door (10:1); however, the sheep will know the true shepherd and avoid the false ones (10:2-5).

---

37. Mary Katharine Deeley, "Ezekiel's Shepherd and John's Jesus: A Case Study in the Appropriation of Biblical Texts," in *Early Christian Interpretation of the Scriptures of Israel: Investigations and Proposals*, ed. C. A. Evans and J. A. Sanders, JSNTSup 148 (Sheffield: Sheffield Academic Press, 1997), 252–64 (253). Deeley argues for a parallel between John 8–11 and Ezek. 33–37.

38. At points in the Ezekielian text, especially in 34:16, we see motifs similar to Isa. 61:1-3.

39. Ezekiel blurs the lines between Yahweh and David as shepherds. For a similar comparative list, see Dodd, *The Interpretation of the Fourth Gospel*, 358–59.

Here John notes that the disciples did not understand the metaphor, thus requiring Jesus to unpack it for them (10:6). Jesus identifies himself as the true "door" (10:7) unlike the shepherds who came before him who were thieves and robbers (10:8). Indeed, where false shepherds came to steal and kill (10:9), Jesus promises to lead his flock to a good "pasture" and give them life (10:10).[40] John next juxtaposes the actions of the evil shepherds/hirelings with those of the "good shepherd" (i.e., Jesus; 10:10-13), who is known by his flock, and more importantly, by God (10:14-16). John ends his presentation of Jesus as the "good shepherd" by breaking from the Ezekielian text and adding a new motif. Unlike the unrelenting picture of hope in Ezek. 34, the "good shepherd" in John lays down his life for his flock; however, that is not the end, for he also has the authority to take it up again (10:17-18).

Now, while one should not expect a one-to-one parallel for every verse, for this would remove the artistic license of John, even a cursory glance at the two pericopae, nonetheless, yields a number of parallels: 1) shepherd/sheep imagery, 2) evil shepherds vs. a Good Shepherd, 3) the sheep know their shepherd,[41] 4) protection and provision by the Good Shepherd vs. evil shepherds who are rapacious with the flock, 5) the True Shepherd lays down his life for the flock vs. the exploitation of the flock by evil shepherds, 6) one Good Shepherd vs. many evil shepherds, and 7) the one Good Shepherd is from God/is God vs. evil earthly shepherds.

While Ezekiel's prophecy includes aspects of the Second Advent of Christ, John focuses on the fulfillment of the prophecy from a "first" advent perspective. This of course is most evident in the "laying

---

40. Rudolf Schnackenburg, *The Gospel according to St. John Vol. II: Commentary on Chapters 5–12*, HTCNT, trans. Kevin Smyth (London: Burns & Oates, 1980), 293, suggests that the "rich pastures" are a metaphor for deliverance from the Gentiles.
41. In Ezek. 34, the prophet uses one phrase to show ownership and recognition between the sheep and the shepherd: צֹאנִי/ṣō'nî ("my flock/sheep"; 34:6, 8, 10, 11, 12, 15, 17, 19, 22, 31).

down" of the Good Shepherd's life (John 12:17-18; cf. 6:51). In this vein, Ezekiel does not present Yahweh as one who will die for the people, a motif that is not fitting to Ezekiel's overall rhetorical focus. John, however, takes the exalted nature of Yahweh in Ezekiel and applies it to Jesus moving beyond Ezekiel's focus in order to present Jesus as the One who will lay down his life for his flock (John 6:51; 10:11, 15, 17).[42] In this vein, C. K. Barrett comments, "We should not expect to read that an O.T. shepherd died for his flock; but once the shepherd had been identified with Jesus this development was inevitable."[43] Of course, standing this side of the church councils, this is in keeping with a more "Trinitarian" bent, something that was well beyond Ezekiel's purview.

Also of importance are the clear messianic overtones in both texts. Even though other Old Testament prophets speak about the Davidic messianic figure (e.g., Isa. 9:7 [Hebrew 9:6]; 16:5; 22:22; Jer. 23:5; 30:9; 33:15, 17; Amos 9:11), it is Ezekiel who notes that "David" will be the shepherd and "prince" of Yahweh's flock.[44] Interestingly, in John 7:42, John records the people's connection of the Messiah with the line of David. This Davidic messiah motif will also appear again in Ezek. 37, which John will develop in John 17–20 (see more in chapter 6 below). For John's readers, David's willingness to risk his life for his sheep (1 Sam. 17:34-37) certainly would be vital in drawing the comparisons between the Old Testament and the New Testament understanding of Jesus' actions on the cross and his teaching in John 10.[45]

---

42. Cf. Dodd, *Interpretation of the Fourth Gospel*, 360; and Barrett, "Old Testament in the Fourth Gospel," 163.
43. Barrett, "Old Testament in the Fourth Gospel," 163.
44. See Moloney, *Signs and Shadows*, 137–39.
45. So too Manning, *Echoes of a Prophet*, 118–19. See also comments of Fowler, "Background to the Good Shepherd Discourse," 148.

Moreover, it is clear that Ezekiel has in mind "one shepherd" (רעה אחד/rōʻeh ʼeḥād; cf. Ezek. 34:23). This minimizes the comparisons to other texts like those of Jeremiah, who sees a plurality of shepherds (e.g., Jer. 23:4).[46] Contextually, even though John sets the pericope of the Good Shepherd apart from what follows in John 10:22-42, the overall message needs to be read as a unity. Indeed, the recapitulation of the "sheep" motif in John 10:26-27 demands as much. Therefore, Jesus' audience makes the obvious messianic connections being presented in John 10 when they ask Jesus directly, "If you are the Christ, tell us plainly" (John 10:24; cf. Mark 14:61). When he responds that he is the "Son of God" (υἱὸς τοῦ θεοῦ εἰμι/huios tou theou eimi) they charge him with blasphemy (John 10:33).

In light of such vitriol, it is also important to note that the evil "shepherds" in both texts are the rulers of the people.[47] This is clear from Ezekiel's context (e.g., Ezek. 8:11-12; 9:6; 13-14; 17; 19; 20:1-3; 22:6, 25-31), and, based upon the reaction of the religious elite throughout John, especially John 9:40-41, the Pharisees are the central focus of Jesus' accusations (John 1:24; 3:1; 4:1; 7:32, 45, 47, 48; 8:3, 13; 9:13, 15, 16, 40; 11:46, 47, 57; 12:42; 18:3).[48] Conversely, the good "shepherds" in Ezekiel and John are Yahweh and Jesus respectively. Not surprisingly, within this very chapter John records Jesus' words that he and God are to be equated: Jesus says, "I and the father are one" (ἐγὼ καὶ ὁ πατὴρ ἕν ἐσμεν; John 10:30; cf. John 10:38).

---

46. Daniel I. Block, *Beyond the River Chebar: Studies in Kingship and Eschatology in the Book of Ezekiel* (Eugene, OR: Cascade, 2013), 79.
47. See Francis J. Moloney, *Signs and Shadows: Reading John 5–12* (Minneapolis: Fortress Press, 1996), 133–37. There is some irony in the use of "prince"/nasi in the messianic overtones due to the fact that the leader of the Sanhedrin was known as the "nasi," the very ones coming against Jesus, the true Nasi (see Ḥag. 2:2).
48. So too the conclusion of Dodd, *Interpretation of the Fourth Gospel*, 359; and Eduard Schweizer, "What about the Johannine 'Parables'?," in *Exploring the Gospel of John: In Honor of D. Moody Smith*, ed. R. Alan Culpepper and C. Clifton Black (Louisville: Westminster John Knox, 1996), 209.

The picture of judgment in both texts is also of central importance to both authors. For Ezekiel, judgment would come in the form of exile with the hope of a return for the remnant to a renewed land of Israel (Ezek. 34–48). In John's case, judgment upon the evil shepherds would be no less real. As C. H. Dodd states,

> His [Jesus'] gift of life and light is met with rejection. Those who reject it are shown in the very act of bringing down upon themselves the inevitable judgment of God on those who prefer darkness to light. But in that same act they are preparing the death of Christ, through which He gives life to the world. By a slight shift of thought, His death is itself a judgment upon those who compassed it through their rejection of the light, as the heroic death of the noble shepherd arraigns both the greed of the robber and the craven desertion of the hireling.[49]

In Ezekiel's day, he too had seen the unabashed greed and wanton rebellion of the leaders and in turn saw Yahweh separating the metaphorical sheep from the goats through the curses of the covenant and ultimately exile (Ezek. 34:16b-21; cf. Ezek. 6:1-10; 33:24-33). Jesus' death, burial, and resurrection, would serve a similar function. Those who rejected his message and sacrifice would/will be judged at the end of days (John 5:22, 27; 8:16; 12:31; cf. Rom. 2:5; 14:10; 2 Cor. 5:10; 1 Tim. 5:24; Heb. 9:27; 10:27; James 3:1; 2 Peter 2:9; 1 John 4:17). Not surprisingly, Ezekiel ends chapter 34 with the recognition formula "then they will know that I, Yahweh their God, am with them and the house of Israel is my people" (Ezek. 34:30; see more below on the recognition formula). In the Fourth Gospel, the revelation of Jesus to the "house of Israel" is this moment of introduction that initiates the messianic Kingdom—indeed, Jesus' sheep know the Shepherd's voice (John 10:14, 27).[50]

---

49. Dodd, *Interpretation of the Fourth Gospel*, 360–61.
50. So too Manning, *Echoes of a Prophet*, 115.

Finally, the themes of shepherding and scattering are resumed, albeit in a subdued way, in John 11:52 and Ezek. 37:21-26. Similar to Ezek. 34:23-24, Ezek. 37:24-25 addresses the role of David as shepherd all in the context of the new covenant of peace (37:26; cf. Ezek. 34:25). In John 11:52, John once again draws an allusion to the scattered sheep of Ezek. 34 and the fact that Jesus would be the one doing the gathering.[51] This motif of unification is of course the dominant theme of Ezek. 37:15-28. We will return to this unity theme again in the next chapter.

Before leaving this discussion it is perhaps fitting to briefly note another unique feature of John that may be explained by this "I Am" Saying and its parallels to Ezekiel. As we have seen the dominant motif in both of these passages has been the servanthood of Yahweh and Jesus as attending shepherds. They tend to the flock and the physical needs of the sheep as any "good" shepherd would. It is possible that this could be the reason why John records the footwashing ceremony, which is omitted by the other gospel writers (John 13:1-17). This is about service to the "sheep." This is also reinforced in the putative appendix in John 21[52] where Jesus cooks breakfast for his disciples and then renders the threefold call to Peter to "feed/tend my lambs/sheep" (John 21:15-17).[53]

---

51. Ibid., 126–27.
52. Most recognize chapter 21 as being from a later time or from a different writer. Cf. Howard M. Teeple, "Methodology in Source Analysis in the Fourth Gospel," *JBL* 81, no. 3 (1962): 279–86, esp. 279; William Baird, *History of New Testament Research, Volume One: From Deism to Tübingen* (Minneapolis: Fortress Press, 1992), 10 (here Baird is noting the position of Hugo Grotius); and Francis J. Moloney, *The Resurrection of the Messiah: A Narrative Commentary on the Resurrection Accounts in the Four Gospels* (New York: Paulist, 2013), 117. See also the article by Beverly Roberts Gaventa, "The Archive of Excess: John 21 and the Problem of Narrative Closure," in *Exploring the Gospel of John: In Honor of D. Moody Smith*, ed. R. Alan Culpepper and C. Clifton Black (Louisville: Westminster John Knox, 1996), 240–52. Conversely, P. S. Minear, "The Original Functions of John 21," *JBL* 102, no. 1 (1983): 85–98, argues persuasively that chapter 21 was always a part of the Gospel. See also comments by Richard Bauckham, *The Testimony of the Beloved Disciple* (Grand Rapids: Baker, 2008), 78, 123, where he ascribes the term "epilogue" to this chapter.

I Am the Resurrection and the Life

The importance of this "I Am" Saying of Jesus cannot be overstated. It is at once a declaration of hope to those mourning Lazarus's death while also having prophetic impetus for both Jesus' own resurrection and the resurrection of those who believe (John 11:24; cf. Matt. 27:52; 1 Cor. 15).[54] It also has multiple points of contact with Ezekiel. For example, in our previous chapter, we saw that the Lazarus event had many parallel motifs with one of Ezekiel's last sign acts: the loss of his wife (Ezek. 24:15-27; cf. John 11:25). And, as we will see in our next chapter, this "I Am" Saying also has import for the metaphorical resurrection of the nation of Israel if they will only believe (Ezek. 37:1-14; cf. Dan. 12:1-3).[55] The pregnant motif of resurrection in Ezek. 37:1-14, and what that meant for all people, is utilized by John both here and in the resurrection scene in John 20:1-17 (see more on this in the next chapter).

Even though the context of Ezek. 37:1-14 is speaking of metaphorical resurrection, there are a few further points that need to be made in light of Jesus' declaration that he is in fact the Resurrection and Life here in John 11. First, the three days of despair that preceded the resurrection of Lazarus is a fitting parallel to the despair sensed by Ezekiel in viewing the valley of dry bones. Yahweh asks Ezekiel "can these bones live?" (Ezek. 37:3). Ezekiel responds by acknowledging that only Yahweh knows such things. Similarly, Jesus asks Martha a question regarding her belief in his abilities to raise Lazarus (John 11:26). Martha, like Ezekiel, is cautious in her response. Finally, in both cases the command to the dead to rise is given by God—Yahweh through the prophet and Jesus to Lazarus. Jesus makes

---

53. Moloney, *The Resurrection of the Messiah*, 121–23, draws a direct link between the Good Shepherd narrative and Peter's call to tend the "sheep."
54. Hassell Bullock, "Ezekiel: Bridge between the Testaments," *JETS* 25, no. 1 (1982): 30.
55. Manning, *Echoes of a Prophet*, 165, also draws connections to Ezek. 37:1-14.

it clear that his actions mirror those of Yahweh. In fact, in John 5:21 Jesus states, "For just as the Father raises up the dead and makes them alive, in the same way the Son also gives life to whom he desires." Interestingly, the implication will play itself out in full view when Jesus, after the resurrection, gives new "life" to the disciples, that is, to *whom he desires* (cf. John 20:22).

I Am the Way the Truth and the Life

The connections of the next "I Am" Saying—I am the Way, the Truth, and the Life (ἐγώ εἰμι ἡ ὁδὸς καὶ ἡ ἀλήθεια καὶ ἡ ζωή; John 14:6)—to the previous two "I Am" Sayings are self-evident. As such many of the overlapping points of John 14 will not be rehashed here. John uses the idea of life (ζωή/*zōē*) forty-seven times in the Fourth Gospel (e.g., 3:15-16; 8:12; 10:10; 13:37-38; 17:2-3).[56] He goes out of his way to present Jesus as the way to eternal life and fulfillment in God (John 1:4; 3:15-16, 36; 4:14; 5:21, 24, 26, 40; 6:27, 33, 35, 40, 47-48, 51, 53-54, 63, 68; 8:12; 10:10, 28; 11:25; 12:50; 14:6; 17:3; 20:31).[57] Indeed, beginning as early as chapter 1, the themes of life and truth appear (John 1:4, 14 respectively).

Another connection to the life found in Jesus is the λόγος sayings in John 1. Jesus is the incarnate Word and thus to believe in him is to have life (John 1:4). Similarly, as noted in chapter 2 above, there is a direct connection between Jesus becoming the Word and the spoken word of Yahweh through the prophets. For example, the giving of the Ten Commandments was to bring life to those of the covenant, for to disobey and break the covenant (i.e., the "ten words") meant punishment or even death (Exod. 32–34).

---

56. Jeannine K. Brown, "Creation's Renewal in the Gospel of John," *CBQ* 72, no. 2 (2010): 277.
57. With the exception of two indirect references to Jesus bringing life, the Synoptics are silent on this motif (cf. Mark 8:35; Luke 9:24).

In the context of Ezekiel, Fowler comments, "The primary means of securing life in Ezekiel is by turning from wickedness (3:19; 13:22; 18:21-32; 33:9-19), and by keeping, observing, and walking in God's statutes, ordinances and commandments (18:8-28; 20:11-21; 33:15-19). When people do not walk with God as He directs, His wrath is directed towards them (7:8-19; [8:17-9:10]; et al.). Life in Ezekiel is to keep God's word or else know His wrath."[58] The clearest teaching on this is found in Ezek. 20.[59] Three times the prophet declares that if the people listen to and obey Yahweh's statutes, ordinances, and commandments then they will "live" (חיה/ḥāyāh; Ezek. 20:11, 13, 21; cf. Ezek. 18:9, 17, 19, 21, 22, 23, 27, 28, 32; 20:11, 13, 21; 33:15; 37:5, 9, 10, 14). Thus, there is a strong relationship between God's word and life for the individual.[60] There is no less of a strong connection with Jesus as the Word, Life, and Living Water in the Fourth Gospel.[61] Indeed, the comments in 20:30–31 betrays the desire of John to cause belief in Jesus as God and in turn to have life.[62]

In a structural sense, John continues to move in a somewhat canonical sequence through the book of Ezekiel. Much like Ezekiel's chapters of hope (Ezek. 34–48), John's use of this "I Am" Saying here in chapter 14 is forward-looking and makes direct connections to the work of the Spirit in the new covenant (John 14:16-17, 26; cf. Ezek. 36:26-27; 37:14; 39:29; see also Ezek. 11:19). At the same

---

58. Fowler, "The Influence of Ezekiel," 65.
59. See Brian Peterson, "Ezekiel's Perspective of Israel's History: Selective Revisionism?," in *Prophets and Prophecy and Ancient Israelite Historiography*, ed. Mark J. Boda and Lyssa Wray Beal (Winona Lake, IN: Eisenbrauns, 2013), 295–313.
60. J. T. Forestell, "Jesus and the Paraclete in the Gospel of John," in *Word and Spirit: Essays in Honor of David Michael Stanley, S. J. on His 60th Birthday*, ed. Joseph Plevnik (Toronto: Regis College Press, 1975), 151–97 (188).
61. On the living water connection, see Thomas R. Hatina, "John 20:22 in Its Eschatological Context: Promise or Fulfillment?," *Bib* 74, no. 2 (1993): 196–219 (209, 213).
62. Brown, "Creation's Renewal," 278. Brown suggests that "life given through Messiah Jesus" forms an inclusio with John 1. See also Stan Harstine, "The Fourth Gospel's Characterization of God: A Rhetorical Perspective," in *Characters and Characterization in the Gospel of John*, ed. Christopher W. Skinner, LNTS 461 (London: T & T Clark, 2013), 146.

time John draws the reader's attention to the covenant of peace (John 14:27; cf. Ezek. 34:25-26; 37:26) that will be addressed post-cross in John 20. This is further bolstered by the topic with which John begins chapter 14. Here we find Jesus' words of encouragement that in his Father's "house" (οἰκία/*oikia*) there are "many rooms" (μοναὶ πολλαί/*monai pollai*). Jesus goes on to promise that he is preparing a "place" (τόπος/*topos*) for his disciples and followers (John 14:2). The setting of this chapter in the Farewell Discourses serves to offer the disciples the hope of a great future with a tangible dwelling place. The allusions to Ezekiel's message of hope are apparent. Yahweh too is preparing a new temple (with *many rooms*; cf. Ezek. 40–42) and a spacious land for the nation of Israel (Ezek. 47–48).

Finally, John uses the verb "to know" (γινώσκω/*ginōskō*; note also the use of οἶδα *oida*/to know or understand; cf. John 14:4, 5 [2x]) eight times in this chapter in reference to "knowing him and/or the Father (John 14:7 [3x], 9, 17 [2x], 20, 31). As will be demonstrated in our final section below, to know someone connotes covenantal connections. This is indeed fitting in the context of Jesus being the Way, the Truth and the Life. Now while the term "truth" (ἀλήθεια/*alētheia*) may not appear in Ezekiel, the greater implications that Ezekiel and the prophets spoke the truth about Yahweh are certainly present (Ezek. 2:5; 33:33). By accepting the truthfulness of Jesus' and Ezekiel's words and example, the people of both eras could find the "way" to "life."

I Am the True Vine

The last "I Am" Saying—"I am the true Vine" (ἐγώ εἰμι ἡ ἄμπελος ἡ ἀληθινή)—finds a number of Old Testament parallels (e.g., Ps. 80:8-16; Isa. 5:1-10; Jer. 2:21; Ezek. 15:1-5; 17:1-21; 19:10-15; Hos. 10:1; 14:7). Most scholars are quick to point to these Scriptures as influencing John.⁶³ However, in keeping with the numerous Ezekielian parallels we have shown thus far, it only makes sense to see how Ezekiel uses the motif.⁶⁴ Not surprisingly, much like the shepherd metaphor of Ezek. 34, the vine metaphor stands out as an important motif in Ezekiel.⁶⁵ The vine imagery in Ezek. 15 deals with the nation, and both Ezek. 17 and 19 focus heavily on the judgment on the monarchy/Davidic line (cf. Tg. Ezek. 17:22).⁶⁶ Of course, Jesus as the new David figure and corporate head of the nation could fulfill both roles. In this regard Manning notes,

> Jesus' description of himself as the 'true vine' can be explained as his appropriation of the privilege and status of Israel to himself. Jesus was Israel as Israel ought to have been: a choice vine, producing fruit consistent with his identity. Isaiah, Jeremiah, and Ezekiel describe Israel as a vine that had failed to produce grapes, a nation that had been unfaithful to God. John describes Jesus as the 'true vine' who remains faithful to the Father and produces fruit through his disciples.⁶⁷

Yet, Ezek. 15:1-8 still seems to play the dominant role in influencing John's analogy.⁶⁸ In chapter 15, although brief, the prophet shows how useless the vine/nation had become.⁶⁹ Unlike Isaiah's metaphor, this is not a "vineyard" per se, but rather a vine that is worthless. This is why Jesus compares himself to a vine and not a vineyard as is typical of Jeremiah and Isaiah. Also, in both Ezekiel and John, the

---

63. For example, Francis J. Moloney, *Love in the Gospel of John: An Exegetical, Theological, and Literary Study* (Grand Rapids: Baker, 2013), 23–24; and Daniel B. Stevick, *Jesus and His Own: A Commentary on John 15–17* (Grand Rapids: Eerdmans, 2011), 186–87.
64. Contra Ridderbos, *Gospel of John*, 515, who asserts that there is no link to a specific Old Testament passage.
65. Thompson, "'Every Picture Tells a Story,'" 259–77 (268, 275–76). Here Thompson points specifically to Ezekiel as John's inspiration.
66. Craig A. Evans, *Word and Glory: On the Exegetical and Theological Background of John's Prologue*, JSNTSup 89 (Sheffield: JSOT, 1993), 37–39.
67. Manning, *Echoes of a Prophet*, 142–43.
68. For a chart and statistical comparison of the linguistic parallels between John 15 and Ezek. 15, 17, 19, Isa. 5:1-5, and Jer. 2:21-22, see ibid., 140–41.
69. So too Köstenberger, *John*, 454; and D. A. Carson, *The Gospel according to John*, PNTC (Grand Rapids: Eerdmans, 1991), 517.

motif of a worthless vine fit for the fire obtains (i.e., branches are pruned [καθαίρω[70]/*kathairō*] and burned; John 15:2, 6//Ezek. 15:4, 7).[71] In Ezekiel, the language evokes covenant parallels. The fact that the nation had acted "unfaithfully" (מעל/*māʿal*; cf. Ezek. 15:8) must be understood from the context of covenant breach.[72] For John, Jesus thus becomes the fulfillment of the covenant for Israel in that he is the true vine, namely, the corporate head of Israel, who keeps covenant perfectly.

At the same time, Jesus urges his disciples to "remain"/"abide" (μένω/*menō*) in him (John 15:4, 6, 7, 9, 10, 16), which denotes association with the new covenant.[73] As will be handled in more detail in chapter 6 below, John desires to draw a direct connection between Jesus' works and the new covenant of peace (cf. Ezek. 34:25; 36:26; 37:26). Jesus serves as the true Vine, and in turn, his followers are the branches that are attached to the Vine. Jesus insists that remaining in him, the true Vine, brings life.[74] The vine imagery in Ezekiel is no less important. Israel, the vine, had failed to remain in covenant in a heartfelt way and thus became nothing more than worthless charred branches fit for the fire.

From a structural perspective, of all the "I Am" Sayings, this final one does not fit the sequential pattern vis-à-vis Ezekiel that we have seen thus far. However, when John 15 is viewed as a whole, John includes a number of other topics related to the Old Testament prophets and specifically Ezek. 34–39. These include: 1) Jesus speaking about abiding in the vine as a means of living securely in the abiding presence of God (John 15:1-17); 2) the concept of God

---

70. For a discussion on the importance of this word in light of John 15 and Ezek. 15, see Manning, *Echoes of a Prophet*, 141.
71. See also comments by Daniel Block, *The Book of Ezekiel: Chapters 1–24*, NICOT (Grand Rapids: Eerdmans, 1998), 720; and Thompson, "'Every Picture Tells a Story," 275.
72. See Peterson, *Ezekiel in Context*, 181–82.
73. Köstenberger, *John*, 453.
74. See Stevick, *Jesus and His Own*, 185.

judging those who do not abide in the vine (John 15:2a, 6); 3) the promise of the Spirit—a reference to the new covenant (John 15:26); and 4) the motif of the world "hating" God's people (John 15:18-25). In the prophetic corpus, Ezekiel included, a sign of the messianic kingdom was the picture of people dwelling securely in the land (Ezek. 28:26; 34:25, 28; 38:8, 11, 14; 39:26), each person sitting under their vine (Micah 4:4), with blessings of fecundity (Ezek. 44–48; cf. Zech. 3:10; 8:12; Mal. 3:11).

However, these concepts in Ezekiel are unlike any of the prophets. In Ezekiel, after the institution of the era of peace and security (Ezek. 34:25, 28; 37:21-28), those who hate Israel amass against her, without a cause, in order to kill and annihilate her (Ezek. 38–39 see esp. 38:8, 11, 14; 39:26). It is into this fray that Yahweh, now at peace and friendship with Israel, will come and defend the nation.[75] The mentioning of the giving of the Spirit both before and after these hostile events is telling (cf. Ezek. 37:14; 39:29). The covenant of peace is initiated (Ezek. 34:25; 37:26), yet a period of tribulation/hostility follows (Ezek. 38–39) before complete peace and security can be realized (Ezek. 40–48). The similarities with John 15 are striking. The disciples are promised life and protection in the Vine, yet hostility awaits them after the new covenant is initiated (John 15:17-27; cf. Acts 7, 12, 21). Jesus even points out that they hated them without a cause (John 15:25; cf. Pss. 35:19; 69:4). Nevertheless, just as in Ezekiel, in the end God will judge those hostile towards his people (John 12:48//Ezek. 38:22; 39:21).[76]

---

75. Note the dominant use of עמי (*'ammi*/my people) in these chapters to denote possession and protection of Israel (Ezek. 34:30; 36:8, 28; 37:12-13, 23, 27; 38:14, 16; 39:7; cf. 11:20).

76. The concept of an inaugurated eschatology (i.e., an "already but not yet" concept) seems apparent here.

The "I Am" Sayings in John Juxtaposed with the Larger Message of Ezekiel

To summarize what we have covered thus far, when one looks at the basic Johannine teaching of the "I Am" Sayings, they spell out for the reader how to have eternal life. According to John, belief in Jesus, the *Door* and *Good Shepherd* (John 10), would bring spiritual *Light* (John 8:12; 9:5) and sustenance (i.e., as the *Bread* of life cf. John 6:35, 41, 48, 50, 51, 58) to those who accepted him. Jesus offered himself as the *Way*, the *Truth*, and the *Life* (John 14:6), and as the *Resurrection* and the *Life* (John 11). For those choosing to accept Jesus' sacrifice and to abide in the true *Vine* (John 15:4, 6, 7, 9, 10), streams of *Living Water* flowing forth from the believer awaited them (John 4:10; 7:38). This abiding in the *Vine* while on earth would translate into an eternal abiding with Jesus in heaven (John 14:1-3). From this it is clear that John's "I Am" Sayings had both terrestrial and eschatological implications.

Ezekiel's message was no different. Abiding in the covenant with Yahweh and following the *way* of Yahweh's commandments brought *life* and not death (Ezek. 20:11, 13, 21). Those who caught a glimpse of the *Light* of Israel (Ezek. 1:27-28), and would listen to the *truth* plainly displayed through the words and visions of the prophet, could be assured that in the context of exile, even for a charred and worthless *vine* (Ezek. 15:1-8), there was hope (Ezek. 18:23, 32). Yahweh would *resurrect* them from their metaphorical graves (Ezek. 37:1-14) to a blessed and rejuvenated land (Ezek. 47:13—48:35) with a new temple (Ezek. 40:1—43:5) and a new "good" *Shepherd* to lead them (Ezek. 34, 46 cf. Ezek. 45:8; 46:1-3). Then the people could come to the *door* of the new temple and bask in *living water* that brings *life* to the deadest of lands (Ezek. 47:1-12). Unlike John, however, for the classical prophets, Ezekiel included, the terrestrial and the eschatological were blurred in light of Old Testament thought and milieu.⁷⁷ Nevertheless, as we have demonstrated, Ezekiel still seems to be the most obvious literary garden from which the Johannine "I Am" Sayings sprang forth.

The Recognition Formula: Then They Will Know: Knowledge of Yahweh and Jesus

Before leaving our discussion of the "I Am" Sayings, one final important feature of the use of ἐγώ εἰμι ("I am") needs to be addressed due to its relevance to our theory concerning John's use of Ezekiel. Apart from the "I Am" Sayings with the predicate nominative (e.g., "I am the true vine"), we also have a series of "absolute" "I Am" Sayings throughout the Fourth Gospel (e.g., "I am *he*"; cf. John 4:26; 6:20; 7:34, 36; 8:21, 24, 58; 13:19; 17:24; 18:5, 6, 8).⁷⁸ The combination of these absolute sayings and the "I Am" Sayings serve to bring attention to the reality of Jesus' identity: the people need to "recognize" that he is God! In essence, John was employing a form of the Old Testament recognition formula ("then they/you will know that I am Yahweh"). In fact John actually uses the phrase in John 8:28.

John had a number of possible places in the Old Testament to find the motif of bringing belief through knowledge. For example, as Martin Hengel comments, Isa. 43:10 "sounds completely Johannine: ἵνα γνῶτε καὶ πιστεύσητε . . . ὅτι ἐγώ εἰμι; 'that *you may know and believe that I am*'" (italics original).⁷⁹ However, the recognition formula is used predominantly within Exodus and Ezekiel.⁸⁰ Not

---

77. So too Bullock, "Ezekiel," 29–30.
78. See Paul N. Anderson, *The Riddles of the Fourth Gospel: An Introduction to John* (Minneapolis: Fortress Press, 2011), 14.
79. Martin Hengel, "The Prologue of the Gospel of John as the Gateway to Christological Truth," in *The Gospel of John and Christian Theology*, ed. Richard Bauckham and Carl Mosser (Grand Rapids: Eerdmans, 2008), 265–92 (280).

surprisingly, Ezekiel once again dominates with a total of sixty-three occurrences.[81] The Johannine "I Am" Sayings are in essence metaphors,[82] and as such find a suitable "home" being perhaps inspired from the one Old Testament prophetic book with the longest of any Old Testament metaphors: Ezek. 16 and 23.

The connection between knowledge/knowing and covenant in the ancient Near East was understood.[83] For Ezekiel's audience they required a re-education of who exactly their Suzerain was, the one with whom they had entered into covenant at Mt. Sinai. Because they had forgotten about that relationship and had rather settled for a life of religiosity and temple attendance devoid of a changed heart, Ezekiel formats his work, especially from chapters 1–39 with the focus on this re-education process. Even in the midst of judgment the people failed to come to the saving knowledge of Yahweh even though Yahweh offered hope if they repented (Ezek. 18).

The parallels with Jesus' day are evident. Even the language used in each book is similar. In Ezekiel the verb used in the LXX for "know" is γινώσκω (*ginōskō*). This is the same verb used throughout the Fourth Gospel to point out people's knowledge of who Jesus was or their lack of it (John 1:10, 48; 3:10; 5:42; 6:69; 7:17, 26; 8:27, 28, 32, 43, 55; 10:14, 15, 27, 38; 13:7, 35; 14:7, 9, 17, 20; 16:3; 17:3, 7, 25). Throughout the Fourth Gospel, this verb is used in connection

---

80. Robert Houston Smith, "Exodus Typology in the Fourth Gospel," *JBL* 81, no. 4 (1962): 329–42, esp. 341–42, connects John's usage to the Exodus passages (cf. Exod. 7:5, 17; 8:22; 10:2; 14:4, 18; 16:12; 29:46; 31:13). The other books where this phrase appears are: Deut. 29:6; 1 Kgs. 20:13, 28; Isa. 49:23; Joel 3:17.
81. There are several variations of this form in Ezekiel: e.g., "To make myself known to them" (20:5, 19); "I am the Lord your God" (20:7, 19); they will "know the Lord has spoken" (5:13; 17:21; 37:14); they will "know the Lord does the smiting" (7:9; 21:2; 22:22); they will "know I have not done this in vain" (14:23); they will "know the Lord is with them" (34:30); they will know "the Lord has heard" (35:12); and the nations will know "that the Lord has rebuilt the ruined places" (36:36).
82. Schweizer, "What about the Johannine 'Parables,'" 214–15.
83. See for example Herbert B. Huffmon, "The Treaty Background of the Hebrew *Yāda'*," *BASOR* 181 (1966): 31–37; and Peterson, *Ezekiel in Context*, 257–63.

with believing in order to identify those who come to a knowledge of who Jesus is and what his mission was. In the end, those who truly "know" him will enter into covenant with him (i.e., be saved). Again, Hassell Bullock rightly notes,

> Jesus describes his own obedience in terms of this purpose, that the world might be brought to a recognition of his love for the Father: "But I do as the Father has commanded me, so that the world may know that I love the Father" (John 14:31). And most significantly he describes eternal life in terms of the knowledge of God and his relationship to him: "And this is eternal life, that they know thee, the only true God, and Jesus Christ whom thou hast sent" (John 17:3).[84]

To this we can add the words of Stan Harstine: "Not only is God/Father the source of all that is, but knowing God/Father is the desired endgame for the text."[85]

Even though the exile had made Israel a people of the "book" (i.e., they knew the law cf. John 3:10), for John, their heart was far from God. As in the days of Ezekiel, they had settled on religiosity and temple service without a changed heart (John 2:13-22). It is into this context that John's Jesus comes preaching and ministering. John therefore used the signs and the "I Am" Sayings to teach and bring about belief in the people that Jesus was in fact the promised Messiah and, in turn, divine/God.[86] Bullock says it best when he concludes, "The point we are making is that Jesus used the same method and recognition formula in John's gospel as did Ezekiel to establish the recognition of his relationship to the Father. The goal of his life and work, as with the prophet Ezekiel, was to bring men to the knowledge of God. According to John's presentation the knowledge of Jesus' nature was to be gained in his actions."[87]

---

84. Bullock, "Ezekiel," 26.
85. Harstine, "Fourth Gospel's Characterization of God," 146.
86. So too the conclusion of Bullock, "Ezekiel," 25–27.
87. Ibid., 27.

Closely associated with the recognition of Jesus as *the* I Am, is his sheer authority and otherness. Jesus' God-like attributes, as opposed to his humanity, are stressed by John as evinced in the almost complete absence of suffering in the Passion narrative.[88] On this Judith Lieu notes that the Johannine Jesus is "more spiritual and less fleshly . . . Jesus . . . suffers no agony in the Garden, or dereliction on the Cross . . . can at the moment of his arrest fell his opponents to the ground with a theophanic 'I am' (18.5-6).'"[89] As with the majesty and glory of Yahweh in Ezekiel, John's Jesus is God, the I Am.

Conclusion

Throughout this chapter we have noted the numerous parallels between John's use of the seven "I Am" Sayings and their connection to Ezekiel. Further, we have seen that throughout John 6–15, John follows a fairly close canonical sequence with many of the themes and motifs present in Ezek. 12–39. John appears to be showing how Jesus, as the corporate representative and messianic figure for Israel, reflects and fulfills that which Ezekiel had prophesied and had hoped for, namely, that Israel would come to know their Suzerain. In this vein, the "I Am" Sayings and John's use of the recognition formula (John 8:28) again finds affinity with Ezekiel. Jesus' generation would come to know who Jesus was if they believed his testimony and his signs. Of course the greatest of these "signs" was Jesus' resurrection. It was this event that solidified, all that Jesus had told his disciples, into

---

88. Schnackenburg, *Gospel according to St. John Vol. II*, 398, also points up the absence of Jesus' suffering in the Passion Narrative because of John's desire to show the glorification of Jesus not the scandal of the cross (cf. John 7:39; 12:16; 13:31-32; 17:1). See also Ernst Käsemann, *The Testament of Jesus: A Study of the Gospel of John in Light of Chapter 17*, trans. Gerhard Krodel (London, SCM, 1968), 10.
89. Judith M. Lieu, "How John Writes," in *The Written Gospel*, ed. Markus Bockmuehl and Donald A. Hagner (Cambridge: Cambridge University Press, 2005), 171–83 (171). See also Moloney, *The Resurrection of the Messiah*, 101–106.

the belief that he was in fact God—even for a doubting Thomas (John 20:24-29). It is to the post-resurrection scene that we now turn.

6

John 17, 20, and Ezekiel 37

Unity, Resurrection, and the Insufflation

Thus far we have looked at a number of structural and thematic connections between Ezekiel's prophetic work and the Fourth Gospel. On the macro-structural level some of Ezekiel's ordering seems to have been followed by John especially where these connections have related to Ezekielian themes, sign acts, and the visionary "peaks" noted in my chart in chapter 1. For example, John's introduction of Jesus reflects Ezekiel's introduction of Yahweh in his first vision (cf. John 1//Ezek. 1–3); John's placement of Jesus' early cleansing and departure of the temple mirrors the defiled temple and the departure of Yahweh in Ezekiel's second vision (cf. John 2:13-22//Ezek. 8–11); several of Ezekiel's sign acts parallel Jesus' signs (e.g., the death of Ezekiel's wife and the raising of Lazarus); and finally, there are numerous echoes of Ezek. 12–39 in the "I Am" Sayings in John.

As both books draw to a close, a number of Ezekielian motifs again appear to be intentionally drawn upon by John. Ezek. 37, which just happens to contain the third vision/peak in the structure of Ezekiel, is one chapter in particular that has a number of connections with the closing chapters of the Fourth Gospel (viz., John 17–20). The unique presentation of Jesus' prayer of unity in John 17;[1] the absence of the Eucharistic meal; and John's presentation of the resurrection and insufflation in John 20 are foremost in these overlapping motifs.

In light of these points of contact, in this chapter I will begin by handling the close thematic connections between John's resurrection scene, including the insufflation, and the valley of dry bones in Ezek. 37:1-14.[2] I will also argue that Jesus' three-fold greeting of peace during the insufflation scene and the absence of the institution of the communion meal must be read in light of Ezekiel's promised covenant of peace (cf. Ezek. 34:25; 37:26). Finally, I will look at the connections between Jesus' prayer of unity in John 17, and the sign act of Ezek. 37:15-28. At the same time it is important to bear in mind that while the motifs in these closing chapters of John find the most affinity with Ezek. 37, the precise ordering of the Ezekielian motifs vis-à-vis the Johannine material in John 12–20 follows a looser ordering than those demonstrated in my previous chapters. Again, the words of C. K. Barrett bear repeating and remain true here: ". . . though John uses the O.T. he uses it in a novel manner, collecting its sense rather than quoting."[3] Moreover, because the Passion narrative

---

1. For a discussion on structure and content of the unity prayer, see Francis J. Moloney, *Love in the Gospel of John: An Exegetical, Theological, and Literary Study* (Grand Rapids: Baker, 2013), 122–33.
2. Others have seen this connection but fail to develop it to its logical end. See for example, Gail R. O'Day, "The Gospel of John: Introduction, Commentary and Reflections," in *New Interpreter's Bible: A Commentary in Twelve Volumes*, ed. Neil Alexander (Nashville: Abingdon, 1995), 9:846; John W. Pryor, *John: Evangelist of the Covenant People: The Narrative and Themes of the Fourth Gospel* (Downers Grove, IL: InterVarsity, 1992), 89; and Andrew T. Lincoln, *Truth on Trial: The Lawsuit Motif in the Fourth Gospel* (Peabody, MA: Hendrickson, 2000), 255.

is unlike anything in the Old Testament, we must allow room for John to exercise literary license to develop this event. Yet, even in this once-in-history moment, John's "literary license" does not answer why his presentation is so unique. Once again, an appeal to his reliance on Ezekielian motifs appears to be the best solution to this dilemma.

Parallels between John 20 and Ezekiel 37

John 20 records the resurrection scene with Mary Magdalene, Peter, and the other disciple, "whom Jesus loved," arriving and inspecting the empty tomb. After the disciples' departure, Mary then has an encounter with the resurrected Jesus (John 20:1-18). This scene is followed by Jesus' miraculous appearance, twice, in a locked room; first to ten of the disciples (Thomas being absent), and a second time when Thomas is present (John 20:19-31). During the first appearance Jesus "breathes" on the disciples and tells them to "receive the Holy Spirit" (λάβετε πνεῦμα ἅγιον; John 20:22). In our parallel text of Ezek. 37, two pericopae dominate the chapter: the valley of dry bones (Ezek. 37:1-14), and the sign act depicting the union of the two sticks (Ezek. 37:15-28). In the latter section we find the prophecy about the covenant of peace (Ezek. 37:26), which will be developed in our next section. I will begin, however, by listing the common elements that appear in both John 20 and Ezek. 37:1-14. After listing these I will discuss them seriatim.

John 20 and Ezek. 37:1-14 Parallels

1. Both scenes begin with a setting of death (a tomb and a valley of dry bones).
2. Both scenes depict resurrection (at least the aftermath of it in John).

---

3. Charles K. Barrett, "The Old Testament in the Fourth Gospel," *JTS* 48, no. 2 (1947): 155–69 (156).

3. In both accounts, belief in God's ability to resurrect is questioned; by Ezekiel himself (Ezek. 37:3) and by Thomas (John 20:27-29).
4. In both accounts, divine-human interaction takes place; Mary with the angels, Mary and the disciples with a resurrected Jesus (e.g., John 20:13), and Ezekiel with Yahweh (Ezek. 37:3-6, 9, 11-14).
5. In both accounts, physical appearance plays a key role as evidence for the resurrected person(s); Jesus shows his hands and his side as evidence (John 20:20, 25, 27), and Ezekiel sees the decomposed bodies come back to life (Ezek. 37:7-8).
6. In both cases, "life" comes by breathing into/onto people; Jesus breathes on his disciples to bring spiritual life (John 20:22), and, through Ezekiel's prophecy, Yahweh breathes spiritual life into Israel's metaphorical corpses (Ezek. 37:10).

In both of the chapters in question, the setting is one of death or a graveyard. Ezekiel's "graveyard" is an unnamed valley where no doubt a battle took place.[4] The theological and spiritual significance of the two scenes should not be overlooked. In 586 B.C.E., the nation of Israel lost a physical battle with Nebuchadnezzar of Babylon because of a broken covenant with both their earthly suzerain as well as their heavenly Suzerain (Ezek. 6:12; 11:10-11; 17:21; 21; Jer. 52:8).[5] As a result, many men ended up either dying or going into exile (Ezek. 33:21). Moreover, the scene of Ezek. 37:1-14 is one of cursing.[6] In the ancient Near East, it was a common practice to leave the corpses of dead soldiers on the battlefield as a testimony to the conqueror's might.[7] Non-burial was the worse curse that could

---

4. Johannes Herrmann, *Ezechiel übersetzt und erklärt*, KAT 11 (Leipzig: A. Deichert, 1924), 235, identifies the scene as a battlefield ("Schlachtfeld"). So too the conclusion of Charles R. Biggs, *The Book of Ezekiel* (London: Epworth, 1996), 117; W. Baumgartner, *Zum Alten Testament und seiner Umwelt* (Leiden: Brill, 1959), 361; and William H. Brownlee, *Ezekiel 1–19*, WBC 28 (Waco, TX: Word Books, 1986), xxxi. This conclusion is also implied by A. W. Streane, *The Book of the Prophet Ezekiel* (repr., Cambridge: Cambridge University Press, 1924), 290; and Marvin A. Sweeney, "Ezekiel: Zadokite Priest and Visionary Prophet of the Exile," SBLSP 39 (Atlanta: SBL, 2000), 728–51, esp. 746.
5. A battle is intimated in the text.
6. See similar comments by Christopher J. H. Wright, *Old Testament Ethics for the People of God* (Downers Grove, IL: InterVarsity Press, 2004), 82.

be enacted upon a person after death (cf. Deut. 28:25-26; cf. Lev. 26:30).[8]

The spiritual parallels are evident, parallels that John may have picked up on. The very reason for Jesus' burial before sundown on the day of his crucifixion was to avoid breaking the law of God (i.e., the Sabbath) and bringing God's wrath upon the people (John 19:31), for every man who is hung upon a tree is cursed under the law (Deut. 21:22-23). Therefore, prior to both settings, a curse had been enacted on the subjects. Israel's army had been left unburied and as a result were nothing but dry bones, and Jesus had suffered the curse of being hung on a "tree" and now was laid in a tomb (John 19:38-42). As noted immediately above, in Ezekiel's day, leaving someone unburied on a field of battle showed the might of the suzerain. Similarly, in John's day, Satan desired to show his power over Jesus by bringing about his death (John 13:27). However, in both cases the power of the "suzerain" is superseded by the power of God evinced in the reversal of the curse through resurrection. This leads to our second parallel.

Both scenes record the resurrection of those accursed. The resurrection of the corpses in the valley of dry bones served as a curse reversal, something unparalleled in the ancient world.[9] Similarly,

---

7. See Brian Neil Peterson, *Ezekiel in Context: Ezekiel's Message Understood in Its Historical Setting of Covenant Curses and Ancient Near Eastern Mythological Motifs*, PTMS 182 (Eugene, OR: Pickwick Publications, 2012), 232–42; Stanley Gevirtz, "Curse Motifs in the Old Testament and in the Ancient Near East" (PhD diss., The University of Chicago, 1959), 171–90, esp. 171–72; Charles F. Fensham, "The Curse of the Dry Bones in Ezekiel 37:14 Changed to a Blessing of Resurrection," *JNSL* 13 (1987): 59–60; and Francesca Stavrakopoulou, "Ezekiel's Use and Abuse of Corpses," (paper presented at the annual meeting of the SBL. Boston, MA, November 24, 2008).

8. Seth Richardson, "Death and Dismemberment in Mesopotamia: Discorporation between the Body and Body Politic," in *Performing Death: Social Analyses of Funerary Traditions in the Ancient Near East and Mediterranean*, ed. Nicola Laneri, UCOIS 3 (Chicago: OIUC, 2007), 189–208, esp. 200.

9. Cf. Herbert M. Wolf, "The Transcendent Nature of Covenant Curse Reversals," in *Israel's Apostasy and Restoration: Essays in Honor of Roland K. Harrison*, ed. R. K. Harrison and Avraham Gileadi (Grand Rapids: Baker, 1988), 319–325. See also Peterson, *Ezekiel in Context*, 247–53.

Jesus' resurrection brought about the reversal of the curse of death and the cross. Also, Ezek. 37:1-14 must be understood in light of Ezek. 38–39 and the fact that the curse of non-burial is removed from the nation of Israel and placed upon her enemies (Ezek. 39:4, 12-20).[10] Jesus' resurrection not only reversed the curse of death effected by Adam's sin (Gen. 3; Rom. 5:12-16; 1 Cor. 15), but also allowed his disciples to have the authority of Jesus over their enemy, Satan (see John 12:31; 16:11; 20:23; cf. Eph. 6:12; Col. 2:15).

Third, Yahweh's question to Ezekiel: "Can these bones live?" (Ezek. 37:3a), evokes a veiled response from Ezekiel: "only you know Lord" (Ezek. 37:3b). In light of the bleakness of the scene, this response clearly reflected Ezekiel's doubts. In John's account, Thomas questions the validity of Jesus' resurrection as relayed to him by his fellow disciples (John 20:27-29). In both cases it takes a miracle from God to convince the doubting party. Yahweh commands Ezekiel to prophesy over the bones, but before Ezekiel does so, Yahweh relates how he is going to bring life into the bones (Ezek. 37:4-6). For Thomas, Jesus had to reappear in a locked room in order for the doubt to be removed. In both cases, seeing is believing!

Fourth, closely connected to our previous parallel, are the interactions between humans and the divine. Mary Magdalene interacted with the angels and a resurrected Jesus, as do the disciples in the latter case. Similarly, throughout Ezek. 37, Yahweh and the prophet dialogue with one another. The close encounters of humans with the heavenly sphere in both accounts shows the importance of the event.

Fifth, much like the third example above, the physical appearance of the resurrected individual(s) serves as a key linking motif. The resurrected physical bodies thus become the evidence of the

---

10. On the parallels between Ezek. 37 and 38–39, see Peterson, *Ezekiel in Context*, 271–76.

miraculous event (John 20:20, 25, 27//Ezek. 37:7-8). In the case of Ezekiel, the visionary resurrection had both physical and spiritual import. The vision depicted the reality of a future hope of return/revivification of Israel as a nation (Ezek. 37:11-14), but also had a spiritual nuance that promised a renewed spiritual awakening (37:26). In John, Jesus' resurrection had both spiritual and physical import. The resurrected body showed Jesus' divinity, but more importantly, it offered the physical hope of future resurrection. The resurrected Jesus also inaugurated the new covenant, namely, the covenant of peace spoken about by the prophets, none more so than Ezekiel (Ezek. 34:25; 37:26; cf. 11:19; 36:26).

Finally, in both pericopae, life is imparted by the inbreathing of God. In Ezekiel, it metaphorically depicts the spiritual rebirth of the nation under the new covenant; in John, it symbolizes the spiritual birth of the church/new Israel under the new covenant of peace. In this vein, Thomas Hatina rightly notes the parallels between the Targum of Ezekiel and John 20:22 when he states,

> The Targum of Ezek. 37:14 comes even closer to John 20:22, for it describes God's *memra* [word] as the agent who decrees the giving of the Spirit; "And I will put My Spirit into you, and you shall live, and I will make you dwell upon your land, and you shall know I, the Lord, have decreed it by *My Memra*." It is possible that John may be recalling this synagogue teaching in his description of God's Word as the giver of the Spirit" (italics original).[11]

Hatina goes on to note the close parallels with targumim Pseudo-Jonathan, Onqelos, and Neofiti at Gen. 2:7.[12] These, he concludes, were the textual impetus for John. Nevertheless, even though these

---

11. Thomas R. Hatina, "John 20:22 in Its Eschatological Context: Promise or Fulfillment?," *Bib* 74, no. 2 (1993): 217. For the Targum text, see Samson H. Levey, *The Targum of Ezekiel* (Collegeville, MN: The Liturgical Press, 1990), 104. Note also the direct reference to Ezek. 37:14 when commenting on Gen. 2:7 in *Midrash Rabbah Genesis*, vol. 1, trans. Rabbi H. Freedman (London: The Soncino Press, 1983), 116.

may have been part of the literary milieu of John, the threefold announcement of peace in the insufflation scene pushes against the direct Genesis parallels and toward the Ezekiel text (see discussion immediately below).

Insufflation/In-Breathing

This discussion on the revivification of the corpses in Ezekiel's valley leads naturally to the importance of the event of the insufflation in John 20:22. What actually took place during this event has been hotly debated. Did it mark the beginning of the new life in Christ? Was this merely John's Acts 2 event? Is the notation of "breathing" on the disciples simply an exhalation of Jesus' earthly breath and nothing more? (I will return to these questions shortly.) While affirmative responses to each of these questions have been given, the important thing to notice is that in the context of Ezekielian motifs, the spiritual and prophetic significance must not be overlooked.

To begin, many initiate their discussion of John 20:22 by looking to Gen. 2:7, one of only seven appearances of the verb ἐμφυσάω (*emphusaō*/"to breathe") in the LXX (Ezek. 21:36, 37:9; 1Kgs. 17:21; Job 4:21; Nah. 2:2; Wis. 15:11).[13] Most go on to conclude that because Genesis language first appeared in John 1:1 and now is recapitulated here, Genesis must be the point of origin for John here in 20:22. Unfortunately, once these parallel motifs are noted, rarely do scholars consider other possible connections, which, as we will see, favor Ezek. 37:9 over Gen. 2:7. For indeed, both of

---

12. Hatina, "John 20:22 in Its Eschatological Context," 217–18. Hatina (218) concludes that Jesus is giving the disciples "his words and understanding of eternal life." One is left wondering how far afield of the concept of regeneration this conclusion really falls (see more below).
13. The four other appearances of the verb do not connote creation activity, perhaps with the exception of Elijah's breathing life into the dead boy in 1 Kgs. 17:21. On the assimilation of the *nu* to a *mu* before a labial as seen in the alternate forms of ἐμφυσάω and ἐνεφύσησεν, see William Mounce, *The Morphology of Biblical Greek* (Grand Rapids: Zondervan, 1994), 37.

these texts present the creation motif.[14] Now, while the Gen. 2 link is correct to a degree, it fails to satisfy the context completely. The author of Gen. 2:7 speaks of breathing the *breath* of life into humanity by using the term πνοὴν (*pnoēn*/"breath") not πνεῦμα (*pneuma*/"breath" or "spirit").[15] It is only Ezek. 37:9 and John 20:22 that use ἐμφυσάω and πνεῦμα together! Also, most fail to make the simultaneous connection between the inbreathing of life and the comments about the covenant of peace found in Ezek. 37:26 (cf. Ezek. 34:25), something that is absent in the Genesis passage (see more on this below). This seems to clarify for the reader which Old Testament text is being employed by John. Therefore, while connections can be made to the book of Genesis, I believe it was not the central focus of the Evangelist. Yes, John wanted to draw the connection between Jesus and Yahweh as creator (John 1:1)—one who has authority to create both physical and spiritual life. But in light of John's use of Ezekielian motifs, Ezek. 37 also needs to come into view, especially the context of instituting the new covenant of peace.

It goes without saying that Ezekiel's presentation of the inbreathing was meant to depict a new creation of the nation; Yahweh himself says as much (Ezek. 37:11-14). Similarly, in John, Jesus' inbreathing of his Spirit into the disciples is the moment when the "new Israel"/church is birthed. In this regard, Saeed Hamid-Khani aptly notes, "The passage in Ezekiel 37 looks to the *regeneration* of Israel immediately prior to the establishment of the Messianic kingdom" (italics mine).[16] Thus, in John 20:22, this is not necessarily the Spirit-equipping scene as recorded by Luke in Acts 2; it may

---

14. Jeannine K. Brown, "Creation's Renewal in the Gospel of John," *CBQ* 72, no. 2 (2010): 282.
15. So too Gary T. Manning, *Echoes of a Prophet: The Use of Ezekiel in the Gospel of John and in Literature of the Second Temple Period* (London: T & T Clark, 2004), 166.
16. Saeed Hamid-Khani, *Revelation and Concealment of Christ: A Theological Inquiry into the Elusive Language of the Fourth Gospel*, WUNT 120 (Tübingen: Mohr Siebeck, 2000). 361.

very well be the moment when the disciples are *regenerated*, when they finally come to complete faith and are brought into eternal communion with Christ (cf. 1 Cor. 12:3; see discussion below).[17] John sees in the act of the inbreathing the spiritual completion of the resurrection of the dry bones of Ezekiel promised in Ezek. 37:9; the church (and disciples) is now ready, as Max Turner puts it, "to embark on its new life."[18]

To help demonstrate this point, one can also draw connections between the events of John 20 and those of John 3 in light of the dual promises of Yahweh of cleansing and spiritual renewal handled respectively in Ezek. 36 and 37.[19] In John 3, Jesus told Nicodemus that he must be born of "water and the spirit" (John 3:5). Now, while the meaning of this phrase has been debated *ad nauseum*[20] and will not be rehashed here, there may be a simple solution to the meaning rooted in the promises of Yahweh in Ezek. 36:25-27 and 37:14 (cf. Isa. 44:3-5). Ezek. 36:25-27 reads,

> Then I will sprinkle clean water on you, and you will be clean; I will cleanse you from all your filthiness and from all your idols. Moreover, I will give you a new heart and put a new spirit within you; and I will remove the heart of stone from your flesh and give you a heart of flesh. And I will put My Spirit within you and cause you to walk in My statutes, and you will be careful to observe My ordinances (NASB).

---

17. See also comments by I. De La Potterie, "Parole et Esprit dans S. Jean," in *L'Évangile de Jean, Sources, Rédaction, Théologie*, ed. M. De Jonge (Leuven: Gembloux and Leuven University Press, 1977), 176–201 (196).
18. Max Turner, *The Holy Spirit and Spiritual Gifts* (Peabody, MA: Hendrickson, 1999), 99. Turner (101) calls this giving of the Spirit in John 20:22 the coming of the "charismatic wisdom and understanding." This does not seem to be that helpful in light of Bennema's (see n31 below) well-argued presentation for something along the lines of a "relational" experience.
19. See discussion by Manning, *Echoes of a Prophet*, 186–89.
20. That is, does it refer to natural birth and spiritual birth, or is it referring to water baptism and spirit baptism? See for example the conclusions of Zane C. Hodges, "Water and Spirit—John 3:5," *BSac* 135, no. 539 (1978): 206–20. For an excellent overview of the competing interpretations, see Linda Belleville, "Born of Water and Spirit," *TJ* 1, no. 2 (1980): 125–41, esp. 125–34.

In dealing with this text and Ezek. 37, Hamid-Khani notes,

> This prophecy [Ezek. 36:25-27] points to a time of Israel's coming restoration, when the nation shall 'be born in a day' (Isa. 66:8). In the next chapter [Ezek. 37], Ezekiel pictures this great national revival as the bringing of the dead to new life by the word of the Lord, and employs the figure of wind to picture the life-giving activity of the Spirit of God. Thus, in the first part of the prophecy, the figure of water is employed in connection with the cleansing away of filthiness; and in the latter portion, the figure of the wind is introduced for the giving of new life.[21]

These events were two sides of the same proverbial coin and depicted the completed work of Jesus and the giving of the new birth/life.[22] Thus, one could argue that in the same way Jesus was expecting Nicodemus, a teacher in Israel, to know his own Scriptures (John 3:10),[23] John is expecting his readers to draw a direct link to the Nicodemus event and the fulfillment of these Ezekielian prophecies in the life of Jesus.[24] Jesus came to give both spiritual purification (i.e., the image of the water in Ezek. 36:25-27; cf. Ezek. 39:29; *Jub.* 1:22) and spiritual new life (i.e., the image of the resurrection in Ezek. 37:1-14).[25] These terms thus serve as a hendiadys depicting the same event.

This concept, clearly rooted in Ezekiel, was also present at Qumran. The Manual of Discipline states:

> Then, too, God will purge all the acts of man in the crucible of His truth, and refine for Himself all the fabric of man, destroying every spirit of perversity from within his flesh and cleansing him by the holy

---

21. Hamid-Khani, *Revelation and Concealment of Christ*, 364.
22. See also comments by J. Ramsey Michaels, *The Gospel of John*, NICNT (Grand Rapids: Eerdmans, 2010), 102; and Belleville, "Born of Water and Spirit," 140–41.
23. So too the conclusions of Hodges, "Water and Spirit," 217.
24. Ibid., 219. Here Hodges draws an interesting parallel between the fact that Jesus came from heaven and would return to heaven. In his use of "water and spirit/wind" Jesus was speaking of the two elements that also come from the natural heavens/atmosphere. Thus, Jesus may have been using these natural images as an object lesson for the new birth.
25. So too Belleville, "Born of Water and Spirit," 138–39.

spirit from all the effects of wickedness. Like waters of purification He will sprinkle upon him the spirit of truth, to cleanse him of all the abominations of falsehood and of all pollution through the spirit of filth; to the end that, being made upright, men may have understanding of transcendental knowledge and of the lore of the sons of heaven, and that, being made blameless in their ways, they may be endowed with inner vision.[26]

Yahweh had promised new life for the nation of Israel (Ezek. 37:11-14), an event only foreshadowed in the return of 538 B.C.E.[27] And, as just noted, this new life was to be both physical and spiritual (physical: Ezek. 37:14, 21, 25; spiritual: Ezek. 37:23 cf.; 39:29). For John, Ezekiel's visionary resurrection of Israel can be seen exemplified in the institution of the Church (rooted in its Jewish/Israelite setting); the spiritual life is what is instituted when Jesus "breathed" on the disciples in John 20:22. Jesus makes it clear that he is actually copying his Father in giving life, perhaps an allusion to Ezek. 37 (John 5:21).

The Institution of the Covenant of Peace

One of the other peculiarities about John is his failure to depict the Eucharistic meal with the full institution of the new covenant rites (i.e., bread and wine). This "lacuna" may again be explained by John's reliance on Ezekiel's presentation of the covenant of peace. We see that the institution of the covenant is still a central focus even for John when Ezekielian parallels are considered.[28] Instead of concentrating on the pre-cross institution of the sacrament of the new covenant—language reminiscent of Jeremiah (Jer. 31:31 cf. Matt.

---

26. Theodor H. Gaster, *The Dead Sea Scriptures*, third ed. (Garden City, NY: Doubleday & Co., 1976), 50–51. See also 1QS 3:6-8; 4:21-24; 7:6; 9:32;11:10-14; 12:12; 16:12; 17:20, as noted by Belleville, "Born of Water and Spirit," 140n85.
27. Some see the return of the Jews to Israel in 1948 as the more appropriate fulfillment of this prophecy. While this is a topic of heated debate (i.e., Zionism), there is a large portion of Christendom, both past and present, that see Israel's return to their ancient land a fulfillment of Ezek. 37.
28. Andreas J. Köstenberger, *John*, BECNT (Grand Rapids: Baker, 2004), 572.

26:28; Mark 14:24; Luke 22:20; 1 Cor. 11:25; Heb. 12:24)—John instead focuses on the completed work of Jesus and the covenant of peace, clear Ezekielian terminology (Ezek. 34:25; 37:26).[29] We see this implicitly in John 20 where Jesus gives the threefold pronouncement of "peace with you" (εἰρήνη ὑμῖν; cf. John 20:19, 21, 26). The only parallel to this phrase in the Synoptic Gospels is in Luke 24:36. In Matt. 10:13 and Luke 10:5-6, the word εἰρήνη is found on the lips of Jesus, but in both cases this is Jesus' instructions for a formal greeting between people (cf. Mark 5:34//Luke 8:48; Luke 7:50; 19:42). This being noted, regarding John's use of the phrase, Raymond Brown correctly points out that we "should not assume that 'Peace to you' is an ordinary greeting."[30]

Earlier in the Fourth Gospel, the author introduces the motif of "peace" that is developed here in chapter 20 (cf. John 14:27; 16:33). Whereas some rightly connect the term "peace" used in chapter 20 with John 14:27 and 16:33, they fail to give an explanation of where this terminology originates.[31] Moreover, some fail to see its importance at all.[32] Others have seen the value of connecting Jesus' words in John 14:27 with Ezekiel's covenant of peace but fail to move beyond that to its appearance in John 20:19, 21, 26.[33] In light of the

29. The phrase "covenant of peace" appears two other places in the Hebrew text: Num. 25:12 and Isa. 54:10. However, in both of these cases different constructions are used. In Num. 25:12 it is "my covenant of peace" (ברית שלום/*berîtî šālôm*) speaking about the covenant between Yahweh and Phinehas. In Isa. 54:10 it is "the covenant of my peace" (ברית שלומי/*berît šelômî*) referring to Yahweh's covenant with Israel in general by using Noahic covenantal language.
30. Raymond E. Brown, *The Gospel according to John XIII–XXI*, AB 29a (New York: Doubleday, 1970), 1021. Contra, Köstenberger, *John*, 572, who suggests it was a greeting to alleviate the disciples' fear. However, Köstenberger (443) rightly notes the Old Testament connections in his earlier comments concerning the phrase.
31. Cornelius Bennema, "The Giving of the Spirit in John's Gospel—A New Proposal," *EvQ* 74, no. 3 (2002): 195–213 (211); and Gail O'Day and Susan E. Hylen, *John*, WBCom (Louisville: Westminster John Knox, 2006), 195, all connect the term "peace" used here in chapter 20 with John 14:27 and 16:33.
32. Typical of how commentators handle the three occurrences of "peace" is Frederick Dale Bruner, *The Gospel of John: A Commentary* (Grand Rapids: Eerdmans, 2012), 1160, 1162, 1186–87, who quickly passes over the occurrences. He does not even comment on the third appearance.

numerous Ezekielian connections up to this point it seems likely that the institution of the new covenant of peace is in view here. The triple use of "peace" in the context is a means of drawing the reader's attention to that connection.

Now while some may argue that in Ezekiel the covenant of peace is mentioned only two times (Ezek. 34:25; 37:26) as opposed to the three appearances in John, this concern is easily allayed when we examine the Johannine context. When one looks at Jesus' first appearance to the disciples after the resurrection, he uses the phrase two times (John 20:19, 21), the second somewhat awkwardly clearly indicating its specific importance to the context. However, the third time is a separate occasion for the purpose of including Thomas in this new covenant of peace (John 20:26). Thus the last two usages serve the same purpose.

In this vein, it is the second appearance of the phrase in 20:21 that pushes against the interpretation of a simple greeting. In John 20:21, Jesus says "Peace to you" right before he breathes on the disciples. This seems odd if it is a mere greeting. Instead one must see the connection to the issuance of the Ezekielian covenant of peace. Jey Kanagaraj correctly connects Jesus' breathing on the disciples with Ezek. 37:7, but then quickly goes to the default text of Gen. 2:7 because, he concludes, Ezek. 37:9-10 deals with the resurrection of the dead.[34] However, Kanagaraj has failed to keep in mind the metaphorical and eschatological function of Ezek. 37:1-14. Yes, the picture is of a valley of dry bones, and yes, this is resurrection, but

---

33. E.g., see Jey J. Kanagaraj, *John*, NCCS (Eugene, OR: Cascade Books, 2013), 150. On the other hand, Craig S. Keener, *The Gospel of John: A Commentary*, 2 vols (Peabody, MA: Hendrickson, 2003; repr., Grand Rapids: Baker, 2012), 2:1201, rightly points out the threefold appearance of the phrase and even connects it to imparting "actual peace to his disciples" but fails to see any further covenantal significance in the context.

34. Kanagaraj, *John*, 199.

more importantly, this is new spiritual life being given to the nation of Israel! The new covenant is in view here.

The Inbreathing: An Alternate Proposal

As noted previously, the picture of Jesus' breathing on the disciples and his call to receive the Holy Spirit has been a difficult picture to interpret with a number of proposals proffered:[35] this is John's Acts 2 moment;[36] this is merely symbolic anticipating of Pentecost to come;[37] this is the gift of the Spirit for preaching the gospel;[38] or this was for the disciples only, for empowerment to forgive sins.[39] Now while some of these positions do have a level of merit (e.g., this was empowerment to forgive sins), the dominant scholarly position that this was John's Acts 2 event does not seem tenable. To begin, even though John is not above disregarding chronology and specific details for a greater theological purpose (e.g., the cleansing of the temple; although his chronology for this event may in fact be more accurate), it hardly seems likely that John, writing late in the first century, would not be aware of Luke's presentation of Pentecost in Acts.[40] Moreover, one also has to contend with the fact that John's

---

35. Bennema, "Giving of the Spirit," 201–11, lists seven different perspectives of what may be going on in 20:22.
36. This is the majority position within Johannine scholarship. E.g., Brown, *John XIII–XXI*, 1038–39; Martin Hengel, "The Old Testament in the Fourth Gospel," *HBT* 12, no. 1 (1990): 30; and Murray Rae, "The Testimony of Works in the Christology of John's Gospel," in *The Gospel of John and Christian Theology*, ed. Richard Bauckham and Carl Mosser (Grand Rapids: Eerdmans, 2008), 295–310 (299). For a fuller bibliographic list, see Bennema, "Giving of the Spirit," 202n36; or Lincoln, *Truth on Trial*, 255.
37. Brown, *John XIII–XXI*, 1038, notes that Theodore of Mopsuestia proposed this view and was soundly condemned at the Second Council of Constantinople (553 C.E.). Köstenberger, *John*, 574; and D. A. Carson, *The Gospel according to John*, PNTC (Grand Rapids: Eerdmans, 1991), 652–55, hold to a symbolic act here, which looks forward to Acts 2. For a refutation of Carson's position and argument, see Hatina, "John 20:22 in Its Eschatological Context," 196–219.
38. E. Schweizer, "Πνεῦμα, πνεθματικός," in *TDNT*, 6:332–51 (442–44, esp. 444).
39. Leon Morris, *The Gospel according to John*, NICNT rev. ed. (Grand Rapids: Eerdmans, 1995), 461–62.
40. Contra O'Day, "Gospel of John," 9:848, who says that "the distance between Easter and Pentecost is collapsed."

audience as well would have been aware of the chronology of the events leading up to the watershed moment of Pentecost. Second, it doubtful that, after receiving the Holy Spirit, the disciples would remain behind locked doors (John 20:26)[41] and then go off fishing (John 21:3); this is hardly the picture of Acts 2. In light of these concerns, it is my firm belief that based upon my thesis the clearest reason for John's inclusion of the insufflation is perhaps best explained by Jesus' threefold reference to "peace."[42]

The giving of the Spirit here in John may serve as the inauguration of the new covenant of peace, which just happens to find close parallels with Ezekielian motifs. In Ezek. 37:1-14, Yahweh revives Israel by Yahweh's life-giving breath and then inaugurates the covenant of peace (Ezek. 37:26). Similarly, Jesus' first act after completing his work on the cross was to come and welcome the disciples into the fullness of the new covenant of peace by the act of inbreathing spiritual life into them, that is, offering them regeneration and birth into the new covenant. Cornelis Bennema's and Max Turner's positions help explain this point.[43]

Bennema, drawing on the work of Turner notes, "Within Jesus' earthly ministry, people (including the disciples) could already have 'foretastes' or experiences of the life-giving Spirit, but authentic Christian faith became a reality only after the cross, the resurrection and the gift of the Spirit (in 20:22). Indeed texts such as 7:39 and 16:7 seem to suggest that the disciples still had to wait for the coming of the Spirit (-Paraclete) (and hence salvation) till after Jesus' glorification."[44] Bennema is indeed correct to take John 7:39 and 16:7

---

41. So Kanagaraj, *John*, 200.
42. Wilson Paroschi, *Incarnation and Covenant in the Prologue to the Fourth Gospel (John 1:1-18)* (Frankfurt am Main: Peter Lang, 2006), 153–55, argues that covenant is in view from the opening verses of the Prologue.
43. Cf. Turner, *Holy Spirit*, 97–102.
44. Bennema, "Giving of the Spirit," 196. Contra Pryor, *John: Evangelist of the Covenant People*, 89, who follows the status quo and calls this the coming of the Paraclete. Marianne Meye

seriously in interpreting this passage. These two passages seem to present two completely different aspects to the giving of the Spirit: the first relational, the second functional. Thus, the new experience here in 20:22 is "a relationship with the Spirit that secures and sustains their salvation."[45] Similarly, James Dunn seems to hold to the position that this is the moment when the disciples were regenerated.[46] C. H. Dodd claims this is "a moment in history when men received the Spirit as they had not received it before, and this moment is represented by the incident of the 'insufflation,' which is securely anchored to the empirical history of the Church by the commission to forgive sins—a commission strictly relative to the existence of the Church in time."[47] However, contra Dodd, who intimates that this is the Johannine version of Acts 2,[48] it appears that this was a once-in-history event that initiated the disciples' "salvation" and the church age.[49] Acts 2 would be the moment when the Spirit would be given to empower them/the church for witnessing to the world.[50] As noted immediately above, John had a solid scriptural basis to draw from when viewed in light of Ezekiel. No less than on four separate

---

Thompson, "The Raising of Lazarus in John 11: A Theological Reading," in *The Gospel of John and Christian Theology*, ed. Richard Bauckham and Carl Mosser (Grand Rapids: Eerdmans, 2008), 233–44 (237), notes that Jesus' actions bring to the disciples "the promised new birth."

45. Bennema, "Giving of the Spirit," 211–12.
46. James D. G. Dunn, *Baptism in the Spirit*, second ed. (London: SCM, 2010), 178–82. See also comments by Craig L. Blomberg, *The Historical Reliability of John's Gospel: Issues and Commentary* (Downers Grove, IL: InterVarsity, 2001), 266–67.
47. C. H. Dodd, *The Interpretation of the Fourth Gospel* (Cambridge: Cambridge University Press, 1953), 442. Rudolf Schnackenburg, *The Gospel according to St. John Vol. III: Commentary on Chapters 13–21*, HTCNT, trans. David Smith and G. A. Kon (London: Burns & Oates, 1982), 325–26, seems to suggest that Jesus' inbreathing is for the bestowal of life and the forgiveness of sins for the church, as I hold. He goes on to suggest that the sending of "the Paraclete is not yet focused upon" (326). However, he tempers this with the assertion that Luke's Pentecost in Acts 2 was not for all believers, but rather the "exception" to the rule—on this point I would argue the opposite. Herman Ridderbos, *The Gospel of John*, trans John Vriend (Grand Rapids: Eerdmans, 1997), 643, suggests that these are two separate events and that John's version is for the immediate disciples only.
48. Dodd, *Interpretation of the Fourth Gospel*, 227.
49. So too Dunn, *Baptism in the Spirit*, 178.
50. So too Bennema, "Giving of the Spirit," 213.

occasions Ezekiel records the promise of the giving of the Spirit at a future date as a means of enabling the true followers of Yahweh to live in fullness with Yahweh (Ezek. 11:19; 36:26-27; 37:14; 39:29).

The relational interpretation makes the most sense of these Ezekielian connections. Israel had a covenantal relationship/connection to Yahweh in the Old Testament, much like the disciples had a relationship with Jesus while he ministered on earth. Israel had the temple/tabernacle, the priests, sacrifices, and the Torah. Through these God-given institutions they had communion with Yahweh. Similarly, while Jesus was in the flesh, the disciples had communion with him, had access to him and his words, and in turn experienced a level of relationship with God (John 6:63, 68). However, none of this was the end goal of Yahweh or Jesus (John 14:2-3//16-26). Yahweh knew that someday the relational aspect of the covenant between Yahweh and Yahweh's people would indeed change (Ezek. 11:19; 36:26). The vision of Ezek. 37:1-14 is a picture of the moment that that relationship changes into a more personal one through spiritual regeneration, that is, through the revivification of the metaphorical "dry bones" of Israel. John draws upon that imagery and here instills it with new life as the disciples and the church become the new Israel[51] and are now enabled to have the completeness of what was only begun with Jesus' earthly ministry. The Passion Week events brought forth the full glorification of Jesus that enabled the giving/inbreathing of the regenerative work of the cross (John 7:39).

---

51. I use this term very cautiously so as not to imply some form of hyper replacement theology. The prophecy of Ezek. 37 must be understood in light of chapters 38–39, which seem to connote a future work with the nation of Israel. Paul says as much in Rom. 9–11. Therefore, there may be a double fulfillment in view or a *sensus plenior* for the last days/eschaton.

Jesus' Prayer of Unity and Ezekiel 37:15-28

Some scholars have already noted that Ezek. 37:15-28 may inform our understanding of aspects of John as a prophecy/fulfillment motif.[52] For example, Mary L. Coloe suggests that there is a literary/theological connection between John 4:1-42 and Ezek. 37:15-28. She proposes that a connection can be made between Jesus' ministry to the Samaritan woman at the well and the Ezekielian promise in 37:15-28 to reunite Ephraim and Judah. Whereas Jacob and Rachel meet at a well where marriage ensues (Gen. 29:1-28), Jesus (a man from Judah) and the Samaritan woman (i.e., representative of Ezekiel's stick named Ephraim) meet at a well for a spiritual "marriage," thus fulfilling the promise of Yahweh in Ezek. 37 to reunite the two "sticks."[53] Even though some of Coloe's connections may be forced,[54] she does present a plausible scenario whereby John has Ezekielian motifs in view. On this I can agree wholeheartedly. This also further supports my assertions in chapter 3 above concerning the ministry of Jesus to outsiders.[55]

However, there is by far a stronger Johannine parallel to Ezek. 37:15-28 found in Jesus' prayer of unity in John 17.[56] The prayer of unity, another unique feature of John, takes the place of the

---

52. Mary L. Coloe, "The Woman of Samaria: Her Characterization, Narrative, and Theological Significance," in *Characters and Characterization in the Gospel of John*, ed. Christopher W. Skinner, LNTS 461 (London: T & T Clark, 2013), 182–96.
53. Ibid., 193–96.
54. For example, ibid., 194n44. Here Coloe suggests that the sixth hour of the day is a vital link between the two pericopae. However, in Gen. 29:7 neither the MT nor the LXX mention the time of day specifically as the "sixth" hour, only that it was "high day" (היום גדול /hayyôm gāḏôl), which could possibly be any time during the afternoon. Victor Hamilton, *The Book of Genesis: Chapters 18–50*, NICOT (Grand Rapids: Eerdmans, 1995), 252, translates the ambiguous phrase as "broad daylight."
55. See similar comments by Dorothy A. Lee, "Martha and Mary: Levels of Characterization in Luke and John," in *Characters and Characterization in the Gospel of John*, ed. Christopher W. Skinner, LNTS 461 (London: T & T Clark, 2013), 207.
56. John F. O'Grady, "The Prologue and Chapter 17 of the Gospel of John," in *What We Have Heard from the Beginning: The Past, Present, and Future of Johannine Studies*, ed. Tom Thatcher (Waco, TX: Baylor University Press, 2007), 215–28, draws thematic links to the Prologue.

Gethsemane prayer in the Synoptics.[57] In the prayer of John 17, Jesus draws upon his unity with the Father as an example for the disciples/Church (John 17:1-5, 10, 21, 22, 24, 26), a picture similar to the unity between Yahweh and Israel highlighted in Ezek. 37. Also, Jesus' prayer should be understood in the overall context of his initiation of the new covenant. Not surprisingly, in Ezek. 37:15-28, the sign act of the two sticks is set within the context of an established new covenant of peace (Ezek. 37:26). Beyond these macro similarities there are no less than eight key themes that unite John 17 (dealing with the unity of the disciples/Church)[58] and Ezek. 37:15-28 (dealing with a unified Israel). These include:

1. The once divided nation will be one (Ezek. 37:17, 22) = Jesus prays for the unity of the church (John 17:11, 21, 22, 23).
2. Yahweh will give the nation into the care of one king/David (Ezek. 37:22, 24-25) = The Father has given the church into Jesus'/the Davidic Messiah's care (John 17:6, 9, 11, 12, 24).
3. Yahweh will be the God of Israel (Ezek. 37:23, 26) = The Father is the God of the church (John 17:3, 6, 9, 26).
4. The unified nation will be purified (Ezek. 37:23) = The church is sanctified (John 17:19).
5. God will have communion with his people (Ezek. 37:27) = The disciples have communion with God (John 17:21).
6. Yahweh is with the nation eternally (Ezek. 37:26-28) = Eternal life is promised to the church (John 17:2-3).
7. A unified Israel will cause the world to know that Yahweh is God (Ezek. 37:28) = A unified church will be an example to the world that they may believe (John 17:21, 23).

---

57. Pryor, *John: Evangelist of the Covenant People*, 71, suggests that many of the themes of the Farewell Discourses are present in John 17.
58. I use "church" as representative of the disciples and all who will come after them.

8. The unified nation will follow Yahweh's laws (Ezek. 37:24) = The church will follow God's laws (John 17:6-9, 14).

Even with these numerous parallels one still may postulate that the similarities are only coincidental. However, when all of the other motifs that have been mentioned above are included in the discussion, the weight of evidence pushes one to conclude that John had Ezek. 37:15-28 in mind when he penned this prayer. Once again, the connections to Ezekiel also help explain the peculiarities of the Fourth Gospel.

Conclusion

In this chapter we have examined a number of parallels between John 17/20 and Ezekiel 37. What we have discovered is that a number of the peculiarities of John's presentation of the Passion Week (e.g., the absence of the sacrament of communion and the prayer in the Garden, the inclusion of the prayer of unity, and the insufflation event) may be explained by the Evangelist's reliance on Ezek. 37, which includes the prophet's third structural "peak"/vision of the revivification of Israel (Ezek. 37:1-14), the sign act of the two sticks (37:15-28), and the institution of the covenant of peace (37:26). What is more, chapter 37 falls squarely within the final section of Ezekiel (34–48), which deals with the future hope for Israel. What better way for John to bring hope to what on the surface appeared to be a bleak few days in the life of Jesus and the disciples. Similar to Ezekiel's message of hope to the remnant in the desperate situation of the exile, John borrows many of Ezekiel's themes and breathes new life into them, no doubt seeing in the life of Jesus the fulfillment of many of Ezekiel's prophecies. Taken on their own, many of the similarities between these motifs could be adjudicated as coincidence. When taken together, however, the accumulation of evidence begins to force one to consider actual intent on the part of John. Yet John still has one more key connection to make as he closes out the Fourth Gospel: the reconstruction of the "temple" of Jesus' body, which Jesus himself had prophesied (John 2:19). The "reconstruction" of the temple of Jesus' body and his "return" to Jerusalem to encourage his disciples serves a fitting literary balance to Jesus' earlier enigmatic sign (John 2:19, 22). Of course these motifs and structural devices once again find an exact parallel in the final "peak"/vision of the book of Ezekiel. Here in the closing chapters of Ezek. 40–43 the eschatological temple is rebuilt and the *kāḇôḏ*/glory of Yahweh returns to the holy city, thus bringing a literary and theological balance to the departure of Yahweh depicted in Ezek. 8–11. It is to this final, but all-important motif, that we now turn to complete our investigation.

7

Jesus' Rebuilt "Temple" and Ezekiel 40–43

The last of the peaks of Ezekiel's structure depicts his fourth vision. This final vision is similar to the prophet's first two visions of Yahweh's glory/*kābôd*. However, this time the vision portrays the glorious return of Yahweh's *kābôd* to a cleansed (Ezek. 42:20), purified (Ezek. 43:26), holy (Ezek. 42:13-14; 43:12) and rebuilt temple (Ezek. 40–42),[1] no doubt built by the hand of Yahweh.[2] Of course these Ezekielian motifs are strikingly similar to Jesus' prophetic words to rebuild the "temple" in three days in John 2:19 (cf. Ezek. 40:1—43:5).[3] As a part of these corresponding motifs, one should not miss the importance of Jesus' triumphal entry as playing a vital role in the parallels between Jesus' and Yahweh's entry/return to the city of Jerusalem. With these similar motifs in mind, in this penultimate

---

1. So too Craig A. Evans, "Jesus' Action in the Temple: Cleansing or Portent of Destruction?," *CBQ* 15, no. 2 (1989): 251.
2. See Brian Neil Peterson, "Ezekiel's Rhetoric: ANE Building Protocol and Shame and Honor as the Keys in Identifying the Builder of the Eschatological Temple," *JETS* 56, no. 4 (2013): 707–31; and 4QFlorilegium 1:1-13.
3. One could argue that even though Jesus was sinless, through the Passion event, his body was "cleansed" of its earthly limitations and the corruption of death.

chapter we will look at two key similarities. First, we will examine the pre- and post-cross returns of Jesus to Jerusalem to inaugurate the new covenant of peace vis-à-vis Yahweh's return to Yahweh's abode to inaugurate the eschatological hope of Israel as envisioned by Ezekiel. Second, we will point out a few of the parallels between the benefits of Jesus' rebuilt "temple" as the wellspring of spiritual blessings to the church and Yahweh's rebuilt temple in Ezekiel as the source of bounty to a renewed Israel. However, before addressing these concerns, it seems appropriate to consider how John is adopting the final vision of Ezekiel in light of eschatological issues.

John's and Ezekiel's Eschatology

One of the more difficult issues to deal with in both books is the eschatological outlook of each author. Much of this has to do with the authors' blurring of the eschatological and present realities in both books. In the case of the Fourth Gospel, on the one hand John presents the completed work of Jesus through the initiation of the new covenant of peace. On the other hand, there is still a dimension that awaits fulfillment when Jesus will come and dwell in the midst of his people as the eschatological temple.[4] In other words, John's Jesus has both an incarnate reality that must be considered as well as an eternal dimension. John's eschatological perspective oscillates between a realized eschatology (John 5:24) and an inaugurated eschatology (cf. John 5:28-29; 14:3; 21:22), thus allowing John's Jesus to bring life in the immediate earthly setting (John 20:31) while giving hope for an eternity with God (John 14:3). Similarly, Ezekiel also speaks of present realities of the exile (Ezek. 1–24) while blending

---

4. So too the conclusion of Steven M. Bryan, "Consumed by Zeal: John's Use of Psalm 69:9 and the Action in the Temple," *BBR* 21, no. 4 (2011): 479–94 (480). Note also that Revelation 19–22 develops in detail the motif of Jesus' dwelling in the eschatological city.

them with eschatological hope when Yahweh would dwell in their midst in the rebuilt temple (Ezek. 34–48).

For Ezekiel, Yahweh will be the triumphal King who returns to the temple after its destruction. Ezekiel portrays that clearly in Ezek. 43:1-5. This moment allowed for the abundance of Yahweh's blessings to flow to the nation of Israel (Ezek. 44–48). Yet, even though some of the words of hope in Ezek. 34–48 may have relevance for the events associated with the return in 538 B.C.E. and the rebuilding of the temple in 516 B.C.E., many aspects seem to have future importance as well. Similarly, in John's presentation, Jesus' return to Jerusalem, both before and after the resurrection and rebuilding the "temple" of his body, did not have immediate fulfillment in some present hope of an earthly kingdom even though that may have been the disciples' hope (cf. John 21:23; Acts 1:6). For John, his eschatological presentation had to take into account the Passion Week, something well beyond Ezekiel's purview. On account of this, John blended the present and future realities by first presenting Jesus as the promised "King of Israel" (ὁ βασιλεὺς τοῦ Ἰσραήλ) through the triumphal entry and only later (after the Passion) as the resurrected and rebuilt Temple.

The Triumphal Entry

The return of Jesus to Jerusalem beginning in John 12 dominates the last nine chapters of the book of John and its aftermath (John 12–20). Likewise, the last nine chapters of Ezekiel deal with the return of Yahweh's glory/kāḇôḏ to Jerusalem and the aftermath of that event (40–48; see esp. 43:1-5). John's work ends with a hope for the future era of Jesus' reign when he would permanently return to the earth (John 21:22; cf. 14:1-3; 16:28). In the same way, Ezekiel's book ends with a future-looking, permanent return and reign of Yahweh from an earthly abode, an abode where both city and temple are blended into one (Ezek. 40:2).⁵ Interestingly, in Rev. 21:22, a similar picture emerges in the coming eschatological reign of Jesus: city and temple are one. In fact, no temple appears in the New Jerusalem, for Jesus obviates this facet. Such connections are not uncommon within scholarship. John's understanding of the role that Jesus plays as superseding and replacing the temple is evident in a number of scholarly works.⁶ Indeed, Paul Hoskins concludes that, "The cumulative evidence from 1:14, 1:51, and 4:20-24 leads one to posit that Jesus fulfills and replaces the Temple as the locus of God's presence, glory, revelation, and abundant provision."⁷

Further, as we saw with the context of John 17 and 20 in our previous chapter, the triumphal entry must be read in light of the inauguration of the covenant of peace, which occurs prior to this utopian depiction, which both Ezekiel and the book of Revelation address. For Ezekiel, the covenant of "peace" will be overseen by none other than David, Yahweh's "prince" (נשיא/*nāśiʾ*; Ezek. 34:23-24; 37:24-25), a picture that John seeks to present in the triumphal-entry scene: Jesus is the new Son of David who will reign in Jerusalem as King of Israel if the people accept him.

John records that when Jesus entered Jerusalem the crowd lauded him as "the King of Israel" (ὁ βασιλεὺς τοῦ Ἰσραήλ; see John 12:13).⁸ The phrase ὁ βασιλεὺς τοῦ Ἰσραήλ is used in the Synoptics only twice, and in both cases it is placed on the lips of people in a derisive manner while Jesus hangs on the cross (cf. Matt. 27:42;

---

5. While Ezekiel later makes a distinction between the city and temple (cf. Ezek. 45:6-7; 48), the city is nonetheless connected directly to the holy allotment of Yahweh. Note also that the temple is depicted as being "like" a city in 40:2.
6. Paul M. Hoskins, *Jesus as the Fulfillment of the Temple in the Gospel of John* (Great Britain: Paternoster, 2006); and Saeed Hamid-Khani, *Revelation and Concealment of Christ: A Theological Inquiry into the Elusive Language of the Fourth Gospel*, WUNT 120 (Tübingen: Mohr Siebeck, 2000), esp. 280–85. Hoskins (1–37) argues for a typological fulfillment in Jesus.
7. Hoskins, *Jesus as the Fulfillment*, 195.
8. See more on this in Edwin D. Freed, "The Entry into Jerusalem in the Gospel of John," *JBL* 80, no. 4 (1961): 329–338 (332). Note also 1 Macc. 13:51.

Mark 15:32). However, in John, the phrase is used twice in an inclusio-like manner for the public ministry of Jesus. In both cases it is uttered by people identifying Jesus as the King of Israel in an attitude of praise, not derision; the first recognition by Nathaniel, and the second at Jesus' triumphal entry (John 1:49; 12:13; cf. John 6:15).[9] Now, while Luke records a variation of the Johannine phrase, namely, "blessed is *the king* who comes in the name of the Lord" (εὐλογημένος ὁ ἐρχόμενος ὁ βασιλεὺς ἐν ὀνόματι κυρίου), he does not add the second notation about the "King of Israel" (ὁ βασιλεὺς τοῦ Ἰσραήλ). In John, the word "king" (ὁ βασιλεὺς) is removed from the first phrase εὐλογημένος ὁ ἐρχόμενος ἐν ὀνόματι κυρίου and is placed in the second clause forming the genitive phrase "King of Israel" (ὁ βασιλεὺς τοῦ Ἰσραήλ). Thus, John has the people declaring Jesus as not just any "king" (i.e., a messiah figure only) but the "King of Israel!"[10] As noted above, this is in keeping with John's theme of presenting Jesus as the promised messianic Davidic "king."[11] But more importantly, Jesus will be "King" of Israel whether the elites agree to it or not—the rejection of Jesus' claims to leadership/authority being another common motif in John (e.g., John 2:18; 7:32; 8:59; 10:31-39; 11:45-53; 18:2-14; 19:7).

Similarly, throughout the book of Ezekiel, the prophet seeks to present Yahweh as the true King and Sovereign over Israel (see chapter 2 above). However, Israel had a long history of rejecting

---

9. John also notes the derisive statements by the people but he only uses the term "king" or "King of the Jews" (John 12:3, 12).
10. Contra, C. H. Dodd, *The Interpretation of the Fourth Gospel* (Cambridge: Cambridge University Press, 1953), 370, who suggests Luke's and John's presentations are the same. These are clearly different in the inclusion of the term "Israel." Moreover, Freed, "Entry into Jerusalem," 332, fails to see the importance of this addition by calling the phrase an "afterthought." However, Maarten J. J. Menken, "Observations on the Significance of the Old Testament in the Fourth Gospel," in *Theology and Christology in the Fourth Gospel: Essays by the Members of the SNTS Johannine Writing Seminar*, ed. Gilbert van Belle, Jan G. Van Der Watt, and Petrus J. Maritz, BETL 184 (Leuven: Leuven University Press, 2005), 173, rightly sees the importance placed upon this phrase in John.
11. Freed, "Entry into Jerusalem," 332, 334.

Yahweh's claim to kingship and those whom Yahweh had sent as messengers (e.g., 1 Sam. 8).[12] They opted for their own devices and rejected Yahweh's claims. It is for this reason that Yahweh states unequivocally through the prophet Ezekiel, "As I live declares the Lord Yahweh, surely with a strong hand and with an outstretched arm and with outpoured rage, I will be king over you!" (Ezek. 20:33). One could say that in John, despite the plans of the religious elite and the rulers to do their own thing, Jesus will be Messiah/King over Israel, even with a strong hand and an outstretched arm (cf. John 2:13-21; 18:36). Indeed, Jesus, himself, acknowledges his role as king and his eternal kingship in John 18:36.

John also quotes Zech. 9:9 (John 12:15; cf. Matt. 21:5) for the purpose of linking Jesus' entry into Jerusalem to the prophetic promise of a messianic king. As pointed out above, the kingly line would be none other than David's. When one reads Ezek. 34 and 37, we find references to the coming "Davidic king" (Ezek. 34:23-24; 37:22-25) in the period of restoration. That is, when the covenant of peace will be instituted (Ezek. 37:26). As highlighted in chapter 6 above, Ezekiel goes on to note that "David will be king over" the people (Ezek. 37:24). And, that "David, my servant, will be their prince forever" (Ezek. 37:25).[13] For John, Jesus is the coming Davidic king who will usher in the new age/covenant. It is very likely that John uses the attribution for Jesus as "King of Israel" to form an inclusio to Jesus' earthly ministry and to inaugurate the covenant of peace that takes place during the Passion Week of John 12–20. There can be little doubt that John included this as a pivotal text. He

---

12. See Brian Peterson, "Ezekiel's Perspective of Israel's History: Selective Revisionism?," in *Prophets and Prophecy and Ancient Israelite Historiography*, ed. Mark J. Boda and Lyssa Wray Beal (Winona Lake, IN: Eisenbrauns, 2013), 295–313; and idem, "Stephen's Speech as a Modified Rîḇ Formula," *JETS* 57, no. 2 (2014): 351–69.
13. It appears that John has the Hebrew text in mind because in both places where "king" (מלך/*melek*) appears in the Hebrew text (i.e., Ezek. 37:22, 24) the LXX uses ἄρχων (*archōn*/"ruler") instead of βασιλεὺς (*basileus*).

makes this clear by the parenthetical aside immediately following the triumphal entry:[14] "These things His disciples did not understand at the first; but when Jesus was glorified, then they remembered that these things were written of Him, and that they had done these things to Him" (John 12:16; NASB).

Jesus as the Restored/New Temple

As we noted in chapter 4 above, the cleansing of the temple was the impetus for Jesus' prophetic words that he would rebuild/restore the "temple" of his body in three days. Andreas Köstenberger has rightly noted that the destruction of the first temple afforded John the opportunity to present Jesus as its spiritual replacement.[15] This theme governs the trajectory of the Fourth Gospel as John's end goal is to bring belief in the people that Jesus is the Son of God (John 20:31). He did this through Jesus' signs, the most notable of which, one could argue, was the death burial and resurrection of Jesus' "temple"/body. Of the classical prophets, Ezekiel is the most notable for the motif of temple restoration (Ezek. 37:26; 40–42).[16] There can be little doubt that these chapters were in mind as John wrote.

On the other hand, Mark Matson has argued that John's numerous allusions to Zechariah 9–14 are the basis for his eschatological hope, specifically Zech. 14.[17] In particular, the temple cleansing pericope

---

14. So too Dodd, *Interpretation of the Fourth Gospel*, 370.
15. Andreas J. Köstenberger, "The Destruction of the Second Temple and the Composition of the Fourth Gospel," in *Challenging Perspectives on the Gospel of John*, ed. John Lierman, WUNT 2.219 (Tübingen: Mohr Siebeck, 2006), 69–108, esp. 78–82, 85, 94–108. See also Stephen Motyer, *Your Father the Devil?: A New Approach to John and 'the Jews'* (Carlisle, UK: Paternoster, 1997), 36–42, esp. 40–41; Mary L. Coloe, *God Dwells with Us: Temple Symbolism in the Fourth Gospel* (Collegeville, MN: The Liturgical Press, 2001); and A.R. Kerr, *The Temple of Jesus' Body: The Temple Theme in the Gospel of John*, JSNTSup 220 (Sheffield: Sheffield Academic, 2002).
16. Hassell Bullock, "Ezekiel: Bridge between the Testaments," *JETS* 25, no. 1 (1982): 29.
17. Mark A. Matson, "The Contribution of the Temple Cleansing by the Fourth Gospel," SBLSP 31 (Atlanta: Scholars, 1992): 489-506 (502–504). See also idem, "The Temple Incident: An Integral Element in the Fourth Gospel's Narrative," in *Jesus in Johannine Tradition*, ed. Robert T. Fortna and Tom Thatcher (Louisville: Westminster John Knox Press, 2001), 145–53 (151).

at John 2:16 references Zech. 14:21. It seems clear that John makes allusions to these types of texts; however, one must keep in mind that this does not a priori exclude John's allusions to Ezekiel, especially chapters 40–48. Interestingly, some have even noted the high degree of probability that Zechariah is commenting on these chapters of Ezekiel as he is writing his book![18] As we have demonstrated throughout, there are by far more allusions and direct connections to Ezekiel than most have been willing to concede. Further, Raymond Brown rightly notes that, during the first century, Ezek. 40–48, with its focus on a rebuilt temple and the period of Messiah, was well known in the Qumran community and was expected even after the destruction of the Herodian temple.[19] Of course John worked within this context. And part of the expectation of the messianic era was the promise of abundance and blessings.

The "return" of Jesus to Jerusalem after his resurrection allowed for the initiation of the abundant blessings associated with the completed work on the cross. The triumphal entry had been rejected by the nation, but the post-cross return served as the moment when Jesus became the new "temple" and Savior for the burgeoning Church. As we noted in our discussion concerning Ezek. 34 and the Good Shepherd, Ezekiel did not in any way depict the event of the cross. Therefore, John's literary need and license allowed for the insertion of the crucifixion, but John quickly resumes the triumphal nature of Jesus' "return" as the rebuilt temple after the vital crucifixion event.

---

18. Cameron Mackay, "Zechariah in Relation to Ezekiel 40–48," *EvQ* 40 (1968): 197–210, suggests that Zechariah is the first "expositor" of Ezek. 40–48 as reflected in his post-exilic prophecy. For a similar conclusion, see Otto Plöger, *Theocracy and Eschatology*, trans. S. Rudman (Oxford: Basil Blackwell, 1968), 88–96; and S. Tuell, "Haggai-Zechariah: Prophecy After the Manner of Ezekiel," SBLSP 39 (Atlanta: SBL, 2000), 263–86, esp. 268–72.
19. Raymond E. Brown, *The Gospel according to John I–XII*, AB 29 (New York: Doubleday, 1966), 122. See also Brian Peterson, "Ezekiel's Rhetoric," 707–31. Cf. 1 En. 90:29; Jub. 1:17, 27–29; and 11Q Temple Scroll 29:8–10. See further comments by Yigael Yadin, *The Temple Scroll* (New York: Random House, 1985), 113–15.

Abundance as the Hallmark of Life When Deity Is Present

Throughout the ancient Near East, long before Ezekiel's era, a new or restored temple with the deity at rest in his/her abode assured blessings.[20] This ubiquitous motif is adopted by Ezekiel and fleshed out for more than six chapters as the prophet shows the blessings for those who trust in Yahweh. Indeed, the general setting of Ezek. 43–48 is one of blessings and renewal for the land, the priesthood, and food stocks. Ezekiel shows that when Yahweh is present in a renewed temple, blessings abound at all levels.[21] As I have noted elsewhere in relation to Ezek. 47,

> The reversal of curses dealing with the lack of food and water also plays out in these final chapters. In 4:16-17, God tells Ezekiel that the people will be forced to limit their daily intake of water and food because of the siege and war. In 47:1-5 we see this reversed with water so plentiful in the renewed land that there is water to swim in and a river that cannot be crossed. Also, while famine once prevailed and food was scarce (cf. 4:16; 5:12, 16-17; 7:15, 19; 12:16; 14:13, 21), in 47:12 plenty is the norm in the restoration (cf. also Joel 2). Fish, an important part of Israel's former economy and diet, will be in abundance and offer a means of employment for many (47:9-10) even to the level of marine stocks equaling the "Great Sea." Finally, where the charred trees and vines served as a negative metaphor for the nation (cf. 15:6) in 47:7 and 12 we see them as a source of abundant food and for healing.[22]

---

20. See Diane Sharon, "A Biblical Parallel to a Sumerian Temple Hymn?," *JANES* 24 (1996): 99–109, and her treatment of the Dream of Gudea (c. third millennium B.C.E.). See also the hope of blessing expected in the period of Haggai and Zechariah when the temple was rebuilt as discussed by Mark J. Boda, "From Dystopia to Myopia: Utopian Re(visions) in Haggai and Zechariah 1–8," in *Utopia and Dystopia in Prophetic Texts*, ed. Ehud Ben Zvi and Michael Floyd, PFES (Helsinki/Winona Lake: Finnish Exegetical Society/University of Helsnki/Eisenbrauns, 2006), 211–49.
21. See Brian Neil Peterson, *Ezekiel in Context: Ezekiel's Message Understood in Its Historical Setting of Covenant Curses and Ancient Near Eastern Mythological Motifs*, PTMS 182 (Eugene, OR: Pickwick Publications, 2012), 319–26.
22. Ibid., 324. Second Baruch 29:4-6 picks up on the motif of the plenteous amount of food in the end times.

As we noted in chapter 5 above when dealing with the "I Am" Sayings, Jesus had embodied many of these promised blessings in an inaugurated fashion. He had offered healing, food, and living water for his flock while on earth (John 2–11). Not surprisingly, others have already seen the important Ezekielian symbolism in the theme of living waters spoken about in John 7:37-39 (cf. Ezek. 47:1-5).[23] No less important is the reality that when Jesus appeared to the disciples as the resurrected temple, blessings are immediately evident. The gift of the new covenant of peace and the Holy Spirit are given (John 20:22; see discussion in chapter 6 above), the power to forgive sins is imparted (20:23), and the symbolic sign of abundance in the miraculous catch of fish (John 21:4-11), all show affinity with Ezek. 47:1-12. In the latter case, this adds support to the argument that John 21 was an original part of the Fourth Gospel. Indeed, if J. A. Emerton, Bruce Grigsby, and Paul Trudinger and others are correct, Ezekielian motifs continue to play a vital role even into John 21.[24]

Finally, John's focus on the feasts of Israel so heavily centralized in the temple—Tabernacles (John 7:37-39; 8:12), Passover (John 2:13; 6:4; 11:55), and Dedication (John 10:22; cf. 2 Macc. 1:18—2:18)—points to the role that Jesus plays as the Passover Lamb,

---

23. Bruce H. Grigsby, "Gematria and John 21:11—Another Look at Ezekiel 47:10," *ExpTim* 95, no. 6 (1984): 177–78.
24. See comments by William Glenn Fowler, "The Influence of Ezekiel in the Fourth Gospel: Intertextuality and Interpretation" (PhD diss., Golden Gate Baptist Theological Seminary, 1995), 202–207. See further J. A. Emerton, "The Hundred and Fifty-three Fishes in John XXI.11," *JTS* 9, no. 1 (1958): 86–89, who offers intriguing speculations related to *gematria*, viewing 153 as equalling the reference to En Gedi and Englaim from Ezek. 47:10. Cf. Heinz Kruse, "Magni Pisces Centum Quinquaginta Tres," *VD* 38 (1960): 129–48; Grigsby, "Gematria," 177–78; Paul Trudinger, "The 153 Fishes: A Response and a Further Suggestion," *ExpTim* 102, no. 1 (1990): 11–12; Kenneth Cardwell, "The Fish on the Fire: John 21:9," *ExpTim* 102, no. 1 (1990): 12–14; Neil J. McEleney, "153 Great Fishes (John 21:11)—Gematriacal Atbash," *Bib* 58 (1977): 411–17; and Joseph A. Romeo, "Gematria and John 21:11—The Children of God," *JBL* 97, no. 2 (1978): 263–64, who makes a loose connection to Ezek. 34:11-16 and suggests that the gematria interpretation should reflect the Hebrew phrase בני האלהרם ("the children of God"). These sources as noted by Fowler, "Influence of Ezekiel in the Fourth Gospel," 202.

sustainer of the feasts in a spiritual sense, and the one who will grant abundance once the temple is destroyed.[25] On this Paul Hoskins notes, "Looking at the Temple in particular, he [Jesus] fulfills and replaces it as the place of sacrifice and the place from which God pours out his abundant provision upon his people."[26] To be sure, prior to Jesus' Second Advent, this is most readily apparent in the spiritual abundance and provision that Christians experience thanks to Jesus' death, burial, and resurrection. However, John's audience, especially in a post-70 C.E. and post-temple context, also had a future hope when all of earth's troubles would end and Jesus would be the source of blessings in the here and now, a picture depicted best in the book of Revelation.

Revelation: The Fullness of Eschatological Hope

One cannot leave this important topic without considering the role that the book of Revelation plays in light of Johannine thinking, especially in relation to the book of Ezekiel. Now, while Mark Matson contends that the lack of extended eschatological expectation in John may be attributed to a later redactor's "blunting" of this hope, this need not be the case if John (or the putative Johannine "School") knew that the apocalyptic work of Revelation would/had covered this topic in detail.[27] Whereas John leaves the disciples awaiting the heavenly return of Jesus (John 14:1-3; 21:23), the author of Revelation picks up on the concept and makes it an eschatological reality. As Hoskins notes, ". . . in the book of Revelation, one finds the consummation of God's promise do dwell among his people. As the

---

25. For a discussion on Jesus as a replacement of the feasts, see Hoskins, *Jesus as the Fulfillment*, 160–81. Hoskins (160–61) connects John 7:37-39 and 8:12 with the Feast of Dedication.
26. Ibid., 196.
27. Matson, "Contribution of the Temple Cleansing," 503–505. Much of Matson's theory is an argument from silence, that is, what is not present in the text or what has been removed by a later redactor. See especially his concluding comments on pages 504–505.

Fourth Gospel anticipated, the union between Christ and the people of God comes to fruition in the New Jerusalem when God's people are finally with God in the city of God (21:3). In that city, they are able to behold Father and Son who are its Temple."[28]

Thus, it makes sense why John's portrayal of Jesus as the fulfillment of Ezek. 40–48 in an eschatological sense does not find complete fulfillment in the Fourth Gospel; the book of Revelation would address these concerns in detail. Yet, this in no way diminishes the abundant Ezekielian connections in John that we have addressed in our preceding chapters. If this shows us anything, it is that John and/or the Johannine School found in Ezekiel ready-made motifs that resonated with the life of Jesus, a preference that appears to have extended beyond the Fourth Gospel to the Apocalypse. As we have pointed out in our first chapter, the author of Revelation also relied heavily on Ezekiel for his depiction of the consummation of the final age (e.g., four living creatures: Rev. 4:6, 8, 9; 5:6, 8, 11, 14; 6:1, 6; 7:11; 14:3; 15:7; 19:4; swallowing the scroll: Rev. 6:14; the Gog and Magog oracles: Rev. 20:8; the appearance of the new Jerusalem: Rev. 21:1-27; river imagery: Rev. 22:1-2; and the tree of life: Rev. 22:2). However, the numerous parallels between these latter two books is perhaps best reserved for a future monograph when proper attention can be given to the continued Johannine parallels and the book of Ezekiel.

Conclusion

In this chapter we have shown that John's reliance on Ezekiel continues in his presentation of Jesus as the new temple. Ezekiel focuses nine chapters on the role that the rebuilt temple would play in light of Yahweh's returned *kāḇôḏ*. Blessings, both spiritual and

---

28. Hoskins, *Jesus as the Fulfillment*, 201.

earthly, accompany the eternal presence of Yahweh in the city and temple. In John's view, when Jesus made his triumphal entry/return into Jerusalem to complete his earthly work, both before and after the cross, he inaugurated this Ezekielian reality through which the church could presently begin to experience the untold blessings of having God dwelling in their midst. For John, through the death, burial, and resurrection of Jesus, Jesus became the new temple from which all the blessings of the godhead may flow to the believer. John drew the Fourth Gospel to a close by highlighting just a few of these blessings as a foretaste of the glory yet to come in the eschaton. The author of Revelation, be that John, his "School," or some other person, picked up on this hope and completed the picture and parallels, which John had initiated in the Fourth Gospel.

8

Conclusions and Implications

Throughout the previous chapters I have attempted to draw connections between the Fourth Gospel and the book of Ezekiel. While it may be argued that some of the connections are only coincidental, what we have seen is that on numerous occasions, John has drawn upon Ezekielian motifs, and in some cases, even his structural layout. Most of these parallels are rooted in the basic message and content of the four visions, which highlight the structure of Ezekiel: Ezekiel 1–3 (Yahweh's self-revelation); chapters 8–11 (Yahweh's anger over the polluting of Yahweh's temple); chapter 37 (Yahweh's metaphorical resurrection of the nation of Israel and the promise of unity within the covenant of peace); and chapters 40–48 (Yahweh's return to Jerusalem and the rebuilt temple as the sign of the eschaton). We have shown that in numerous situations John has relied heavily on these unifying motifs.

For example, after noting several of John's unique features in chapter 1, in chapter 2 we looked at eighteen points of contact between John's presentation of the glory of Jesus as the Son of Man/

God incarnate and Ezekiel's vision of Yahweh's glory/kāḇôḏ. We determined that the reason John chooses to start his Gospel in such a unique way compared to the Synoptic writers was due to his intent on drawing a direct link between Ezekiel's vision of the awesome splendor of Yahweh when Yahweh was revealed to Ezekiel, and the self-revelation of Jesus as God's Word/λόγος.

In chapter 3, I continued my comparisons by arguing that John's choice of signs to prove to a religious first-century Jewish nation that Jesus was who he said he was—God's Messiah—could be structurally and thematically tied to Yahweh's command to Ezekiel to use sign acts as a way of demonstrating that he was indeed sent by Yahweh to the rebellious house of Israel. In both cases, neither Ezekiel's nor Jesus' audiences chose to believe the signs, except for a "remnant." Many of the signs performed by Jesus had direct thematic connections to the sign acts of Ezekiel, especially when comparing the raising of Lazarus with the sign act of the death of Ezekiel's wife (John 11//Ezek. 24).

In chapter 4, I continued to draw connections to Ezekiel by examining the oft-debated temple-cleansing pericope of John 2:13-22. I proposed that John's rhetorical reasons for placing the temple cleansing early in his Gospel, contra the Synoptic writers, may again best be explained by John's reliance on Ezekiel's second structural "peak"—the vision of the defiled Jerusalem temple and the subsequent departure of Yahweh from the temple (Ezek. 8–11). Moreover Jesus' cleansing of the temple sets the tone for the rest of the book, as does Ezekiel's second vision. Also, Ezekiel's second vision showed that Yahweh was free to minister outside of the geographical boundaries within which Israel had confined Yahweh. No less poignant is John's presentation of Jesus' phased departure from the temple and Jerusalem to Samaria and Galilee to minister to "outsiders" (i.e., Nicodemus, the Samaritans, and a foreign [?] official) who were not within the accepted classes of Israel's hyper-religious elite.[1]

CONCLUSIONS AND IMPLICATIONS

In chapter 5, I addressed the numerous connections between the "I Am" Sayings and the similar motifs in Ezekiel. These included John's depictions of Jesus as reversing the curses against Israel by giving bread (and living water) to the masses—both literally and spiritually. For John, Jesus became the Light of God to a spiritually, and in select cases, literally blind nation—a fitting Ezekielian parallel to the spiritual and literal blindness of Israel's king Zedekiah and the nation (Ezek. 12). Jesus declared himself the Good Shepherd and the True Vine in fulfillment of the oracles of Ezek. 34 and 15 respectively, while letting the nation know that he was the only Door to heaven. Finally, through a blending of motifs of the Resurrection, the Way, the Truth, and the Life, Jesus' resurrection of Lazarus prefigured his own resurrection as a primary sign that the new age had dawned. In Ezekiel's third vision in 37:1-14, John found a ready-made parallel, which also depicted the coming new age through metaphorical resurrection—Yahweh's word being the way and the truth, that in turn brought life (Ezek. 20).

Drawing upon the third visionary "peak" of Ezek. 37:1-14, in chapter 6, I examined how the insufflation of John 20:22 was rooted in Yahweh's inbreathing of new life into the covenant community, which I argued was fulfilled in John's day. John's recording of Jesus' threefold greeting of "peace" in John 20 alerts the reader to the reality that Jesus had initiated the covenant of peace by the act of insufflation. Also, the anomalous prayer of unity in John 17 finds numerous connections to Ezekiel's sign act of a unified nation in Ezek. 37:15-28. The hallmark of the new age was to be the unification of Yahweh's/Jesus' people.

---

1. While Nicodemus was a part of the religious elite, he was an "outsider" in that he chose, against the majority of his peers, to express belief/interest in Jesus—although silently—out of fear for the Jews (John 7:13; 19:39; 20:19).

Finally, in chapter 7 I looked at the final peak of Ezekiel's fourfold visionary sequence vis-à-vis Jesus' return to Jerusalem for his final days on earth. Here I argued that John's presentation of Jesus' return to Jerusalem for the purpose of inaugurating the new covenant of peace with its ensuing spiritual blessings mirrored in many ways the similar picture of Yahweh's return to the rebuilt temple (Ezek. 43:1-5). Jesus' declaration that he would rebuild the temple in three days (John 2:19), is fulfilled in his death, burial and resurrection. According to John, Jesus becomes the spiritual Temple from which all blessings flow, most appropriately exemplified by the giving of the Spirit for life, the power to forgive sins, and the blessings of abundance (John 20:23; 21:1-11). In a similar fashion, Ezekiel had envisioned this moment of provision and blessing, albeit in a blended/blurred state. That is, Ezekiel saw the completed work of Yahweh in the eschaton whereas John worked within an inaugurated eschatological framework. The book of Revelation would complete the theological picture that John had begun.

Now while many scholars have noted points of contact between Ezekiel and John, none have offered a sustained discussion of these and the numerous other structural, motif, and thematic parallels. Some may posit that John's audience would never have drawn all of these connections; however, John's first-century audience was more astute in their ability to read and draw inter-textual parallels than we often give them credit for.[2] The first-century Jewish society was steeped in the Hebrew Bible. And the hermeneutic of their day

---

2. See also the astute assessment of John's use of Ezekiel in light of Richard B. Hay's seven tests of valid correspondences noted by William Glenn Fowler, "The Influence of Ezekiel in the Fourth Gospel: Intertextuality and Interpretation" (PhD diss., Golden Gate Baptist Theological Seminary, 1995), 209–16. These are 1) Availability, 2) Volume, 3) Recurrence, 4) Thematic Coherence, 5) Historical Plausibility, 6) History of Interpretation, and 7) Satisfaction. Cf. Richard B. Hays, *Echoes of Scripture in the Letters of Paul* (New Haven: Yale University Press, 1989), 29–32. I have argued even more vociferously than Fowler, that John used Ezekiel and that his audience was well aware of the correspondences.

(e.g., pesher and midrash) only makes this argument stronger. Such a conclusion also gives credence to the premise that John's audience was Jewish. Conversely, for a twenty-first-century audience, which is, for the most part biblically illiterate, such a close inter-textual reading appears as an impossibility. However, for a first-century audience fighting for their very literal and spiritual survival amidst persecution from all sides, knowledge of the Text and the subtle allusions authors often drew would have been second nature. The book of Revelation is proof of this fact. Whoever authored the Fourth Gospel (and Revelation), be it John, one of his followers, or a Johannine School, certainly appreciated the message of Ezekiel.

Finally, one can never be certain as to why John chose to fashion his book after Ezekiel's visions, sign acts, and oracles. There may be a very practical reason; John may simply have liked the book of Ezekiel. There could also be the solid possibility that John saw something in the life and experiences of the prophet that resonated with his own day and age. First, Ezekiel ministered in a tumultuous time when Judah had refused to listen to those whom Yahweh had sent—a fact no less true in John's day when the words of Jesus were rejected. Second, Ezekiel's message fell on a spiritually deaf nation that chose exile rather than life—a not so unfamiliar picture for John's audience. In this vein, Ezekiel prophesied, and to a degree, witnessed the destruction of the temple and city—a similar scenario that John experienced with the destruction of Jerusalem and the temple in 70 C.E. Both Ezekiel and John witnessed both sides of that destruction, and may have even shared the hardships of exile, that is, if John the Revelator and the beloved disciple are one in the same. Whatever the reasons are for John's choice of Ezekiel, the words of Hassell Bullock certainly serve as a fitting conclusion to my work,

> We have therefore seen a prophet and priest whose life and work point far beyond himself into the future. Only with difficulty can we write

off the affinities of Ezekiel with the life and work of Jesus. While he was not *the* Son of Man, he was indeed oriented toward his appearance. His obedience, the vicarious nature of his ministry, and the content of his message set our faces toward the NT figure of Jesus and prepare us for the incarnate Son. Ezekiel builds a prophetic bridge between the Testaments and makes the passage far smoother than it would have been without him.[3]

---

3. Hassell Bullock, "Ezekiel: Bridge Between the Testaments," *JETS* 25, no. 1 (1982): 31.

Index of Subjects

Angels/angelic, 57-58, 60, 168, 170
Anti-Judaism/Jewish, 67, 94-96

Babylon/Babylonia, 5, 15-16, 26, 36-37, 51-52, 79, 92, 101, 115, 137, 168
Barrett, C. K., 12-13, 17, 42, 46, 67, 144, 147, 166
Bauckham, Richard, 7, 23, 33, 102, 106, 150, 159, 179, 181
Beasley-Murray, George, 75, 85, 138
Bennema, Cornelius, 28-29, 177, 179-81
Beutler, Johannes, 11-12, 14, 144
Block, Daniel, 18, 45, 52, 72, 76, 119-20, 148, 156
Blomberg, Craig L., 9, 24, 89, 181
Brooke, George J., 13, 21, 69
Brown, Jeannine, 40, 44, 80-81, 86, 152-53, 173

Brown, Raymond E., 12-13, 68, 86, 102-3, 131, 177, 179, 194
Brown, Sherri, 33-34, 37
Bullock, Hassell, 5, 25, 30, 53-54, 60, 67, 82-83, 112, 124, 126, 151, 159, 161, 193, 205-6
Buse, Ivor, 102

Caiaphas, 106, 117
Cana (of Galilee), 62, 76-79, 83, 96-97, 103, 113
Carson, D. A., 10-12, 14, 61, 75-76, 86-87, 101, 109, 139, 155, 179
Carter, Warren, 38
Chariot-throne, 19, 36
Coloe, Mary L., 34, 183, 193
Cooke, F. A., 103
Croy, N. Clayton, 99, 124

David (king), 145, 147, 150, 155, 184, 190, 192

207

Davies, W. D., 11, 65
De Jonge, M., 24, 59, 66, 140, 174
Deeley, Mary Katharine, 144-45
Dodd, C. H., 66, 76, 81, 143, 145, 147-49, 181, 191, 193
Draper, J. A., 13, 99, 111
Dunn, James, 6, 181

Edersheim, Alfred, 74, 106
Ellens, J. Harold, 59-60
Emerton, J. A., 196
Enz, Jacob J., 10
Eppstein, Victor, 106, 117
Essene(s), 10, 17, 107
Eucharist(ic)/communion meal, 9, 80, 166, 176
Evans, Craig A., 10-11, 23, 34, 106-7, 109, 139, 145, 155, 187
Exorcism, 8, 91, 93

Ferguson, John, 105-6
Foot washing, 96
Fortna, Robert, 8, 25, 60, 66, 69, 76, 90, 92, 100, 134, 193
Fowler, William, 1, 129, 135, 142-43, 147, 153, 196, 204

Gnostic/Gnosticism, 11, 35, 38
Grigsby, Bruce, 196
Guthrie, Donald, 65-66, 74

Hamid-Khani, Saeed, 3, 11, 17, 35, 38, 84, 143, 173, 175, 190
Hamilton, Victor, 93, 183
Harstine, Stan, 38, 153, 161
Hatina, Thomas, 78, 153, 171-72, 179
Hellenism/Hellenistic, 35, 39
Hengel, Martin, 12-13, 24, 33, 37-38, 159, 179
Hezekiah, 104
Hodges, Zane C., 174-75
Hoskins, Paul, 190, 197
Hoskyns, Edwyn, 7, 25, 81, 104, 124

"I Am" Saying(s), 9, 22, 41, 75, 83, 128-42, 150-54, 156, 158-62, 196, 203
Insufflation/Inbreathing, 9, 22, 165-66, 171-74, 179-82, 185, 203
Isaiah, 5, 49, 58, 67-69, 82-83, 104, 111, 132-33, 144, 155

Jeremiah, 5, 26, 40, 43, 56, 70-71, 132-33, 141, 148, 155, 177
Jerusalem, 5, 7, 9, 18, 22, 26, 30, 43, 45, 50-52, 56, 77, 79, 81, 84, 86, 88, 95, 97, 100-1, 112,

115-18, 120, 122, 126, 140, 186-92, 194, 198-99, 201-2, 204-5
John the Baptist, 23, 42-44, 50-54
Judaism, 11, 35, 94, 96, 105

Kanagaraj, Jey, 178, 180
Käsemann, Ernst, 46-47, 113, 162
Keener, Craig S., 24-25, 58, 62, 65-66, 78, 105, 118, 143, 178
Keith, Chris, 21
Kiley, Mark, 66
Kling, Sheri, 45
Koester, Craig R., 15-16, 140
Köstenberger, Andreas J., 2, 6, 10, 23-26, 37, 39, 41-42, 46, 59, 69-73, 75-76, 81, 107, 114-15, 120, 139, 143, 155-56, 176-77, 179, 193
Kreitzer, Larry J., 21, 103

Lazarus, 9, 23, 76, 78, 84-87, 103, 151, 165, 202-3
Lee, Dorothy A., 16, 48, 60, 131, 183
Leviticus, 14, 132
Lewis, Karoline, 143-44
Lieu, Judith, 102, 162
Lightfoot, R. H., 58, 79, 104, 108
Lincoln, Andrew, 29, 106, 166, 179

Lindars, Barnabas, 7, 24, 34, 87

Maahs, Kenneth K., 6, 9, 24, 84
Mackay, Cameron, 194
Manning, Gary T., 1, 38, 57-58, 76, 78, 136, 143, 147, 149, 151, 155-56, 173-74
Martin, James, 142
Mary Magdalene, 28, 167, 170
Matson, Mark A., 39, 82, 100, 102, 106, 121-22, 134, 193, 197
Mburu, Elizabeth W., 17
Menken, Maarten J. J., 13, 15, 191
Minear, P. S., 23, 150
Moloney, Francis J., 12-13, 40, 59, 75, 101, 109-10, 113, 127, 147-48, 150-51, 155, 162, 166
Montefiore, Hugh, 78, 103
Moses, 12, 47, 49, 68-69, 78, 92, 143
Muteness (Ezekiel's), 88-90

New Covenant, 14, 22, 115, 128, 135, 141, 150, 153, 156-57, 171, 173, 176-80, 184, 188, 196, 204
Nicodemus, 15-16, 51, 97, 116, 174-75, 202-3

O'Day, Gail R., 11, 25, 45, 60 143, 166, 177, 179

209

Paroschi, Wilson, 34, 68, 180
Passion Week (The), 114, 182, 185, 189, 192
Pentecost, 172-73, 179-81
Perrin, Nicholas, 102, 105, 108-9
Peter (The apostle), 9, 87, 150, 167
Petter, Donna, 55-56, 81, 125
Phillips, Peter M., 3, 21, 34, 39, 49
Philo, 38-39
Pilate, 57, 89
Piper, Ronald, 91
Plumer, Eric, 24, 90-91
Prologue (Johannine), 22, 33-34, 48, 62, 180, 183
Pryor, John W., 57, 60, 94-96, 166, 180, 184

Qumran, 10, 17, 35, 91, 107, 175, 194

Recognition formula (The), 22, 149, 159, 161-62
Rengstorf, Karl Heinrich, 68, 70, 83
Resurrection, 21, 28, 61, 76, 81, 86, 89, 109, 133, 149, 151-52, 158, 162-63, 165-71, 174-76, 178, 180, 189, 193-94, 197, 199, 201, 203-4
Ridderbos, Herman, 144, 155, 181

Riga, Peter, 47, 62, 66, 68, 70, 72, 74, 80, 131
Ringe, Sharon, 37, 39-40

Sabbath, 44, 136, 142, 169
Samaria, 116, 202
Samaritan woman, 16, 28, 74, 116, 136, 183
Samaritan(s), 11, 15-16, 78, 202
Sanders, E. P., 107, 145
Sanhedrin, 106, 117, 148
Schnackenburg, Rudolf, 24, 46, 102, 105, 109, 121, 125, 143, 146, 162, 181
Schuchard, Bruce G., 13, 112, 125, 135, 139
Scott, Ernest F., 101, 107, 124
Seeley, David, 102
Septuagint/LXX, 3, 11-12, 36-37, 39-41, 46-47, 54, 68, 72, 87, 103, 123, 125-27, 131, 143-44, 160, 172, 183, 192
Sign Acts (of Ezekiel), 16, 21, 25, 29, 44, 48-49, 61, 63, 65-68, 70-79, 81-88, 90, 94-97, 101, 111, 114, 119-20, 126, 133, 136-37, 139, 151, 165-67, 184-85, 202-3, 205
Signs (of Jesus), 9-10, 16, 21-22, 25, 29, 44, 49, 53, 62-63, 65-91, 93, 96-97, 102-3,

INDEX OF SUBJECTS

112-13, 119, 133-35, 137, 139, 157, 161-62, 165, 186, 193, 196, 201-3
Smith, Robert Houston, 10, 68-69, 160
Son of Man, 30, 57, 59-62, 201, 206
Sophia, 38
Stegemann, Hartmut, 107
Suzerain, 36, 52, 57, 79, 160, 162, 168-69
Synoptic Gospels/Synoptics, 1, 6-9, 15, 17, 22, 30, 55, 57, 61, 70, 84, 90, 99-102, 111-12, 121-23, 127-28, 152, 177, 184, 190

Tabernacle, 182
Temple, 1, 8, 10, 18-19, 22, 26-27, 46, 50-52, 55-56, 58, 61, 63, 75-76, 78-82, 84, 86, 88-89, 95, 97, 99-128, 130, 133-36, 142, 154, 158, 160-61, 165, 173, 179, 182, 186-205

Temple cleansing (The), 8, 22, 63, 75, 79, 81, 84, 97-128, 133, 187, 193, 202
Thomas (The apostle), 163, 167-68, 170, 178
Thompson, Marianne Meye, 35, 38, 66, 73, 131, 136, 139, 155-56, 181
Triumphal Entry (The), 76, 121, 187, 189-94, 199
Trudinger, Paul, 102, 104, 196
Turner, Max, 174, 180
Twelftree, Graham H., 90-92

Vawter, Bruce, 1, 13, 31, 56, 61, 82
Watty, William, 104, 107-9
Wenham, David, 2, 23, 85, 93
Westcott, B. F., 12, 24, 124
Westermann, Claus, 13, 28, 83, 125-26
Whitely, D. E. H., 3, 24, 90, 94
Wink, Walter, 60

Zimmerli, Walther, 19, 82

Index of Scripture References

Genesis
1…..37, 41
1–2…..44
1:1…..37
1:6…..40
1:9…..40
1:14…..40
1:20…..40
1:24…..40
1:25…..123
1:26…..40
1:28…..36, 40
2…..144, 173
2:7…..171-73, 178
3…..170
3:15…..44
17:1…..131
26:24…..131
28:11-19…..58
28:12-22…..57
29:1-28…..183

29:7…..183
31:13…..131
46:3…..131

Exodus
3–12…..68
3:6…..131
3:12…..69
3:14…..131
3:15…..130
4:8…..69
4:9…..69
4:17…..69
4:28…..69
4:30…..69
6:3…..130
7:3…..69, 72
7:5…..131, 160
7:9…..69
7:17…..160
7:20…..78
8:18…..131

8:19…..69	19:10…..131
8:22…..160	19:12…..131
10:1…..69	19:14…..131
10:2…..69, 160	19:16…..131
11:9…..69, 72	19:18…..131
11:10…..69	19:25…..131
12:13…..69	19:28…..131
13:15…..106	19:30–32…..131
13:21…..41	19:34…..131
14:4…..131, 160	19:36…..131
14:18…..131, 160	19:37…..131
14:20…..41	21:23…..131
16…..83, 135	22:30…..131
16:12…..160	24:22…..131
20:2…..131	25:17…..131
22:29…..106	26:1…..131
28:43…..82	26:13…..131
29:46…..131, 160	26:30…..169
31:13…..160	26:44…..131
32–34…..152	26:45…..131
33:9…..45	27:11…..123
34:20…..106	27:26…..106
40:34…..45	

Leviticus

Numbers

1:2…..123	3:13…..106
7:25…..123	14:18…..82
10:17…..82	18:1…..82
11:44…..131	18:15–18…..106
11:45…..131	18:23…..82
16:22…..82	18:28…..106
	25:12…..177

27…..143
31:30…..123

Deuteronomy
5:9…..132
8:3…..9
12:6-17…..106
14:4…..123
18:15-18…..66, 69
21:22-23…..169
28:25-26…..169
29:6…..160
32:1-25…..29
32:11-12…..39
32:18…..39
32:39…..132

Joshua
6…..108

Judges
6:8…..132

1 Samuel
8…..192
8:7…..67
17:34-37…..147

1 Kings
17:21…..172
17:22…..70
20:13…..160
20:23…..16
20:23-28…..52
20:28…..16, 160

2 Kings
4:35…..70
5…..70
5:17…..52
18:16…..104
20:12-18…..104

2 Chronicles
29:2-8…..104
29:14-19…..104
30:1…..104

Job
4:21…..172

Psalms
23…..66, 143-44
27…..66
27:1…..41
35:19…..157
43:3…..41
44:3…..41
45:11…..132
50…..29
69…..144
69:4…..157
69:9…..101, 103, 123, 125-26

80:8-16…..154
91:4…..39
118:20…..141
131:2…..29
137…..116

Proverbs
8…..39

Isaiah
1:2-20…..29
1:10…..40
2:5…..41
3:13-15…..29
5:1-5…..155
5:1-10…..154
6…..58, 144
6:9-10…..10, 139
6:10…..67, 138-39
8:18…..71
9:2…..41
9:7…..147
10:17…..41
11:2…..49
16:5…..147
19:20…..71
20:1-6…..70
20:3…..70
22:22…..147
35:2…..46
37:30…..71

38:7…..71
39…..104
40:3…..49
40:5…..46
41:4…..132
42:6…..41
42:14…..39
43:10…..132, 159
43:25…..132
44:3-5…..174
45:8…..132
45:18…..132
45:19…..132
45:22…..132
46:4…..132
46:9…..132
48:12…..132
48:17…..132
49:6…..41
49:15…..39
49:23…..160
51:12…..132
52:6…..132
53…..82, 83
53:1…..67
53:6…..82
54:10…..177
55:13…..71
56:7…..123
58:8…..46
60:1…..46

INDEX OF SCRIPTURE REFERENCES

61…..83
61:1-3…..145
66:8…..175
66:13…..39
66:19…..71

Jeremiah
1:2…..40
1:8…..132
1:13-15…..56
1:17…..132
1:19…..132
2:2-37…..29
2:8…..141
2:21…..154
2:21-22…..155
2:26…..141
3:12…..132
4:5-8…..56
4:13-22…..56
4:27-31…..56
5:3…..53
5:13…..141
5:31…..141
6:1-8…..56
6:22-26…..56
7:4…..26, 127, 136
7:11…..123
7:18…..141
8:14-17…..56
9:23…..132

10:2…..71
10:21…..143
10:22…..56
11:1…..40
12:10…..143
13:1-11…..71
14:13-15…..141
15:7…..53
17:24-27…..53
18:1-10…..53
18:1-12…..71
19:1-15…..71
21…..43
23:1-4…..143
23:4…..148
23:5…..147
23:14-32…..141
23:23…..132
24:1…..127
24:7…..132
25:9…..56
26:3-6…..53
26:28…..132
27:1-22…..71
27:9-18…..141
27:17…..53
29…..141
30:9…..147
31:31…..177
32:6-15…..71
32:20…..71

217

32:32…..141
33:15…..147
33:17…..147
35:1-19…..71
37:18…..127
37:19…..141
38:17…..53
38:23…..53
43:8-13…..71
44:17-25…..141
44:29…..71
46:24…..56
49:11…..132
51:59-64…..71
52:6-9…..137
52:8…..168
52:11…..139

Ezekiel
1…..37, 40, 42, 57-58, 60, 79
1–3…..19-20, 24, 30, 34-35, 41, 52, 59, 60-62, 71, 77, 131, 165, 201
1–8…..79
1–11…..18
1–24…..18-19, 188
1–39…..160
1:1…..18, 50, 54, 58-59
1:1-3…..79
1:2…..18
1:2-3…..42
1:3…..40, 42, 51
1:4…..41, 52, 54, 56, 137
1:5…..54
1:5-23…..57
1:7…..54
1:13…..54
1:13-14…..41
1:16…..54
1:18…..54
1:20…..54
1:21…..54
1:22…..54
1:24…..49, 54
1:26…..54
1:27…..54
1:27-28…..41, 137, 158
1:28…..46, 49, 54, 80
2…..44, 112
2–3…..55, 60, 79
2–24…..74
2:1—3:11…..42
2:1…..60
2:2…..49, 53
2:3…..60, 74
2:3-7…..29
2:5…..43, 154
2:5-8…..74
2:6…..49, 55, 60
2:7…..42
2:8…..60-61
3…..29, 44

3:1…..60
3:1-3…..24
3:1-4…..61
3:1-11…..112
3:3…..49, 60
3:4…..60
3:7…..42
3:8…..16, 74
3:9…..74
3:10…..60
3:11…..42, 72
3:12…..46, 49, 80
3:13…..49
3:14…..36, 49, 61
3:15…..47, 51, 72
3:16…..18, 40
3:17…..49, 60, 141
3:19…..153
3:22…..49
3:23…..46, 51-52, 80
3:24…..49
3:25…..60
3:26…..74
3:26-27…..88
3:27…..42, 49, 61, 74, 88
4…..16, 50
4–5…..63, 70, 72, 79, 114
4–24…..19, 72, 88, 95
4:1-3…..72-73, 77, 81, 119
4:1-17…..82
4:1—5:4…..81

4:3…..68, 71-73
4:4-6…..60, 73, 77, 119
4:4-15…..61
4:5-6…..82
4:7…..81
4:7-8…..119
4:8…..81-82
4:9-17…..73, 77, 119
4:12…..49
4:15…..49
4:16…..135, 195
4:16-17…..195
4:17…..135
5…..16, 126
5:1-4…..72-73, 77, 126
5:1-17…..119
5:6-7…..126
5:9…..126
5:11…..126
5:12…..195
5:13…..22, 126, 160
5:16…..135
5:16-17…..195
5:17…..135
6–7…..80
6:1…..40
6:1-10…..149
6:9…..26
6:11…..135
6:12…..135, 168
7:1…..40

7:6.....132
7:8-19.....153
7:9.....22, 160
7:15.....135, 195
7:19.....195
7:26.....51-52
7:27.....138
8.....26, 80, 109, 112, 116-17
8–10.....51, 109-10, 136
8–11.....19-20, 30, 34, 99, 110, 116, 121-22, 124-25, 128, 136, 165, 186, 201-2
8–12 136
8:1.....18, 43, 51, 72, 89, 119
8:1-3.....60
8:1-18.....141
8:3-5.....117
8:4.....80
8:4-18.....125
8:7-12.....117
8:10.....122-23
8:11-12.....148
8:12.....117, 127
8:12a.....41
8:12b.....41
8:14.....117, 127, 141
8:16.....117, 127
8:17.....127
8:17—9:10.....153
8:18.....125
9.....116, 122

9–10.....52
9–11.....136
9:1.....124
9:1-2.....117, 124
9:2.....56, 117
9:3.....80, 118, 127
9:5-6.....118
9:6.....127, 148
9:7.....127
10.....24, 55, 116
10:1-20.....57
10:2.....117-18
10:3.....127
10:4.....46, 80, 118, 127
10:12.....54
10:17.....54
10:18.....46, 80, 118, 127
10:19.....80
11.....114, 116, 137
11:7-13.....118
11:10-11.....168
11:14.....40
11:14-21.....27
11:16.....45, 115, 136
11:16-20.....115
11:17-21.....137
11:19.....115, 136, 153, 171, 182
11:20.....115, 157
11:21.....26, 53
11:22-23.....53, 80, 137
11:23.....30, 46, 116, 118

INDEX OF SCRIPTURE REFERENCES

11:25…..72
12…..16, 70, 114, 136-39, 142, 203
12–24…..18
12–39…..162, 165
12:1…..40
12:1-7…..61
12:1-16…..119
12:1-20…..73, 77
12:1-28…..110
12:2…..48, 74, 138-39
12:3…..74
12:3-7…..139
12:3-11…..97
12:6…..71-73, 137, 139
12:7…..137, 139
12:8…..40
12:9…..74, 138-39
12:10…..138
12:11…..71-73
12:12…..137-39
12:12-13…..137
12:13…..139
12:14…..137
12:16…..135, 195
12:17…..40
12:17-20…..61
12:18…..135-36
12:18-19…..49
12:18-20…..77
12:19…..135-36

12:21…..40
12:22…..138-39
12:25…..74
12:26…..40
12:27…..138-39
12:28…..139-40
13…..114, 141-42
13–14…..148
13–24…..80, 114, 134
13:1…..40
13:1-16…..141
13:5…..141
13:17-23…..141
13:22…..153
14…..51, 114
14:1…..43, 51-52, 72, 89
14:2…..40
14:3…..26
14:5…..26
14:12…..40
14:13…..135, 195
14:21…..135, 195
14:23…..22, 160
15…..1, 13, 71, 133, 155, 157, 203
15:1…..40
15:1-5…..154
15:1-8…..155, 158
15:4…..156
15:6…..195
15:7…..156
15:8…..156

221

16…..20-21, 48, 95, 160	20:1-3…..148
16:1…..40	20:1-4…..52
16:42…..27	20:2…..40
16:51-63…..27	20:3…..16, 51
17…..114, 148, 155	20:4…..30, 60-61
17:1…..40	20:5…..22, 160
17:1-21…..154	20:7…..22, 160
17:11…..40	20:11…..153, 158
17:12-24…..110	20:11-21…..153
17:21…..22, 160, 168	20:13…..153, 158
17:22-24…..27, 134	20:19…..22, 160
18…..53, 160	20:21…..153, 158
18:1…..40	20:30…..57
18:2…..49	20:31…..16
18:8-28…..153	20:33…..57, 96, 192
18:9…..153	20:39-44…..27
18:14-23…..27	20:45…..40
18:17…..153	20:49…..61, 67
18:19…..153	21…..168
18:21…..153	21:1…..40
18:21-32…..153	21:2…..22, 160
18:22…..153	21:8…..40
18:23…..153, 158	21:11…..61
18:27…..153	21:12…..61
18:28…..153	21:18…..40
18:32…..95, 153, 158	21:17…..138
19…..114, 148, 155	21:19-23…..30
19:1…..138	21:19-26…..110
19:10-15…..154	21:25…..138
20…..95, 153, 203	21:30…..138
20:1…..18, 43, 51-52, 72, 89	21:36 (LXX) …..172

22…..142
22:1…..40, 61
22:2…..30, 60
22:6…..138, 148
22:17…..40
22:22…..22, 160
22:23…..40
22:25…..141
22:25-31…..141, 148
22:27…..142
22:28…..141
22:30…..141
23…..20, 21, 48, 95, 160
23:1…..40
23:36…..30, 60
24…..16, 50, 70, 72, 114, 202
24:1…..18, 40
24:1-14…..110
24:3…..74
24:3-24…..74
24:15…..40
24:15-18…..77
24:15-24…..61
24:15-27…..151
24:16…..85-87, 120
24:16-18…..27
24:19…..66, 97
24:20…..40
24:23…..87
24:24…..61, 71-73, 77
24:27…..71-73, 77, 85, 88

25–32…..18-19, 45, 85, 134
25–48…..19-20
25:1…..40
26:1…..18, 40
27:1…..40
27:35…..87
28:1…..40
28:11…..40
28:20…..40
28:22-24…..132
28:26…..132, 157
29:1…..18, 40
29:6…..132
29:9…..132
29:16…..132
29:17…..18, 40
29:21…..132
30:1…..40
30:8…..132
30:19…..132
30:20…..18, 40
30:25…..132
30:26…..132
31:1…..18, 40
32:1…..18, 40
32:15…..132
32:17…..18, 40
33…..45, 53, 134
33–37…..145
33–39…..18-19
33–48…..18

33:1…..40
33:6-7…..141
33:9-19…..153
33:11…..95
33:15…..153
33:15-19…..153
33:21…..18, 53, 74, 168
33:21-22…..110
33:22…..85, 88, 90
33:23…..40
33:24-33…..149
33:29…..132
33:32…..16, 44, 68, 114
33:33…..43, 71, 154
34…..1, 13, 71, 133-34, 141-46, 150, 155, 158, 192, 194, 203
34–39…..156
34–48…..88, 149, 153, 185, 188-89
34:1…..40
34:1-8…..145
34:6…..146
34:8…..146
34:9-12…..145
34:10…..146
34:11…..146
34:11-16…..196
34:12…..146
34:12-13…..145
34:14…..84, 145
34:15…..132, 145-46

34:16…..145
34:16a…..145
34:16b-21…..149
34:16b-22…..145
34:17…..146
34:18…..84
34:19…..146
34:22…..146
34:23…..142, 145, 148
34:23-24…..135, 150, 190, 192
34:24…..138, 142
34:25…..128, 134-35, 145, 150, 156-57, 166, 171, 173, 177-78
34:25-26…..154
34:27…..132
34:28…..157
34:29…..84, 135
34:30…..22, 132, 149, 157, 160
34:31…..146
35:1…..40
35:4…..132
35:9…..132
35:12…..22, 132, 160
35:15…..132
36…..174
36:1…..40
36:8…..157
36:8-12…..84
36:11…..132
36:16…..40
36:23…..132

INDEX OF SCRIPTURE REFERENCES

36:25-27…..14, 174-75
36:26…..156, 171, 182
36:26-27…..135, 153, 182
36:28…..157
36:29…..135
36:29-30…..84, 135
36:36…..22, 160
36:37-38…..145
37…..20, 144, 147, 166-67, 170, 173-76, 182-85, 192, 201
37:1…..60
37:1-14…..19, 71, 151, 158, 166-68, 170, 175, 178, 180, 182, 185, 203
37:3…..151, 168
37:3a…..170
37:3b…..170
37:3-6…..168
37:4…..136
37:4-6…..170
37:5…..153
37:6…..132
37:7…..178
37:7-8…..168, 171
37:9…..136, 153, 168, 172-74
37:9-10…..178
37:10…..153, 168
37:11-14…..168, 171, 173, 176
37:12…..136
37:12-13…..157
37:13…..132

37:14…..22, 61, 153, 157, 160, 165, 169, 171, 174, 176, 182
37:15…..40
37:15-17…..88
37:15-28…..73, 77, 88, 150, 166-67, 183-85
37:17…..184-85, 203
37:18…..66
37:18-28…..88
37:21…..176
37:21-26…..150
37:21-28…..157
37:22…..184, 192
37:22-25…..192
37:23…..157, 176, 184
37:24…..142, 145, 185, 192
37:24-25…..135, 150, 184, 190
37:25…..145, 176, 192
37:26…..45, 61, 84, 128, 138, 145, 150, 154, 156-57, 166-67, 171, 173, 177-78, 180, 184-85, 192-93
37:26-28…..184
37:27…..157, 184
37:28…..45, 132, 184
38–39…..20, 24, 93, 157, 170, 182
38:1…..40
38:8…..157
38:11…..157
38:14…..157
38:16…..157

225

38:19…..126
38:22…..157
38:23…..132
39:4…..170
39:6…..132
39:7…..132, 157
39:12-20…..170
39:21…..157
39:22…..132
39:26…..157
39:26-29…..84
39:28…..132
39:29…..153, 157, 175-76, 182
40–42…..154, 187, 193
40–43…..34, 46, 86, 186-87
40–48…..18-20, 45, 157, 189, 194, 198, 201
40:1…..60
40:1a…..18
40:1b…..18
40:1—43:5…..148, 187
40:2…..190
40:5…..127
41:1…..127
41:4…..127
41:15…..127
41:21…..127
41:23…..127
41:25…..127
42:20…..187
42:13-14…..187

43–48…..83, 142, 195
43:1-5…..114-15, 189, 204
43:2…..41
43:4…..46
43:5…..46
43:12…..187
43:26…..187
44–48…..80, 157, 189
44:2…..142
44:3…..138
44:4…..46
45:6-7…..190
45:7…..138
45:8…..158
45:16…..138
45:22…..138
46…..138, 158
46:1…..142
46:1-3…..158
46:1-12…..142
46:8…..142
46:10…..142
46:12…..142
47…..78, 103, 195
47–48…..154
47:1-5…..195-96
47:1-6…..24
47:1-12…..78, 84, 158, 196
47:7…..195
47:8…..103
47:8-12…..84

47:9-10…..76, 195
47:10…..196
47:12…..24, 83, 195
47:13—48:35…..158
48…..190
48:21-22…..138
48:35…..115

Daniel
2…..37
7…..37, 59
8:27…..47
12:1-3…..151

Hosea
1:1…..40
5:14…..132
9:15…..103
10:1…..154
11:3-4…..39
11:9…..132
13:8…..39
14:7…..154

Joel
1:1…..40
2…..195
2:27…..132
3:17…..160

Amos
3:1—4:13…..29
9:11…..147
9:11-13…..80

Jonah
1:1…..40

Micah
1:1…..40
4:4…..157
6:1-8…..29

Nahum
2:2 (LXX)…..172

Haggai
1:13…..132
2:4…..132

Zechariah
3:10…..157
8:12…..157
9–14…..193
9:9…..121, 192
11:1-17…..143
14…..193
14:21…..101, 103, 194

Malachi
1:14…..132
3:1-3…..103

3:11…..157

Matthew
3:1-17…..51
3:7…..50
3:16…..58
4:1-11…..8, 92
4:18-22…..55
5–7…..69
5:23-24…..107
10:13…..177
10:15…..30
11:9…..43
11:9-11…..43
11:22…..30
11:24…..30
12:41-42…..30
13:32…..134
13:57…..44
14:5…..43
14:10…..42
14:27…..131
16:21-28…..110
17:1-9…..8
17:1-12…..61
20:18…..117
21:1-14…..121
21:5…..192
21:12-14…..122
21:12-17…..8
21:13…..123, 125, 127

21:26…..43
22:32…..131
23:16…..127
23:17…..127
23:21…..127
23:35…..127
23:37…..39, 120
26…..9
26:26-29…..9
26:28…..177
26:61…..127
26:63…..89
26:64…..89
27:5…..127
27:11…..89
27:12…..89
27:14…..89
27:37…..57
27:40…..127
27:42…..190
27:46…..89
27:50…..89
27:51…..127
27:52…..151
28:9-10…..90
28:17-20…..90

Mark
1:3-8…..51
1:11-13…..8
1:12-13…..92

INDEX OF SCRIPTURE REFERENCES

1:16-20.....55
1:17.....87
3:22-30.....91
4:30-32.....134
5:2-20.....90
5:34.....177
6:1-6.....44
6:27.....42
6:50.....131
8:31-33.....110
8:35.....152
9:2-8.....8
9:2-13.....61
10:32.....117
11:1-17.....121
11:11.....108, 117
11:15-17.....8, 122
11:17.....122-23, 125, 127
11:32.....43, 55
13:1-2.....26
14.....9
14:22-25.....9
14:24.....177
14:58.....127
14:60-61.....89
14:61.....148
14:62.....131
14:63.....89
15:2.....57, 89
15:4-5.....89
15:29.....127
15:32.....190
15:34.....89
15:37.....89
15:38.....127
16:12-20.....90

Luke
1:9.....127
1:21.....127
1:22.....127
3:2-20.....51
3:3.....51
3:7.....50
3:21.....58
3:23.....54
4:1-13.....8, 92
4:24.....44
5:1-11.....76
6:13-16.....55
7:26.....43
7:50.....177
8:29-37.....90
8:48.....177
9:9.....42
9:24.....152
9:28-36.....61
10:5-6.....177
10:14.....30
10:32.....50
11:31-32.....30
13:19.....134

13:34…..39, 120
17:11…..117
19:29-46…..121
19:42…..177
19:44…..110
19:45-46…..8, 122
19:46…..123, 125, 127
20:6…..43
21:5-6…..26
22…..9
22:2…..55
22:17-20…..9
22:20…..177
22:67-70…..89
22:70…..131
23:2…..57
23:3…..89
23:9…..89
23:28-29…..118
23:28-31…..120
23:43…..89
23:45…..127
23:46…..89
24:13-53…..90
24:36…..177
24:39…..131

John
1…..8, 16, 22, 33-35, 37, 42, 44, 47, 58, 60-62, 71, 77, 92, 96, 131, 144, 152-53, 165

1–2…..104
1–12…..21
1:1…..35, 37, 58, 172-73
1:1-5…..34
1:1-14…..79
1:1-18…..34, 68
1:1-51…..34
1:3…..37
1:4…..137, 152
1:4-9…..41
1:5…..41, 51, 137
1:6…..58
1:6-25…..34
1:6-36…..42
1:6-51…..79
1:7…..27, 42-43, 134, 137
1:8…..42, 137
1:9…..137
1:10…..160
1:11…..44, 53, 74, 112
1:12…..27
1:13…..58
1:14…..38, 45, 47-48, 54, 115, 152, 190
1:14a…..45
1:14b…..46
1:15…..35, 42
1:17…..49
1:18…..38, 131
1:19…..42-43, 50-51
1:19-27…..50-51

INDEX OF SCRIPTURE REFERENCES

1:19—12:50…..75
1:21…..43, 49-51, 69
1:21-25…..43
1:23…..49
1:24…..148
1:25…..69
1:26-27…..44
1:28…..51
1:29…..52, 60, 82-83
1:32…..42, 53-54
1:32-33…..49
1:33…..53
1:34…..42-43
1:36…..53, 83
1:37-51…..55
1:41…..74
1:44…..49
1:45…..49
1:46…..56
1:48…..160
1:49…..57, 191
1:50-51…..16
1:51…..57-60, 62, 190
2…..44, 76, 78, 144
2–4…..9, 78, 89, 115
2–11…..196
2–12…..22, 72, 85
2:1-11…..48-49, 76, 79, 113, 119
2:4…..89
2:11…..46-47, 73
2:13…..9, 50, 196

2:13-14a…..116
2:13-15…..124
2:13-21…..192
2:13-22…..8, 26, 56, 79, 99, 101-2, 120-22, 125, 127-28, 135-36, 161, 165, 202
2:13-25…..103
2:14…..123
2:14-15…..122
2:14-17…..76
2:15…..123-24
2:15-16…..117
2:16…..127, 194
2:16-17…..127
2:17…..125
2:18…..73, 112, 136, 191
2:18-20…..97
2:19…..81, 86, 109, 111, 113, 119, 123, 186-87, 204
2:19-21…..127
2:20…..26
2:21…..76, 109
2:22…..12, 113, 118, 186
2:23…..73
2:24-25…..54
3…..14-15, 51, 174
3–4…..116, 136
3–11…..134
3–12…..113
3:1…..148
3:2…..73

231

3:3-4…..97
3:4…..51
3:5…..174
3:5-8…..116
3:10…..51, 160-61, 175
3:13…..59
3:14…..59
3:14-15…..76
3:14-44…..59
3:15-16…..152
3:16…..27, 83
3:17…..30
3:18…..27, 96, 113
3:19…..30
3:19-21…..137
3:26…..43
3:27-36…..42
3:30…..44
3:34…..40
3:35…..38, 131
3:36…..152
4…..15, 52, 76, 78
4:1…..44, 148
4:1-42…..183
4:9-12…..97
4:10…..158
4:10-14…..48
4:14…..152
4:19…..44, 138
4:20-24…..190
4:21…..38, 46, 116

4:21-24…..52
4:23…..38, 116
4:23-24…..46
4:23-26…..116
4:25…..74
4:26…..116, 159
4:28-29…..28
4:29…..54
4:34…..44
4:39…..54
4:41…..27
4:44…..16, 44
4:46-54…..76, 83, 119
4:48…..16, 69, 73
4:54…..73
5…..76, 136-37
5:1-9…..76, 83, 119
5:9…..136
5:9-18…..142
5:10…..136
5:13…..89
5:14…..118
5:16…..136
5:16-18…..28
5:17…..38
5:18…..38, 67, 113, 131, 136
5:19-20…..131
5:21…..152, 176
5:22…..30, 149
5:24…..30, 152, 188
5:24-30…..96

INDEX OF SCRIPTURE REFERENCES

5:25-28…..136
5:26…..152
5:27…..30, 59, 149
5:28-29…..188
5:29…..30
5:30…..30, 136
5:31-38…..28
5:33…..43
5:33-36…..42
5:35…..137
5:36…..44
5:37…..15, 43, 48, 131
5:39…..41
5:40…..28, 152
5:42…..160
5:47…..12
6…..15, 76, 136-37
6–15…..162
6:1-15…..49, 76, 83
6:2…..73
6:4…..9, 50, 196
6:14…..44, 69, 73-74, 138
6:15…..89, 191
6:20…..130, 159
6:26…..73
6:27…..59, 152
6:28-29…..65
6:30…..73
6:31-32…..135
6:32…..135
6:33…..135, 152

6:35…..132, 152, 158
6:37…..131
6:40…..152
6:41…..132, 135, 158
6:44…..131
6:46…..131
6:47-48…..152
6:48…..132, 158
6:48-66…..9
6:49…..135
6:50…..132, 135, 158
6:51…..132, 135, 147, 152, 158
6:53…..59
6:53-54…..152
6:57…..131
6:58…..132, 135, 158
6:62…..59
6:63…..152, 182
6:64…..54
6:68…..152, 182
6:69…..160
7–10…..13, 21, 69
7:1…..67, 89, 113
7:3…..65
7:4…..89
7:6…..89
7:10…..89
7:13…..29, 55, 202
7:14…..118
7:17…..160
7:19…..113

233

7:20.....67, 91
7:24.....30
7:25.....113
7:26.....160
7:28.....118
7:30.....49
7:31.....73-74
7:32.....148, 191
7:33.....46
7:34.....159
7:36.....159
7:37-39.....48, 196-97
7:38.....12, 158
7:38-39.....78
7:39.....162, 180, 182
7:40.....44, 69, 138
7:42.....12, 147
7:44.....49
7:45.....148
7:47.....148
7:48.....148
7:53—8:11.....21
8.....15
8–11.....145
8:2.....118
8:3.....148
8:12.....132, 137-38, 140, 152, 158, 196-97
8:13.....148
8:15-16.....30
8:16.....149

8:17-18.....40
8:18.....43, 130
8:20.....118
8:21.....159
8:24.....130, 159
8:26.....30, 48
8:27.....160
8:28.....59, 130-31, 159-60, 162
8:32.....160
8:37.....67, 113, 160
8:38.....131
8:40.....48, 113
8:43.....160
8:44.....26, 91
8:48-52.....91
8:49.....131
8:54.....131
8:55.....160
8:58.....130, 159
8:59.....44, 89, 118, 120, 191
9.....76, 139-40, 142
9:1.....138
9:1-7.....76, 83, 139
9:1-41.....69, 138
9:2.....139
9:2-3.....138
9:3-4.....139
9:4.....138-40
9:5.....132, 137-39, 158
9:6.....139
9:6-7.....139

INDEX OF SCRIPTURE REFERENCES

9:6-41…..138-39
9:8-34…..139
9:13…..148
9:13-17…..28
9:14-16…..142
9:15…..148
9:16…..28, 73, 148
9:17…..44, 138
9:22…..29, 55
9:24-34…..28
9:34-38…..142
9:35…..59
9:39…..30, 139
9:39-41…..138-40
9:39—10:21…..143-44
9:40…..139, 148
9:40-41…..148
9:41…..139
10…..1, 13, 15, 71, 118, 133, 142-45, 147-48, 158
10:1…..145
10:1-8…..145
10:1-10…..141
10:2-5…..145
10:6…..146
10:7…..146
10:8…..141, 146
10:9…..133, 141, 146
10:10…..146, 152
10:10-13…..146
10:11…..133, 147

10:12…..142
10:14…..149, 160
10:14-16…..146
10:15…..147, 160
10:17…..147
10:17-18…..146
10:18…..131
10:22…..196
10:22-42…..148
10:24…..148
10:26-27…..148
10:27…..149, 160
10:28…..152
10:28-29…..48
10:29…..131
10:30…..38, 92, 131, 148
10:30-39…..28
10:31…..44
10:31-39…..118, 191
10:33…..148
10:35…..12
10:38…..148, 160
10:39…..49
10:41…..42-43, 73
11…..9, 76, 85, 89, 103, 144, 151, 158, 202
11:1-44…..76
11:10…..137
11:14…..54
11:17…..86
11:24…..151

235

11:25…..133, 151-52
11:26…..151
11:31…..87
11:33…..86-87
11:35…..87
11:39…..49
11:40…..46
11:42…..134
11:45-53…..191
11:46…..148
11:47…..148
11:48…..73
11:52…..145, 150
11:53…..67, 113
11:54…..89
11:55…..50, 196
11:55—12:1…..9
11:57…..148
12…..144, 189
12–20…..166, 189, 192
12:1-8…..76
12:3…..49, 191
12:12…..191
12:12-16…..76
12:12-36…..110
12:13…..57, 190-91
12:15…..192
12:16…..162, 193
12:17-18…..147
12:18…..73
12:23…..59

12:28…..43, 62
12:29…..48
12:31…..30, 91-92, 149, 170
12:34…..59
12:35…..46, 137
12:36…..89, 137
12:37…..16, 44, 67, 73-74, 110, 113
12:40…..138-39
12:41…..46, 58
12:42…..29, 55, 148
12:44-45…..40
12:45…..131
12:46…..137
12:47…..30
12:47-48…..27
12:48…..30, 96, 157
12:49…..131
12:50…..40, 131, 152
13–17…..9, 15, 89
13–21…..21, 85, 87
13:1-17…..150
13:3…..131
13:4-16…..96
13:7…..160
13:18…..12
13:19…..130, 159
13:21-26…..54
13:26-29…..110
13:27…..169
13:31…..59

13:31-32…..162
13:33…..46
13:35…..160
13:37-38…..152
14…..152-54
14:1-3…..158, 189, 197
14:1-4…..110
14:2…..154
14:2-3…..46, 114, 182
14:3…..188
14:4…..154
14:5…..154
14:6…..133, 152, 158
14:7…..154, 160
14:7-9…..131
14:9…..15, 38, 154, 160
14:16-17…..114, 153
14:16-26…..182
14:17…..154, 160
14:18…..114
14:19…..46
14:20…..154, 160
14:26…..114, 153
14:27…..154, 177
14:28…..114, 131
14:30…..92
14:31…..131, 154, 161
15…..1, 13, 71, 133, 155-57
15:1…..133
15:1-8…..8
15:1-17…..156

15:2…..156
15:2a…..157
15:4…..156, 158
15:6…..156-58
15:7…..156, 158
15:9…..156, 158
15:10…..156, 158
15:15…..40
15:16…..156
15:17-27…..157
15:18-25…..157
15:18-27…..28
15:24…..15
15:25…..157
15:26…..157
16:3…..160
16:7…..180
16:8…..30
16:11…..30, 92, 170
16:13…..48
16:16…..46
16:16-19…..110
16:17…..46
16:18…..46
16:19…..46
16:28…..189
16:33…..177
17…..22, 165-66, 183-85, 190, 203
17–20…..147, 166
17:1…..162

17:1-5…..184
17:2-3…..152, 184
17:3…..152, 160-61, 184
17:5…..46
17:6…..184
17:6-9…..185
17:7…..160
17:9…..184
17:10…..184
17:11…..92, 184
17:12…..12, 91, 184
17:14…..185
17:19…..184
17:21…..92, 131, 184
17:22…..46, 184
17:23…..184
17:24…..46, 131, 159, 184
17:25…..160
17:26…..184
18–19…..76
18:2-14…..191
18:3…..148
18:5…..130, 159
18:5-6…..162
18:6…..130, 159
18:8…..159
18:10-11…..110
18:15…..25
18:18…..130
18:20…..90
18:20-21…..89

18:22-23…..49
18:23…..89
18:34…..89
18:36…..89, 192
18:36-37…..57
18:37…..89
19:1-30…..44
19:3…..49
19:7…..28, 191
19:9…..89
19:11…..89
19:15…..96
19:17-20…..118
19:24…..12
19:26-28…..89
19:28…..12
19:30…..89
19:31…..169
19:35…..29
19:36…..12
19:37…..12
19:38…..29, 55
19:38-40…..49
19:38-42…..169
19:39…..202
20…..9, 22, 71, 144, 154, 165-67, 174, 177, 185, 190, 203
20–21…..45, 76, 90
20:1-18…..167
20:1-17…..151
20:9…..12

20:11-18…..28
20:13…..168
20:17…..49, 131
20:19…..29, 55, 115, 177-78, 202
20:19-31…..114, 167
20:20…..168, 171
20:21…..115, 131, 177-78
20:22…..9, 130, 152-53, 167-68, 171-73, 176, 179-81, 196, 203
20:23…..170, 196, 204
20:24-29…..163
20:25…..168, 171
20:26…..115, 177-78, 180
20:27…..168, 171
20:27-29…..168, 170
20:30…..65, 73
20:30-31…..73, 75, 153
20:31…..22, 62, 65, 152, 188, 193
21…..9, 76, 150, 196
21:1-11…..76, 87, 204
21:3…..180
21:4-11…..196
21:9…..196
21:11…..196
21:15-17…..87, 150
21:21-24…..27
21:22…..188-89
21:23…..46, 189, 197
21:24…..29
21:25…..10

Acts
1:6…..110, 189
2…..88, 172-73, 179-81
4:36…..50
5:1-10…..54
7…..30, 157
7:56…..58
10:19…..54
11:12…..54
11:28…..54
12…..157
13:2…..54
13:4…..54
16:6…..54
16:7…..54
21…..157
21:4…..54
21:11…..54

Romans
2:5…..149
5:12-16…..170
9–11…..182
14:10…..149

1 Corinthians
6:19…..109
11:25…..177
12:3…..174
15…..151, 170

2 Corinthians
5:10…..149

Ephesians
6:12…..170

Colossians
2:15…..170

1 Timothy
5:24…..149

Hebrews
1…..36
4:14…..83
9:26…..83
9:27…..149
10:12…..83
10:27…..149
12:24…..177

James
3:1…..149

2 Peter
2:9…..149

1 John
1…..36
4:17…..149

Revelation
1:3…..25
4–7…..59
4:6…..24, 198
4:8…..24, 198
4:9…..24, 198
5:6…..24, 198
5:8…..24, 198
5:11…..24, 198
5:14…..24, 198
6…..30
6:1…..24, 198
6:6…..24, 198
6:14…..24, 198
7:11…..24, 198
7:15…..45
11:1-2…..108
12:12…..45
13:6…..45
14:3…..24, 198
14:7…..30
15:7…..24, 198
16:5…..30
16:7…..30
18:8…..30
18:10…..30
18:20…..30
19–22…..188
19:2…..30
19:4…..24, 198
19:11…..30

20…..93
20:8…..24, 198
21:1-27…..198
21:3…..45, 198
21:22…..109, 190
22:1-2…..24, 198
22:2…..24, 198
22:7…..25
22:10…..25
22:18…..25
22:19…..25

Other Texts

Josephus *Antiquities*
8:46-49…..91

Sirach
45:1-5…..47

Wisdom of Solomon
15:11…..172

1 Maccabees
13:51…..190

2 Maccabees
1:18—2:18…..196
10:5-9…..117

Jubilees
1:17…..194

1:22…..175
1:27-29…..194

1 Enoch
90:29…..194

2 Baruch
29:4-6…..195
29:5…..80

1. Sanh.
98a…..74

Hag.
2:2…..148

Qumran
4QFlorilegium
1:1-13…..187

1QS
3:6-8…..176
4:21-24…..176
7:6…..176
9:32…..176
11:10-14…..176
12:12…..176
16:12…..176
17:20…..176

11Q Temple Scroll
29:8-10…..194

www.ingramcontent.com/pod-product-compliance
Lightning Source LLC
Chambersburg PA
CBHW071155070526
44584CB00019B/2801